THE SECOND AND THIRD PARTS OF

KING HENRY THE SIXTH

GENERAL EDITOR ALFRED HARBAGE

THE PELICAN SHAKESPEARE

WILLIAM SHAKESPEARE

THE SECOND AND THIRD PARTS OF KING HENRY THE SIXTH

EDITED BY ROBERT K. TURNER, JR., AND
GEORGE WALTON WILLIAMS

PENGUIN BOOKS

Penguin Books Ltd, Harmondsworth,
Middlesex, England
Penguin Books, 625 Madison Avenue,
New York, New York 10022, U.S.A.
Penguin Books Australia Ltd, Ringwood,
Victoria, Australia
Penguin Books Canada Limited, 2801 John Street,
Markham, Ontario, Canada L3R 1B4
Penguin Books (N.Z.) Ltd, 182–190 Wairau Road,
Auckland 10, New Zealand

First published in *The Pelican Shakespeare* 1967
This revised edition first published 1980

Library of Congress catalog card number: 75-98364

Printed in the United States of America by
Kingsport Press, Inc., Kingsport, Tennessee
Set in Monotype Ehrhardt

CONTENTS

PUBLISHER'S NOTE

Soon after the thirty-eight volumes forming *The Pelican Shakespeare* had been published, they were brought together in *The Complete Pelican Shakespeare*. The editorial revisions and new textual features are explained in detail in the General Editor's Preface to the one-volume edition. They have all been incorporated in the present volume. The following should be mentioned in particular:

The lines are not numbered in arbitrary units. Instead all lines are numbered which contain a word, phrase, or allusion explained in the glossarial notes. In the occasional instances where there is a long stretch of unannotated text, certain lines are numbered in italics to serve the conventional reference purpose.

The intrusive and often inaccurate place-headings inserted by early editors are omitted (as is becoming standard practise), but for the convenience of those who miss them, an indication of locale now appears as first item in the annotation of each scene.

In the interest of both elegance and utility, each speech-prefix is set in a separate line when the speaker's lines are in verse, except when these words form the second half of a pentameter line. Thus the verse form of the speech is kept visually intact, and turned-over lines are avoided. What is printed as verse and what is printed as prose has, in general, the authority of the original texts. Departures from the original texts in this regard have only the authority of editorial tradition and the judgment of the Pelican editors; and, in a few instances, are admittedly arbitrary.

SHAKESPEARE AND
HIS STAGE

William Shakespeare was christened in Holy Trinity Church, Stratford-upon-Avon, April 26, 1564. His birth is traditionally assigned to April 23. He was the eldest of four boys and two girls who survived infancy in the family of John Shakespeare, glover and trader of Henley Street, and his wife Mary Arden, daughter of a small landowner of Wilmcote. In 1568 John was elected Bailiff (equivalent to Mayor) of Stratford, having already filled the minor municipal offices. The town maintained for the sons of the burgesses a free school, taught by a university graduate and offering preparation in Latin sufficient for university entrance; its early registers are lost, but there can be little doubt that Shakespeare received the formal part of his education in this school.

On November 27, 1582, a license was issued for the marriage of William Shakespeare (aged eighteen) and Ann Hathaway (aged twenty-six), and on May 26, 1583, their child Susanna was christened in Holy Trinity Church. The inference that the marriage was forced upon the youth is natural but not inevitable; betrothal was legally binding at the time, and was sometimes regarded as conferring conjugal rights. Two additional children of the marriage, the twins Hamnet and Judith, were christened on February 2, 1585. Meanwhile the prosperity of the elder Shakespeares had declined, and William was impelled to seek a career outside Stratford.

The tradition that he spent some time as a country

teacher is old but unverifiable. Because of the absence of records his early twenties are called the "lost years," and only one thing about them is certain – that at least some of these years were spent in winning a place in the acting profession. He may have begun as a provincial trouper, but by 1592 he was established in London and prominent enough to be attacked. In a pamphlet of that year, *Groats-worth of Wit*, the ailing Robert Greene complained of the neglect which university writers like himself had suffered from actors, one of whom was daring to set up as a playwright:

. . . an vpstart Crow, beautified with our feathers, that with his *Tygers hart wrapt in a Players hyde*, supposes he is as well able to bombast out a blanke verse as the best of you: and beeing an absolute *Iohannes fac totum*, is in his owne conceit the onely Shake-scene in a countrey.

The pun on his name, and the parody of his line "O tiger's heart wrapped in a woman's hide" (*3 Henry VI*), pointed clearly to Shakespeare. Some of his admirers protested, and Henry Chettle, the editor of Greene's pamphlet, saw fit to apologize:

. . . I am as sory as if the originall fault had beene my fault, because my selfe haue seene his demeanor no lesse ciuill than he excelent in the qualitie he professes: Besides, diuers of worship haue reported his vprightnes of dealing, which argues his honesty, and his facetious grace in writting, that approoues his Art. (Prefatory epistle, *Kind-Harts Dreame*)

The plague closed the London theatres for many months in 1592–94, denying the actors their livelihood. To this period belong Shakespeare's two narrative poems, *Venus and Adonis* and *The Rape of Lucrece*, both dedicated to the Earl of Southampton. No doubt the poet was rewarded with a gift of money as usual in such cases, but he did no further dedicating and we have no reliable information on whether Southampton, or anyone else, became his regular patron. His sonnets, first mentioned in 1598 and published without his consent in 1609, are intimate without being explicitly autobiographical. They seem to commemorate the poet's friendship with an idealized youth, rivalry with a more favored poet, and love affair with a dark mistress; and his bitterness when the mistress betrays him in conjunction with the friend; but it is difficult to decide precisely what the "story" is, impossible to decide whether it is fictional or true. The true distinction of the sonnets, at least of those not purely conventional, rests in the universality of the thoughts and moods they express, and in their poignancy and beauty.

In 1594 was formed the theatrical company known until 1603 as the Lord Chamberlain's men, thereafter as the King's men. Its original membership included, besides Shakespeare, the beloved clown Will Kempe and the famous actor Richard Burbage. The company acted in various London theatres and even toured the provinces, but it is chiefly associated in our minds with the Globe Theatre built on the south bank of the Thames in 1599. Shakespeare was an actor and joint owner of this company (and its Globe) through the remainder of his creative years. His plays, written at the average rate of two a year, together with Burbage's acting won it its place of leadership among the London companies.

Individual plays began to appear in print, in editions both honest and piratical, and the publishers became increasingly aware of the value of Shakespeare's name on the title pages. As early as 1598 he was hailed as the leading English dramatist in the *Palladis Tamia* of Francis Meres:

As *Plautus* and *Seneca* are accounted the best for Comedy and Tragedy among the Latines, so *Shakespeare* among the English is the most excellent in both kinds for the stage: for Comedy, witnes his *Gentlemen of Verona*, his *Errors*, his *Loue labors lost*, his *Loue labours wonne* [at one time in print but no longer extant, at least under this title], his *Midsummers night dream*, & his *Merchant of Venice*; for Tragedy, his *Richard the 2*, *Richard the 3*, *Henry the 4*, *King Iohn*, *Titus Andronicus*, and his *Romeo and Iuliet*.

The note is valuable both in indicating Shakespeare's prestige and in helping us to establish a chronology. In the second half of his writing career, history plays gave place to the great tragedies; and farces and light comedies gave place to the problem plays and symbolic romances. In 1623, seven years after his death, his former fellow-actors, John Heminge and Henry Condell, cooperated with a group of London printers in bringing out his plays in collected form. The volume is generally known as the First Folio.

Shakespeare had never severed his relations with Stratford. His wife and children may sometimes have shared his London lodgings, but their home was Stratford. His son Hamnet was buried there in 1596, and his daughters Susanna and Judith were married there in 1607 and 1616 respectively. (His father, for whom he had secured a coat of arms and thus the privilege of writing himself gentleman, died in 1601, his mother in 1608.) His considerable earnings in London, as actor-sharer, part owner of the Globe, and playwright, were invested chiefly in Stratford property. In 1597 he purchased for £60 New Place, one of the two most imposing residences in the town. A number of other business transactions, as well as minor episodes in his career, have left documentary records. By 1611 he was in a position to retire, and he seems gradually to have withdrawn from theatrical activity in order to live in Stratford. In March, 1616, he made a will, leaving token bequests to Burbage, Heminge, and Condell, but the bulk of his estate to his family. The most famous feature of the will, the bequest of the second-best bed to his wife, reveals nothing about Shakespeare's marriage; the quaintness of the provision seems commonplace to those familiar with ancient testaments. Shakespeare died April 23, 1616, and was buried in the Stratford church where he had been christened. Within seven years a monument was erected to his memory on the north wall of the chancel. Its portrait bust and the Droeshout engraving on the title page of the First Folio provide the only likenesses with an established claim to authenticity. The best verbal vignette was written by his rival Ben Jonson, the more impressive for being imbedded in a context mainly critical:

. . . I loved the man, and doe honour his memory (on this side idolatry) as much as any. Hee was indeed honest, and of an open and free nature: had an excellent Phantsie, brave notions, and gentle expressions. . . . (*Timber or Discoveries*, ca. 1623–30)

*

The reader of Shakespeare's plays is aided by a general knowledge of the way in which they were staged. The King's men acquired a roofed and artificially lighted theatre only toward the close of Shakespeare's career, and then only for winter use. Nearly all his plays were designed for performance in such structures as the Globe – a three-tiered amphitheatre with a large rectangular platform extending to the center of its yard. The plays were staged by daylight, by large casts brilliantly costumed, but with only a minimum of properties, without scenery, and quite possibly without intermissions. There was a rear stage gallery for action "above," and a curtained rear recess for "discoveries" and other special effects, but by far the major portion of any play was enacted upon the projecting platform, with episode following episode in swift succession, and with shifts of time and place signaled the audience only by the momentary clearing of the stage between the episodes. Information about the identity of the characters and, when necessary, about the time and place of the action was incorporated in the dialogue. No place-headings have been inserted in the present editions; these are apt to obscure the original fluidity of structure, with the emphasis upon action and speech rather than scenic background. (Indications of place are supplied in the footnotes.) The acting, including that of the youthful apprentices to the profession who performed the parts of women, was highly skillful, with a premium placed upon grace of gesture and beauty of diction. The audiences, a cross section of the general public, commonly numbered a thousand, sometimes more than two thousand. Judged by the type of plays they applauded, these audiences were not only large but also perceptive.

THE TEXTS OF THE PLAYS

About half of Shakespeare's plays appeared in print for the first time in the folio volume of 1623. The others had been published individually, usually in quarto volumes, during his lifetime or in the six years following his death. The copy used by the printers of the quartos varied greatly in merit, sometimes representing Shakespeare's true text, sometimes only a debased version of that text. The copy used by the printers of the folio also varied in merit, but was chosen with care. Since it consisted of the best available manuscripts, or the more acceptable quartos (although frequently in editions other than the first), or of quartos corrected by reference to manuscripts, we have good or reasonably good texts of most of the thirty-seven plays.

In the present series, the plays have been newly edited from quarto or folio texts, depending, when a choice offered, upon which is now regarded by bibliographical specialists as the more authoritative. The ideal has been to reproduce the chosen texts with as few alterations as possible, beyond occasional relineation, expansion of abbreviations, and modernization of punctuation and spelling. Emendation is held to a minimum, and such material as has been added, in the way of stage directions and lines supplied by an alternative text, has been enclosed in square brackets.

None of the plays printed in Shakespeare's lifetime were divided into acts and scenes, and the inference is that the author's own manuscripts were not so divided. In the folio collection, some of the plays remained undivided, some were divided into acts, and some were divided into acts and scenes. During the eighteenth century all of the plays were divided into acts and scenes, and in the Cambridge edition of the mid-nineteenth century, from which the influential Globe text derived, this division was more or less regularized and the lines were numbered. Many useful works of reference employ the act–scene–line apparatus thus established.

Since this act–scene division is obviously convenient, but is of very dubious authority so far as Shakespeare's own structural principles are concerned, or the original manner of staging his plays, a problem is presented to modern editors. In the present series the act–scene division is retained marginally, and may be viewed as a reference aid like the line numbering. A star marks the points of division when these points have been determined by a cleared stage indicating a shift of time and place in the action of the play, or when no harm results from the editorial assumption that there is such a shift. However, at those points where the established division is clearly misleading – that is, where continuous action has been split up into separate "scenes" – the star is omitted and the distortion corrected. This mechanical expedient seemed the best means of combining utility and accuracy.

THE GENERAL EDITOR

INTRODUCTION

During the fifteenth century the English won and lost France, fought a disastrous civil war at home, and brought Henry VII, the first of the Tudor monarchs, to the throne. This period had a special fascination for the Elizabethans. The times were near enough to be influential and well remembered, yet far enough away to be safely idealized. Readily available were extensive historical and legendary accounts devoted wholly or partially to fifteenth-century personages and happenings, among them John Foxe's *Acts and Monuments of Martyrs*, the *Mirror for Magistrates*, Fabyan's, Stowe's, Grafton's, and Holinshed's chronicles, and Edward Hall's *Union of the Two Noble and Illustre Families of Lancaster and York*. Very early in his career, Shakespeare sensed the poetic, dramatic, and patriotic possibilities in these materials and began to shape from them historical dramas designed to edify and delight. He thus became one of the first of the popular dramatists to turn to English history for source material, and it is just possible that he was the first to do so. He may, then, have been the originator, at least as far as the commercial theatre is concerned, of a kind of play that was to figure prominently in the development of the Elizabethan drama.

From Edward Hall particularly, Shakespeare derived not only information about the men, manners, and events of the preceding era but also a theory of history which imposed a unity on diverse and seemingly inexplicable phenomena, for it was Hall (and from him, Holinshed) who expressed most clearly for Renaissance England the doctrine that God's hand is present in human history, that events, while subject to the free will of the participants, are nonetheless overseen ultimately by a Providence through which order will eventually be restored to a world rendered chaotic by sin. In addition, the focus of Shakespeare's history plays was determined by the view taken by Hall and earlier writers of what was historically significant; history for them was chiefly political history, an account of the rise and fall of great men or those who aspired to be great, of statecraft and public affairs, of faction, sedition, rebellion, war and battle – in short, an account of the vicissitudes and triumphs of the state and its prince. In his sources, then, Shakespeare found a great wealth of detail pertaining to character and event pre-selected according to a well-defined concept of significance, and, underlying all the detail, a philosophy of history which allowed the actions of men to stand in the foreground but which saw behind these actions a logic proceeding from the irrevocable, although sometimes obscure, development of God's plan for England's good.

In the works of these chroniclers Shakespeare saw also an interpretation of fifteenth-century history which has been called the "Tudor myth"; he seems not only to have found this interpretation compatible with his own personal beliefs but also to have recognized in it a strong dramatic potential, particularly suited for didactic purposes. The Tudor myth sprang from the Elizabethans' strong sense of cosmic order, of which political order was a part, and their acute discomfort upon the emergence of symptoms construed to indicate a dislocation of order. The political disasters of the fifteenth century were obviously a kind of disorder, which, according to the concept of sin and retribution, could best be understood as a punishment visited by God upon the people of England for some grave wrong. Logic and a sense of justice required that a sin deserving this punishment be identified, and the chroniclers, looking back to 1399 and 1400, settled upon the deposition and murder of Richard II by Henry Bolingbroke as the crucial event. Richard had been a weak and irresponsible ruler but he had been a king, God's anointed, and the theory was developed that to rebel against a king, however bad a monarch he was, was to violate God's will and thus to commit the cardinal political crime. The troubles that attended Bolingbroke's reign as Henry IV were seen as ample proof of God's displeasure with him and with the realm. During the time of the hero-king Henry V there was a temporary respite, but, as justice remained unsatisfied, the subjects of his son Henry VI had to suffer the lawlessness and confusion that marked the Wars of the Roses and a culminating horror in the tyranny of the monstrous Richard III. But as suffering leads to penitence and finally to forgiveness, God at last relented, and in the person of Henry VII, the founder of the Tudor dynasty, He again blessed England with a strong and able leader who brought peace to the land and instituted an enlightened statecraft which was to lead eventually to the glorious reign of his granddaughter, Elizabeth I. So went the myth. It was fostered by the Tudors because in a general way it strengthened the position of the monarch at the same time that it specifically provided a divine sanction for the somewhat questionable legitimacy of Henry VII's claim to the crown. It was accepted by most Elizabethans because, as they looked at the cycle from the vantage point of their own time, it had a fitness and an appealing optimism. That it did not fully accord with historical data was a matter of no very great concern, for historical truth, while comprehending facts, was not regarded as being precisely correspondent to them but correspondent as well to doctrines acceptable to and significant for the present. This view permitted the chroniclers a certain latitude in their accounts of the past, and it also gave Shakespeare the license necessary for the transformation of history into drama.

Although Shakespeare tightened the narrative fabric somewhat by condensing, altering the chronology of events, and changing the age of some of the characters, the span of time covered by *2* and *3 Henry VI* is so large and so crowded with great affairs that the structure of the plays was almost bound to be loose. Such episodic structure had an authority derived from the medieval mystery cycles, and it had been given fresh sanction by Marlowe's *Tamburlaine*; it permitted the inclusion within a single dramatic framework of highly diversified materials which contributed to the effect of copiousness greatly admired in Elizabethan literature. Yet, evidently in an attempt to achieve some unity and to increase the significance of the episodes, Shakespeare also made use of a theme inherited from the morality play and previously employed in the morality-like interlude *Respublica* and in such courtly historical dramas as *King Johan* and *Gorboduc*. This theme worked allegorically to make the realm itself the center of the dramatic action; the plays, then, are not ultimately about Henry VI or York or Edward or the others but about England itself as it suffers through a retributive civil war immediately caused by the weakness of the king and the corruption of the nobility. They are, in addition, part of a series of essays in definition, as Shakespeare explores the attributes of kingship. What makes a strong and happy state? A good king. What makes a good king? This for Shakespeare seems to have been a complicated question to the many branches of which he gave no easy or final answers.

That it was Shakespeare's intention to convey this complex theme is suggested by certain parts of the action which he developed either entirely on his own or from meagre suggestions in his sources and which he rendered in the stylized, ritualistic manner of the morality play, such as the formal alignment of characters in the opening scene of *2 Henry VI*, the representation of the flatly virtuous Iden (*2 Henry VI*, IV, x), the scene depicting the king on the molehill (*3 Henry VI*, II, v), the abuse of Clifford's corpse by the Yorkists (*3 Henry VI*, II, vi), and Edward's wooing of Lady Grey to the accompaniment of Clarence's and Gloucester's mocking commentary (*3 Henry VI*, III, ii). Dramatic action of this kind serves as an articulation of theme rather than as a rendition of events supposed to be true; it directs our understanding toward the internal significance of the entire action rather than to its depiction alone. But his sense of theatre was too keen for Shakespeare to rest content with a rigidly allegorical representation of a doctrinaire political ideology. He entered imaginatively into the life of many of his characters; moreover, he seized whatever opportunity he could to create effects which would be striking in performance at the same time that they contributed to the general ideas upon which the plays were based. A good example is his handling in *2 Henry VI* of the conflict between Queen Margaret and the Duchess of Gloucester. According to history, Queen Margaret did not arrive in England until several years after the Duchess' fall, but Shakespeare departed from his sources to bring the two together, evidently because he thought that dramatic capital could thus be gained. Not only is the clash between the two ambitious and overbearing women intrinsically interesting, but it helps to define the divided loyalties of the nobility, to create the atmosphere of jealous strife which pervades the court, and to foreshadow the ruin of the good Duke Humphrey. An equally good example of Shakespeare's manipulation of his sources for dramatic effect is his treatment of Jack Cade, whose thematic importance is discussed more fully below. We may note here, however, that many of the incidents represented as occurring during Cade's Rebellion Shakespeare found in the chronicle accounts of the Peasants' Revolt of 1381 and that he completely ignored certain favorable traits in Cade's character as it was described by Holinshed because they obviously ran counter to his purposes.

In spite of these efforts to achieve coherence, *2* and *3 Henry VI* remain rather sprawling plays which lack a strongly represented central character, either good or evil, about whom incidents within their complicated plots could have been arranged. The king, to be sure, is present throughout, but he, far from being a dynamic figure, is nearly the perfect symbol of inaction. That he has many private virtues is clear, but they express themselves publicly only as impotence, irresolution, and for all his conscientiousness, an extraordinary indifference to the preservation of England's power and dignity among nations. Duke Humphrey, whose fall from power provides the focal point of the first two acts and part of the third of *2 Henry VI*, has many of the public virtues wanting in the king – particularly a practical shrewdness combined with a vigorous and self-sacrificing dedication to an ideal of service to the realm – but his confidence in the power of his own innocence and good faith makes him a rather easy victim of the queen and the wolvish nobles, who see him as an obstacle to their own acquisition of power. As Duke Humphrey descends, York rises. His claim to the throne is better than Henry's, and, as he has courage, patriotism (self-interested though it may be), and force of character, he would undoubtedly make a better ruler, but his ambition is flagrant and his method of satisfying it Machiavellian. He is further guilty in ignoring the principle that all kings, regardless of the manner in which their crowns were obtained, are inviolate. As a part of his program, he has stimulated Jack Cade's Rebellion, the development and suppression of which occupies the fourth act. By the beginning of the fifth, York has an army in the field and, with the support of his sons and the Nevils, declares for the crown by open rebellion, against the opposition of Queen Margaret and the Cliffords. York's victory at the Battle of

St Albans ensues, yet, as Henry still lives, *2 Henry VI* ends with York still short of achieving the crown.

The action of *3 Henry VI*, which begins immediately after the Battle of St Albans, is set in motion by Henry's proposal that he be allowed to reign during his lifetime at the price of disinheriting his son in favor of York, a compromise which York swears to respect but which causes Queen Margaret to seek military support from the northern barons. During the first act Margaret's army forces the surrender of the city of York; the act closes with York dead, his head impaled upon the battlements of the city. The Lancastrians are temporarily triumphant, but a Yorkist army under Edward and Richard has yet to be encountered. The second act is devoted chiefly to the Yorkists' defeat of Margaret's powers, with Warwick's help, and Edward's subsequent claiming of the crown; and the third to the capture of King Henry, Edward's proposal to Lady Grey and the consequent destruction of a possible French alliance, Margaret's appeal to Lewis of France for aid, and Warwick's shift of allegiance to the Lancastrian cause. In the long and busy fourth act, Edward is overthrown and then regains his power. The fifth is given over to the campaign, replete with alarms and excursions, which culminates in the final Yorkist victory at Tewkesbury and the murder of the Prince of Wales and King Henry. At the end of the play it would seem that the Yorkist cause should be won and that King Edward should be secure upon the throne, but by this time a new contender has appeared in Richard of Gloucester, who vows to wade to majesty through the blood of his brothers and nephews. The plays, then, are of epic scope, and the tentative emergence of York as the central figure of the Second Part and of Edward as the central figure of the Third is obstructed by a shifting emphasis upon a bewildering number of minor characters who strut and fret for a scene or two, sell one another out, and then die their gory deaths at the base of Fortune's relentless wheel. The implication of the historical accounts becomes, in fact, something of an embarrassment to the plays themselves; the tragedy of the times was that no one man was both strong enough and good enough to lead the country, the king being deficient in public virtue and the house of York in private. As yet not even such a villain as Richard of Gloucester was later to prove had come forward with sufficient force to be dominant. Thus no well-defined protagonist was at hand, and the allegorical figure of England was too vague to serve as an agent of dramatic concentration.

Certain episodes, however, are brilliantly rendered and skillfully fitted into the framework of the whole drama. For example, Shakespeare apparently wanted to show that corruption at the top of the state was certain to penetrate to the bottom, that if the nobles were so criminally foolish as to abandon the ideal of loyalty to the king and commonwealth to serve themselves it was only to be expected that the people would behave in a similar way. His vehicle for conveying this important aspect of his theme was the sinister farce of Cade's Rebellion, which not only shows political chaos manifesting itself on a lower social level than that occupied by the nobles but also, in pointing toward the Wars of the Roses, characterizes them as a kind of universal folly that would be ridiculous were its consequences not so grave. In the world of Cade and his followers, ordinary values are completely inverted, manifest impossibility replaces fact, and right reason becomes a series of puns, defective syllogisms, and contradictions in terms. In Cade's England all is in order when most out of order – seven halfpenny loaves will be sold for a penny, the three-hooped pot will have ten hoops, the pissing conduit will run nothing but claret for a year; it is a capital crime to read and write English and high treason to speak Latin. The massive confusion of such a world is shown not only by the brutality of Cade's actions but also by the havoc wrought upon the arts of language when the rebels speak. The dialogue succeeds in being very funny while simultaneously serving sternly serious purposes, among them the reflection of such cruelty as Clifford's murder of Rutland and such false logic as Warwick's legalistic argument in support of York's claim to the throne (*2 Henry VI*, II, ii, 53–62).

What emerges most strongly from such scenes is a powerful irony. The characters in the plays are living, all unaware, within a web of significance which connects individual actions. The law of cause and effect is always operating, but the individual, having lost his hold upon moral realities because of pride, selfishness, or weakness, cannot see beyond the moment. With morality gone, the old values which make for goodness in men and stability in the state become perverted. The keeping of oaths becomes a matter of expediency. Family loyalty breeds only revenge, which breeds only counter-revenge. Caught up in circumstances which are very imperfectly understood, fathers kill their sons and sons their fathers. Desire for the sweet fruition of an earthly crown leads only to a molehill like that upon which an actual king is to sit and wish that he were anything but a king. Justice becomes confused with self-interest, piety becomes cowardice, and good reasons replace right reason. The ultimate origin of this anarchy lies behind, in history; its ultimate outcome lies ahead, and no character can perceive it except dimly in very occasional moments of foreboding or prophesy. Within the plays certain incidents provide ironical commentaries on others (as, for instance, the mock-heroic combat of the drunken Horner and the frightened Peter casts an ironic light on the hollow chivalry of the nobles), but throughout both our perspective is modified by the discrepancy between our historical knowledge of the outcome of it all and the characters' more limited vision.

It is no doubt impossible to read or to see *2* and *3 Henry VI* without thinking of the Shakespeare that was to come, for in them many things are attempted that were later to be better done. Their language is sometimes stilted and inflexible, adorned with elaborate conceits which are more ornamental than integral; their psychology does not often inquire very far beyond the self-love to which Renaissance moralists conventionally attributed man's corruption. It is a mistake, however, to underrate them. When they were written, there was only one other playwright, Marlowe, who just might have done the job more expertly, and there is no real assurance that he could have managed so well. The mature Shakespeare is noted, among many other things, for unsurpassed skill in dramatic design, for language so pregnant and beautiful that one can only wonder at it, for characters so admirably conceived that they never release their holds upon the imagination, and for as deep an insight into the mystery of things as any writer ever achieved. All these virtues are present, at least in embryonic form, in *2* and *3 Henry VI*.

University of Wisconsin   ROBERT K. TURNER, JR
Milwaukee

Duke University   GEORGE WALTON WILLIAMS

NOTE ON THE TEXTS

The Second and Third Parts of King Henry the Sixth were printed in the folio of 1623, evidently from a manuscript in Shakespeare's hand except for a few brief passages, and the folio text has been closely followed in the present edition. The version of Part Two printed in quarto in 1594 and the version of Part Three printed in octavo in 1595 are discussed in Appendix B, with an explanation of the use made of them in this edition. A list of all substantive departures from the folio text is included in this Appendix. Neither the quarto–octavo nor the folio versions are divided into acts and scenes. The act–scene division here supplied marginally is that of earlier editors. (The present editors have collaborated closely on all portions of this edition, with Professor Turner drafting the Introduction, Professor Williams collating the text, and both writing the glosses.)

THE SECOND PART
OF KING HENRY
THE SIXTH

King Henry the Sixth
Humphrey, Duke of Gloucester, his uncle
Henry, Cardinal Beaufort, Bishop of Winchester,
    great-uncle to the King
Richard Plantagenet, Duke of York
Edward and Richard, his sons
Edmund Beaufort, Duke of Somerset
William de la Pole, Duke of Suffolk
Humphrey Stafford, Duke of Buckingham
Thomas, Lord Clifford
Young Clifford, his son John
Richard Nevil, Earl of Salisbury
Richard Nevil, Earl of Warwick, his son
Thomas, Lord Scales
Sir James Fiennes, Lord Say
Sir Humphrey Stafford
William Stafford, his brother
Sir John Stanley
Vaux
Matthew Goffe
A Lieutenant, Master, Mate, and Walter Whitmore
Two Gentlemen, prisoners with Suffolk
Alexander Iden, a Kentish gentleman
John Hume and John Southwell, two priests
Roger Bolingbroke, a conjurer
Thomas Horner, an armorer
Peter Thump, his man
Clerk of Chartham
Mayor of Saint Albans
Saunder Simpcox, an impostor
Jack Cade, a rebel
John, Dick the butcher, Smith the weaver, and other Rebels
Two Murderers
A Spirit

Margaret, *Queen to King Henry*
Eleanor Cobham, *Duchess of Gloucester*
Margery Jourdain, *a witch*
Wife to Simpcox
Lords, Ladies, Attendants, Petitioners, Aldermen, Herald,
    Beadle, Sheriff, Officers, Citizens, Prentices, Falconers,
    Guards, Soldiers, Messengers, *etc.*

Scene : *England*]

THE SECOND PART
OF KING HENRY
THE SIXTH

Flourish of trumpets, then hautboys. Enter King,
Duke Humphrey [of Gloucester], Salisbury,
Warwick, and [Cardinal] Beaufort [of Winchester],
on the one side ; the Queen, Suffolk, York,
Somerset, and Buckingham on the other.

SUFFOLK
As by your high imperial majesty
I had in charge at my depart for France,
As procurator to your excellence,   3
To marry Princess Margaret for your grace,
So, in the famous ancient city Tours,
In presence of the Kings of France and Sicil,   6
The Dukes of Orleans, Calaber, Bretagne, and Alençon,
Seven earls, twelve barons, and twenty reverend bishops,
I have performed my task and was espoused ;
And humbly now upon my bended knee
In sight of England and her lordly peers
Deliver up my title in the queen
To your most gracious hands, that are the substance
Of that great shadow I did represent :
The happiest gift that ever marquess gave,
The fairest queen that ever king received.

KING
Suffolk, arise. Welcome, Queen Margaret.

I, i The royal palace in London   s.d. *Flourish* fanfare, more elaborate
than a sennet (see I, iii, 98 s.d., n.)   3 *procurator* legal agent, proxy   6
Sicil i.e. Sicily ; Queen Margaret's father, Reignier

18   I can express no kinder sign of love
  Than this kind kiss. O Lord, that lends me life,
  Lend me a heart replete with thankfulness.
  For thou hast given me in this beauteous face
  A world of earthly blessings to my soul,
  If sympathy of love unite our thoughts.

QUEEN

  Great King of England and my gracious lord,
25   The mutual conference that my mind hath had,
  By day, by night, waking and in my dreams,
  In courtly company or at my beads,
28   With you, mine alderliefest sovereign,
29   Makes me the bolder to salute my king
  With ruder terms, such as my wit affords
31   And over-joy of heart doth minister.

KING

  Her sight did ravish, but her grace in speech,
33   Her words yclad with wisdom's majesty,
  Makes me from wond'ring fall to weeping joys,
  Such is the fullness of my heart's content.
  Lords, with one cheerful voice welcome my love.

ALL *(kneel)*

  Long live Queen Margaret, England's happiness!

QUEEN

  We thank you all.
      Flourish.

SUFFOLK

  My Lord Protector, so it please your grace,
  Here are the articles of contracted peace
  Between our sovereign and the French king Charles,
  For eighteen months concluded by consent.

43 GLOUCESTER *(reads)* 'Inprimis, It is agreed between the
  French king Charles and William de la Pole, Marquess

18–19 *kinder ... kind* more natural .. loving 25 *mutual conference*
intimate intercourse 28 *alderliefest* most dear 29 *salute* greet 31
minister suggest 33 *yclad* clad 43 *Inprimis* imprimis, first (marks the
first point agreed upon in a contract; subsequent points are signalled by
item, 'similarly,' as at l. 50)

of Suffolk, ambassador for Henry King of England, that
the said Henry shall espouse the Lady Margaret,
daughter unto Reignier King of Naples, Sicilia, and
Jerusalem, and crown her Queen of England ere the
thirtieth of May next ensuing.
'*Item*, that the duchy of Anjou and the county of Maine
shall be released and delivered to the king her father' –
    [Gloucester lets it fall.]

KING
Uncle, how now?

GLOUCESTER   Pardon me, gracious lord,
Some sudden qualm hath struck me at the heart,
And dimmed mine eyes that I can read no further.

KING
Uncle of Winchester, I pray read on.   55

CARDINAL *[reads]* '*Item*, It is further agreed between
them that the duchies of Anjou and Maine shall be
released and delivered over to the king her father, and
she sent over of the King of England's own proper cost
and charges, without having any dowry.'

KING
They please us well. Lord marquess, kneel down.
We here create thee the first Duke of Suffolk
And girt thee with the sword. Cousin of York,
We here discharge your grace from being regent
I' th' parts of France till term of eighteen months
Be full expired. Thanks, uncle Winchester,
Gloucester, York, Buckingham, Somerset,
Salisbury, and Warwick.
We thank you all for this great favor done
In entertainment to my princely queen.   70
Come, let us in, and with all speed provide
To see her coronation be performed.
             Exit King, [with] Queen, and Suffolk.
             Manet [Gloucester, staying all] the rest.

55 *Uncle* i.e. great-uncle (the cardinal was the half-brother of Henry VI's
grandfather, Henry IV)

GLOUCESTER
Brave peers of England, pillars of the state,
To you Duke Humphrey must unload his grief—
Your grief, the common grief of all the land.
76 What? Did my brother Henry spend his youth,
His valor, coin, and people in the wars?
78 Did he so often lodge in open field,
In winter's cold and summer's parching heat,
80 To conquer France, his true inheritance?
And did my brother Bedford toil his wits
To keep by policy what Henry got?
Have you yourselves, Somerset, Buckingham,
Brave York, Salisbury, and victorious Warwick,
Received deep scars in France and Normandy?
Or hath mine uncle Beaufort and myself,
With all the learned council of the realm,
Studied so long, sat in the Council House
Early and late, debating to and fro
90 How France and Frenchmen might be kept in awe,
And hath his highness in his infancy
Crownèd in Paris in despite of foes?
And shall these labors and these honors die?
Shall Henry's conquest, Bedford's vigilance,
Your deeds of war, and all our counsel die?
O peers of England, shameful is this league.
Fatal this marriage, cancelling your fame,
Blotting your names from books of memory.
99 Rasing the characters of your renown,
100 Defacing monuments of conquered France,
Undoing all as all had never been!
CARDINAL
Nephew, what means this passionate discourse,

---

76 *brother Henry* i.e. Henry V 78 *lodge* lie 80 *true inheritance* (through
Henry V's ancestor Isabella of France, wife of Edward II of England; see
Henry V, I, i, 87–89) 90 *awe* reverential obedience 99 *Rasing ... of*
erasing the letters which record 100 *monuments* (1) stones, (2) documents
(preservers of memory)

32

This peration with such circumstance?   103
For France, 'tis ours; and we will keep it still.

GLOUCESTER
Ay, uncle, we will keep it if we can,
But now it is impossible we should.
Suffolk, the new-made duke that rules the roast,   107
Hath given the duchy of Anjou and Maine
Unto the poor King Reignier, whose large style   109
Agrees not with the leanness of his purse.

SALISBURY
Now, by the death of Him that died for all,
These counties were the keys of Normandy.
But wherefore weeps Warwick, my valiant son?

WARWICK
For grief that they are past recovery;
For were there hope to conquer them again,
My sword should shed hot blood, mine eyes no tears.
Anjou and Maine? Myself did win them both;
Those provinces these arms of mine did conquer;
And are the cities that I got with wounds
Delivered up again with peaceful words?
Mort Dieu!   121

YORK
For Suffolk's duke, may he be suffocate,
That dims the honor of this warlike isle.
France should have torn and rent my very heart
Before I would have yielded to this league.
I never read but England's kings have had
Large sums of gold and dowries with their wives,
And our King Henry gives away his own
To match with her that brings no vantages.

GLOUCESTER
A proper jest, and never heard before,
That Suffolk should demand a whole fifteenth   131

103 *circumstance* detail   **107** *rules the roast* domineers   **109** *large style* pompous title   **121** *Mort Dieu* (an oath; literally, by God's death)   **131** *fifteenth* i.e. the proceeds from a tax of this amount on subjects' real property

For costs and charges in transporting her.
She should have stayed in France, and starved in France,
Before—

CARDINAL

My Lord of Gloucester, now ye grow too hot.
It was the pleasure of my lord the king.

GLOUCESTER

My Lord of Winchester, I know your mind.
'Tis not my speeches that you do mislike,
But 'tis my presence that doth trouble ye.
Rancor will out. Proud prelate, in thy face
I see thy fury. If I longer stay,
We shall begin our ancient bickerings.

143   Lordings, farewell; and say, when I am gone,
I prophesied, France will be lost ere long.

     Exit Humphrey [Duke of Gloucester].

CARDINAL

So, there goes our Protector in a rage.
'Tis known to you he is mine enemy;
Nay more, an enemy unto you all,
And no great friend, I fear me, to the king.

149   Consider, lords, he is the next of blood
And heir apparent to the English crown.
Had Henry got an empire by his marriage
And all the wealthy kingdoms of the west,
There's reason he should be displeased at it.
Look to it, lords. Let not his smoothing words
Bewitch your hearts; be wise and circumspect.
What though the common people favor him,
Calling him 'Humphrey, the good Duke of Gloucester,'
Clapping their hands and crying with loud voice
'Jesu maintain your royal Excellence!'
With 'God preserve the good Duke Humphrey!'

---

143 *Lordings* my lords   **149** *next of blood* (since Henry VI has no child as yet, the crown would pass, in the event of his death, to Gloucester, his uncle and nearest blood relative)

I fear me, lords, for all this flattering gloss,   161
He will be found a dangerous Protector.

BUCKINGHAM
Why should he then protect our sovereign,
He being of age to govern of himself?
Cousin of Somerset, join you with me,
And all together with the Duke of Suffolk,
We'll quickly hoise Duke Humphrey from his seat.   167

CARDINAL
This weighty business will not brook delay;   168
I'll to the Duke of Suffolk presently.   *Exit Cardinal.* 169

SOMERSET
Cousin of Buckingham, though Humphrey's pride
And greatness of his place be grief to us,
Yet let us watch the haughty cardinal;
His insolence is more intolerable
Than all the princes' in the land beside.
If Gloucester be displaced, he'll be Protector.

BUCKINGHAM
Or thou or I, Somerset, will be Protector
Despite Duke Humphrey or the cardinal.
                    Exeunt Buckingham and Somerset.

SALISBURY
Pride went before, ambition follows him.   178
While these do labor for their own preferment,
Behooves it us to labor for the realm.
I never saw but Humphrey Duke of Gloucester
Did bear him like a noble gentleman.
Oft have I seen the haughty cardinal,
More like a soldier than a man o' th' church,
As stout and proud as he were lord of all,
Swear like a ruffian and demean himself
Unlike the ruler of a commonweal.

161 *flattering gloss* specious praise   167 *hoise* hoist   168 *brook* endure
169 *presently* immediately   178 *Pride . . . ambition* i.e. the cardinal . . .
Buckingham and Somerset

Warwick my son, the comfort of my age,
189 Thy deeds, thy plainness, and thy housekeeping
Hath won the greatest favor of the commons,
Excepting none but good Duke Humphrey.
192 And, brother York, thy acts in Ireland
In bringing them to civil discipline,
Thy late exploits done in the heart of France
When thou wert regent for our sovereign,
Have made thee feared and honored of the people.
Join we together for the public good,
In what we can to bridle and suppress
The pride of Suffolk and the cardinal
With Somerset's and Buckingham's ambition;
And, as we may, cherish Duke Humphrey's deeds
While they do tend the profit of the land.

WARWICK
So God help Warwick, as he loves the land
And common profit of his country.

YORK
And so says York – *[aside]* for he hath greatest cause.

SALISBURY
206 Then let's make haste away, and look unto the main.

WARWICK
Unto the main? O father, Maine is lost.
208 That Maine which by main force Warwick did win,
And would have kept so long as breath did last.
Main chance, father, you meant, but I meant Maine,
Which I will win from France or else be slain.
Exeunt Warwick and Salisbury. Manet York.

YORK
Anjou and Maine are given to the French,
Paris is lost; the state of Normandy
214 Stands on a tickle point now they are gone.

---

189 *housekeeping* hospitality, management of personal affairs   192 *brother*
i.e. brother-in-law   206 *main* most important stake (a term in hazard, a
dice game, to which Warwick alludes further at l. 210)   208 *main*
overpowering   214 *tickle* unstable

Suffolk concluded on the articles,
The peers agreed, and Henry was well pleased
To change two dukedoms for a duke's fair daughter.
I cannot blame them all. What is't to them?
'Tis thine they give away, and not their own.   219
Pirates may make cheap pennyworths of their pillage,   220
And purchase friends, and give to courtesans,
Still revelling like lords till all be gone,   222
While as the silly owner of the goods   223
Weeps over them and wrings his hapless hands   224
And shakes his head and trembling stands aloof
While all is shared and all is borne away,
Ready to starve and dare not touch his own.
So York must sit and fret and bite his tongue   228
While his own lands are bargained for and sold.
Methinks the realms of England, France, and Ireland
Bear that proportion to my flesh and blood
As did the fatal brand Althaea burnt   232
Unto the prince's heart of Calydon.
Anjou and Maine both given unto the French?
Cold news for me! for I had hope of France,
Even as I have of fertile England's soil.
A day will come when York shall claim his own;
And therefore I will take the Nevils' parts,   238
And make a show of love to proud Duke Humphrey,
And when I spy advantage, claim the crown,
For that's the golden mark I seek to hit.
Nor shall proud Lancaster usurp my right,   242
Nor hold the sceptre in his childish fist,
Nor wear the diadem upon his head,
Whose churchlike humors fits not for a crown.

219 *thine* (York addresses himself in the second person) 220 *pennyworths*
bargains 222 *Still* continually 223 *silly* helpless 224 *hapless* un-
lucky 228 *bite his tongue* hold his tongue 232 *fatal brand* (the prince of
Calydon, Meleager, died when his mother, Althaea, in a rage burned a
piece of wood [brand] upon which the Fates had said his life depended)
238 *Nevils'* i.e. Salisbury's and Warwick's 242 *Lancaster* (Henry VI was
also Duke of Lancaster)

Then, York, be still awhile, till time do serve.
Watch thou and wake when others be asleep,
To pry into the secrets of the state,
Till Henry, surfeiting in joys of love,
With his new bride and England's dear-bought queen,
251   And Humphrey with the peers be fallen at jars.
252   Then will I raise aloft the milk-white rose,
With whose sweet smell the air shall be perfumed,
And in my standard bear the arms of York
To grapple with the house of Lancaster;
256   And force perforce I'll make him yield the crown
Whose bookish rule hath pulled fair England down.

Exit York.

*

I, ii   *Enter Duke Humphrey [of Gloucester] and his wife*
         Eleanor.

ELEANOR

Why droops my lord like over-ripened corn
2   Hanging the head at Ceres' plenteous load?
Why doth the great Duke Humphrey knit his brows,
As frowning at the favors of the world?
Why are thine eyes fixed to the sullen earth,
Gazing on that which seems to dim thy sight?
What seest thou there? King Henry's diadem,
8   Enchased with all the honors of the world?
9   If so, gaze on and grovel on thy face
Until thy head be circled with the same.
Put forth thy hand, reach at the glorious gold.
What, is't too short? I'll lengthen it with mine;
And having both together heaved it up,
We'll both together lift our heads to heaven

---

251 *be … jars* quarrel   252 *milk-white rose* (the symbol of the house of York)   256 *force perforce* by violent force
I, ii The Duke of Gloucester's house   2 *Ceres* goddess of agriculture   8 *Enchased* adorned   9 *grovel … face* i.e. in adoration

And never more abase our sight so low
As to vouchsafe one glance unto the ground.

GLOUCESTER

O Nell, sweet Nell, if thou dost love thy lord,
Banish the canker of ambitious thoughts.   18
And may that thought, when I imagine ill
Against my king and nephew, virtuous Henry,
Be my last breathing in this mortal world.
My troublous dreams this night doth make me sad.

ELEANOR

What dreamed my lord? Tell me, and I'll requite it
With sweet rehearsal of my morning's dream.

GLOUCESTER

Methought this staff, mine office-badge in court,
Was broke in twain, by whom I have forgot,
But as I think, it was by th' cardinal;
And on the pieces of the broken wand
Were placed the heads of Edmund Duke of Somerset
And William de la Pole, first Duke of Suffolk.
This was my dream; what it doth bode, God knows.

ELEANOR

Tut, this was nothing but an argument   32
That he that breaks a stick of Gloucester's grove
Shall lose his head for his presumption.
But list to me, my Humphrey, my sweet duke.
Methought I sat in seat of majesty
In the cathedral church of Westminster;
And in that chair where kings and queens were crowned,
Where Henry and Dame Margaret kneeled to me
And on my head did set the diadem—

GLOUCESTER

Nay, Eleanor, then must I chide outright.
Presumptuous dame, ill-nurtured Eleanor,   42
Art thou not second woman in the realm,
And the Protector's wife, beloved of him?

18 *canker* ulcer   32 *argument* proof   42 *ill-nurtured* ill-bred

Hast thou not worldly pleasure at command
Above the reach or compass of thy thought?
47   And wilt thou still be hammering treachery
To tumble down thy husband and thyself
From top of honor to disgrace's feet?
Away from me, and let me hear no more.

ELEANOR
What, what, my lord? Are you so choleric
With Eleanor for telling but her dream?
Next time I'll keep my dreams unto myself
54   And not be checked.

GLOUCESTER
Nay, be not angry. I am pleased again.
    Enter Messenger.

MESSENGER
My Lord Protector, 'tis his highness' pleasure
You do prepare to ride unto Saint Albans,
Where as the king and queen do mean to hawk.

GLOUCESTER
I go. Come, Nell, thou wilt ride with us?

ELEANOR
Yes, my good lord, I'll follow presently.
    Exit Humphrey [with Messenger].
Follow I must; I cannot go before
While Gloucester bears this base and humble mind.
Were I a man, a duke, and next of blood,
I would remove these tedious stumbling blocks
And smooth my way upon their headless necks;
And being a woman, I will not be slack
To play my part in Fortune's pageant.
68   Where are you there? Sir John! Nay, fear not, man.
We are alone; here's none but thee, and I.
    Enter Hume.

HUME
Jesus preserve your royal majesty.

---

47 *hammering* hammering out, devising   54 *checked* rebuked   68 *Sir* (the
title of respect given priests as well as knights)

ELEANOR
>What say'st thou? Majesty? I am but grace.   71

HUME
>But by the grace of God and Hume's advice
>Your grace's title shall be multiplied.

ELEANOR
>What say'st thou, man? Hast thou as yet conferred
>With Margery Jourdain, the cunning witch,
>With Roger Bolingbroke, the conjurer?
>And will they undertake to do me good?

HUME
>This they have promisèd, to show your highness
>A spirit raised from depth of under ground
>That shall make answer to such questions
>As by your grace shall be propounded him.

ELEANOR
>It is enough. I'll think upon the questions.
>When from Saint Albans we do make return
>We'll see these things effected to the full.
>Here, Hume, take this reward; make merry, man,
>With thy confederates in this weighty cause.

Exit Eleanor.

HUME
>Hume must make merry with the duchess' gold.
>Marry and shall! But how now, Sir John Hume?   88
>Seal up your lips and give no words but mum;
>The business asketh silent secrecy.
>Dame Eleanor gives gold to bring the witch;
>Gold cannot come amiss, were she a devil.
>Yet have I gold flies from another coast:
>I dare not say, from the rich cardinal
>And from the great and new-made Duke of Suffolk;
>Yet I do find it so; for, to be plain,
>They (knowing Dame Eleanor's aspiring humor)   97

71 *grace* (only monarchs could be addressed as 'majesty'; 'grace' was the proper appellation for a duke or duchess)   88 *Marry and shall* indeed he will   97 *humor* inclination

Have hirèd me to undermine the duchess
99   And buzz these conjurations in her brain.
100   They say, 'A crafty knave does need no broker';
Yet am I Suffolk and the cardinal's broker.
Hume, if you take not heed, you shall go near
To call them both a pair of crafty knaves.
Well, so it stands; and thus, I fear, at last
105   Hume's knavery will be the duchess' wrack
106   And her attainture will be Humphrey's fall.
107   Sort how it will, I shall have gold for all.   *Exit.*

*

I, iii   *Enter three or four Petitioners, the Armorer's Man*
            [Peter] being one.

1. PETITIONER My masters, let's stand close. My Lord
    Protector will come this way by and by, and then we
3   may deliver our supplications in the quill.
2. PETITIONER Marry, the Lord protect him, for he's a
    good man, Jesu bless him!
        Enter Suffolk and Queen.
1. PETITIONER Here 'a comes, methinks, and the queen
    with him. I'll be the first, sure.
2. PETITIONER Come back, fool. This is the Duke of
    Suffolk and not my Lord Protector.
SUFFOLK How now, fellow? Wouldst anything with me?
1. PETITIONER I pray, my lord, pardon me. I took ye
    for my Lord Protector.
QUEEN For my Lord Protector? Are your supplications
    to his lordship? Let me see them. What is thine?
1. PETITIONER Mine is, an't please your grace, against
    John Goodman, my Lord Cardinal's man, for keeping
    my house, and lands, and wife and all, from me.

---

99 *buzz* whisper   100 *broker* agent   105 *wrack* ruin   106 *attainture*
conviction   107 *Sort . . . will* no matter how it turns out
I, iii The palace   3 *in the quill* (1) in a body, (2) illiterate error for 'in
sequel' (?)

SUFFOLK Thy wife too? That's some wrong indeed.
  What's yours? What's here? *[reads]* 'Against the Duke
  of Suffolk, for enclosing the commons of Melford.'   20
  How now, sir knave?

2. PETITIONER Alas, sir, I am but a poor petitioner of
  our whole township.

PETER *[presents his petition]* Against my master, Thomas
  Horner, for saying that the Duke of York was rightful
  heir to the crown.

QUEEN What say'st thou? Did the Duke of York say he
  was rightful heir to the crown?

PETER That my master was? No, forsooth! My master
  said that he was, and that the king was an usurper.

SUFFOLK Who is there?
        Enter Servant.
  Take this fellow in and send for his master with a pur-   32
  suivant presently. We'll hear more of your matter before
  the king.   *Exit [Servant with Peter].*

QUEEN
  And as for you that love to be protected
  Under the wings of our Protector's grace,
  Begin your suits anew and sue to him.
        Tear the supplication.
  Away, base cullions! Suffolk, let them go.   38

ALL Come, let's be gone.   *Exeunt.*

QUEEN
  My Lord of Suffolk, say, is this the guise,   40
  Is this the fashions in the court of England?
  Is this the government of Britain's isle,
  And this the royalty of Albion's king?   43
  What, shall King Henry be a pupil still,
  Under the surly Gloucester's governance?
  Am I a queen in title and in style
  And must be made a subject to a duke?

---

20 *enclosing the commons* fencing public ground for private use **32**
pursuivant officer **38** *cullions* rascals, scum **40** *guise* manner **43**
Albion's England's

I tell thee, Pole, when in the city Tours
49 Thou ran'st a-tilt in honor of my love
And stol'st away the ladies' hearts of France,
I thought King Henry had resembled thee
52 In courage, courtship, and proportion;
But all his mind is bent to holiness,
54 To number Ave-Maries on his beads;
55 His champions are the prophets and apostles,
56 His weapons holy saws of sacred writ;
His study is his tiltyard, and his loves
Are brazen images of canonized saints.
59 I would the college of the cardinals
Would choose him pope and carry him to Rome
61 And set the triple crown upon his head.
That were a state fit for his holiness.

SUFFOLK
Madam, be patient. As I was cause
Your highness came to England, so will I
In England work your grace's full content.

QUEEN
Beside the haughty Protector, have we Beaufort
The imperious churchman, Somerset, Buckingham,
And grumbling York; and not the least of these
But can do more in England than the king.

SUFFOLK
70 And he of these that can do most of all
Cannot do more in England than the Nevils;
Salisbury and Warwick are no simple peers.

QUEEN
Not all these lords do vex me half so much
As that proud dame, the Lord Protector's wife.

---

49 *ran'st a-tilt* jousted   **52** *courtship* courtliness; *proportion* physique   **54**
Ave-Maries Hail Maries (prayers to the Blessed Virgin)   **55** *champions*
defenders (with reference to valiant fighting men who defend the honor
and title of the king)   **56** *saws* sayings   **59** *college . . . cardinals* the pope's
council   **61** *triple crown* papal crown

She sweeps it through the court with troops of ladies,
More like an empress than Duke Humphrey's wife.
Strangers in court do take her for the queen.
She bears a duke's revenues on her back,
And in her heart she scorns our poverty.
Shall I not live to be avenged on her ?
Contemptuous base-born callet as she is,   81
She vaunted 'mongst her minions t' other day,
The very train of her worst wearing gown
Was better worth than all my father's lands
Till Suffolk gave two dukedoms for his daughter.

SUFFOLK
Madam, myself have limed a bush for her,   86
And placed a choir of such enticing birds   87
And she will light to listen to the lays
That never mount to trouble you again.
So let her rest. And, madam, list to me,
For I am bold to counsel you in this :
Although we fancy not the cardinal,
Yet must we join with him and with the lords
Till we have brought Duke Humphrey in disgrace.
As for the Duke of York, this late complaint
Will make but little for his benefit.
So one by one we'll weed them all at last.
And you yourself shall steer the happy helm.   98

     *Sound a sennet. Enter the King, [York and
     Somerset on both sides of the King, whispering with
     him,] Duke Humphrey [of Gloucester], Cardinal
     [Beaufort], Buckingham, Salisbury, Warwick,
     and [Eleanor] the Duchess [of Gloucester].*

KING
For my part, noble lords, I care not which :
Or Somerset or York, all's one to me.

---

81 *callet* strumpet   86 *limed a bush* put lime on twigs of a bush to catch
birds, i.e. set a trap   87 *enticing birds* i.e. decoys   98 s.d. *sennet* trumpet
call signalling a ceremonial entrance or exit

YORK
  If York have ill demeaned himself in France,
102 Then let him be denayed the regentship.

SOMERSET
  If Somerset be unworthy of the place,
  Let York be regent; I will yield to him.

WARWICK
  Whether your grace be worthy, yea or no,
  Dispute not that. York is the worthier.

CARDINAL
  Ambitious Warwick, let thy betters speak!

WARWICK
  The cardinal's not my better in the field.

BUCKINGHAM
  All in this presence are thy betters, Warwick.

WARWICK
  Warwick may live to be the best of all.

SALISBURY
  Peace, son! and show some reason, Buckingham,
  Why Somerset should be preferred in this.

QUEEN
  Because the king forsooth will have it so.

GLOUCESTER
  Madam, the king is old enough himself
115 To give his censure. These are no women's matters.

QUEEN
  If he be old enough, what needs your grace
  To be Protector of his excellence?

GLOUCESTER
  Madam, I am Protector of the realm,
  And at his pleasure will resign my place.

SUFFOLK
  Resign it then and leave thine insolence.
  Since thou wert king (as who is king but thou?)
  The commonwealth hath daily run to wrack,

102 *denayed* denied   115 *censure* decision

The Dauphin hath prevailed beyond the seas,   123
And all the peers and nobles of the realm
Have been as bondmen to thy sovereignty.

CARDINAL
The commons hast thou racked; the clergy's bags   126
Are lank and lean with thy extortions.

SOMERSET
Thy sumptuous buildings and thy wife's attire   128
Have cost a mass of public treasury.

BUCKINGHAM
Thy cruelty in execution
Upon offenders hath exceeded law,
And left thee to the mercy of the law.

QUEEN
Thy sale of offices and towns in France –
If they were known, as the suspect is great –   134
Would make thee quickly hop without thy head.
                              Exit Humphrey.

        [The Queen drops her fan.]
Give me my fan. What, minion, can ye not?
        She gives the Duchess a box on the ear.
I cry you mercy, madam. Was it you?   137

ELEANOR
Was't I? Yea, I it was, proud Frenchwoman.
Could I come near your beauty with my nails,
I would set my ten commandments in your face.   140

KING
Sweet aunt, be quiet. 'Twas against her will.   141

ELEANOR
Against her will, good king? Look to't in time.
She'll hamper thee and dandle thee like a baby.   143

123 *Dauphin* eldest son of the King of France; here, Charles VII (so called
by the English because they consider Henry VI the true King of France)
126 *racked* taxed exorbitantly (literally, tortured on the rack)   128
sumptuous buildings (Somerset refers specifically to Greenwich Palace)
134 *suspect* suspicion   137 *cry you mercy* beg your pardon   140 *ten
commandments* i.e. fingernails   141 *against her will* i.e. an accident   143
hamper (1) obstruct, (2) cradle

144   Though in this place most master wear no breeches,
       She shall not strike Dame Eleanor unrevenged.

                                          Exit Eleanor.

BUCKINGHAM
    Lord Cardinal, I will follow Eleanor,
    And listen after Humphrey, how he proceeds.
148   She's tickled now ; her fume needs no spurs,
       She'll gallop far enough to her destruction.

                                       Exit Buckingham.
       Enter [Duke] Humphrey.

GLOUCESTER
    Now, lords, my choler being overblown
    With walking once about the quadrangle,
    I come to talk of commonwealth affairs.
    As for your spiteful false objections,
    Prove them, and I lie open to the law ;
    But God in mercy so deal with my soul
    As I in duty love my king and country.
    But to the matter that we have in hand :
158   I say, my sovereign, York is meetest man
       To be your regent in the realm of France.

SUFFOLK
    Before we make election, give me leave
    To show some reason, of no little force,
    That York is most unmeet of any man.

YORK
    I'll tell thee, Suffolk, why I am unmeet :
    First, for I cannot flatter thee in pride ;
    Next, if I be appointed for the place,
    My Lord of Somerset will keep me here
167   Without discharge, money, or furniture
       Till France be won into the Dauphin's hands.
169   Last time I danced attendance on his will
       Till Paris was besieged, famished, and lost.

---

144 *most master* the greatest master (i.e. the queen, who wears no breeches)   148 *tickled* irritated ; *fume* rage   158 *meetest* fittest   167 *furniture* furnishings   169 *Last time* (cf. *1 Henry VI*, IV, iii, 9–11)

WARWICK

    That can I witness; and a fouler fact   171
    Did never traitor in the land commit.

SUFFOLK

    Peace, headstrong Warwick!

WARWICK

    Image of pride, why should I hold my peace?
        Enter [Horner the] Armorer, and his Man
        [Peter, guarded].

SUFFOLK

    Because here is a man accused of treason.
    Pray God the Duke of York excuse himself.

YORK

    Doth any one accuse York for a traitor?

KING

    What mean'st thou, Suffolk? Tell me, what are these?

SUFFOLK

    Please it your majesty, this is the man
    That doth accuse his master of high treason.
    His words were these: that Richard Duke of York
    Was rightful heir unto the English crown
    And that your majesty was an usurper.

KING

    Say, man, were these thy words?

ARMORER An't shall please your majesty, I never said
nor thought any such matter. God is my witness, I am
falsely accused by the villain.

PETER By these ten bones, my lords, he did speak them 188
to me in the garret one night, as we were scouring my
Lord of York's armor.

YORK

    Base dunghill villain and mechanical,   191
    I'll have thy head for this thy traitor's speech.
    I do beseech your royal majesty,
    Let him have all the rigor of the law.

---

171 *fact* deed   188 *ten bones* i.e. fingers   191 *mechanical* manual laborer,
i.e. low person

ARMORER Alas, my lord, hang me if ever I spake the words! My accuser is my prentice; and when I did correct him for his fault the other day, he did vow upon his knees he would be even with me. I have good witness of this. Therefore I beseech your majesty, do not cast away an honest man for a villain's accusation.

KING
Uncle, what shall we say to this in law?

GLOUCESTER
202   This doom, my lord, if I may judge:
Let Somerset be regent o'er the French,
Because in York this breeds suspicion;
And let these have a day appointed them
For single combat in convenient place,
For he hath witness of his servant's malice.
This is the law, and this Duke Humphrey's doom.

SOMERSET
I humbly thank your royal majesty.

ARMORER
And I accept the combat willingly.

PETER Alas, my lord, I cannot fight; for God's sake pity my case. The spite of man prevaileth against me. O Lord have mercy upon me; I shall never be able to fight a blow. O Lord, my heart!

GLOUCESTER
Sirrah, or you must fight or else be hanged.

KING
Away with them to prison! and the day
Of combat shall be the last of the next month.
Come, Somerset, we'll see thee sent away.

Flourish. Exeunt.

❋

---

202 *doom* judgment

Enter [Margery Jourdain] the Witch, the two Priests   I, iv
[Hume and Southwell], and Bolingbroke.

HUME Come, my masters. The duchess, I tell you, expects performance of your promises.

BOLINGBROKE Master Hume, we are therefore provided. Will her ladyship behold and hear our exorcisms?   4

HUME Ay, what else? Fear you not her courage.

BOLINGBROKE I have heard her reported to be a woman of an invincible spirit. But it shall be convenient, Master Hume, that you be by her aloft while we be busy below; and so I pray you go in God's name and leave us. (*Exit Hume.*) Mother Jourdain, be you prostrate and grovel on the earth. John Southwell, read you, and let us to our work.

Enter [Duchess] Eleanor aloft [, followed by Hume].

ELEANOR Well said, my masters, and welcome all. To this gear, the sooner the better.   13

BOLINGBROKE

Patience, good lady; wizards know their times.
Deep night, dark night, the silence of the night,
The time of night when Troy was set on fire,
The time when screech owls cry and bandogs howl   17
And spirits walk and ghosts break up their graves –
That time best fits the work we have in hand.
Madam, sit you and fear not. Whom we raise
We will make fast within a hallowed verge.   21

Here do the ceremonies belonging [to conjuring],
and make the circle. Bolingbroke or Southwell reads:
'Conjuro te,' etc. It thunders and lightens terribly;
then the Spirit riseth.

SPIRIT Adsum.   22

WITCH Asnath,   23

I, iv Gloucester's house   4 *exorcisms* conjurations   13 *gear* business   17 *bandogs* leashed watch-dogs   21 *verge* circle; s.d. *Conjuro te* I conjure you (the beginning of a typical conjuration; it would perhaps continue 'by the infernal powers' and, after these were named, 'to appear')   22 *Adsum* I am here   23 *Asnath* (anagram of 'Sat[h]an'; evil spirits were frequently addressed in anagrams)

By the eternal God, whose name and power
Thou tremblest at, answer that I shall ask;
For till thou speak thou shalt not pass from hence.

SPIRIT

27   Ask what thou wilt. That I had said and done!

BOLINGBROKE *[reads]*

'First of the king; what shall of him become?'

SPIRIT

29   The duke yet lives that Henry shall depose;
But him outlive, and die a violent death.
     [As the Spirit speaks, Southwell writes the answer.]

BOLINGBROKE

'What fates await the Duke of Suffolk?'

SPIRIT

By water shall he die and take his end.

BOLINGBROKE

'What shall befall the Duke of Somerset?'

SPIRIT

Let him shun castles.
Safer shall he be upon the sandy plains
Than where castles mounted stand.

37   Have done, for more I hardly can endure.

BOLINGBROKE

Descend to darkness and the burning lake.

39   False fiend, avoid!   *Thunder and lightning. Exit Spirit*
                              [sinking down again].
     Enter the Duke of York and the Duke of Buckingham,
     with their Guard, and break in.

YORK

Lay hands upon these traitors and their trash.

41   Beldam, I think we watched you at an inch.
What, madam, are you there? The king and common-
     weal

---

27 *That* would that   29–30 *The ... death* (deliberately ambiguous; cf. ll.
60–61)   37 *Have done* finish quickly   39 *False* treacherous (without
reference to the information he has given); *avoid* begone   41 *Beldam*
witch; *at an inch* closely

Are deeply indebted for this piece of pains.
My Lord Protector will, I doubt it not,
See you well guerdoned for these good deserts.   45

ELEANOR
Not half so bad as thine to England's king,
Injurious duke, that threatest where's no cause.   47

BUCKINGHAM
True, madam, none at all. What call you this?
    [Shows her the papers.]
Away with them! Let them be clapped up close   49
And kept asunder. You, madam, shall with us.
Stafford, take her to thee.   51
We'll see your trinkets here all forthcoming.   52
All away!   *Exit [Stafford, those above and those below*
                    following, guarded].

YORK
Lord Buckingham, methinks you watched her well.
A pretty plot, well chosen to build upon.
Now pray, my lord, let's see the devil's writ.   56
What have we here?
    Reads.
'The duke yet lives that Henry shall depose;
But him outlive, and die a violent death.'
Why, this is just 'Aio te, Aeacida,   60
Romanos vincere posse.' Well, to the rest:
'Tell me, what fate awaits the Duke of Suffolk?'
'By water shall he die and take his end.'
'What shall betide the Duke of Somerset?'
'Let him shun castles.

45 *guerdoned ... deserts* rewarded for these worthy actions (ironically)   47
Injurious insulting   49 *clapped up* imprisoned   51 *Stafford* (presumably
the captain of the guard and one of Buckingham's kinsmen)   52 *We'll ...
forthcoming* we'll take charge of your magic gear until it is produced as
evidence against you   56 *devil's writ* devil's writing (as opposed to Holy
Writ)   60 *just* precisely   60–61 *Aio ... posse* (1) I say that you, descendant of Aeacus, can overcome the Romans, (2) I say that the Romans can
overcome you, descendant of Aeacus (the ambiguous answer given by the
oracle to Pyrrhus, king of Epirus, when he asked whether he could conquer
Rome)

Safer shall he be upon the sandy plains
Than where castles mounted stand.'
Come, come, my lords; these oracles

69   Are hardly attained and hardly understood.
The king is now in progress towards Saint Albans,
With him the husband of this lovely lady.
Thither goes these news as fast as horse can carry them –
A sorry breakfast for my Lord Protector.

BUCKINGHAM

Your grace shall give me leave, my Lord of York,
To be the post, in hope of his reward.

YORK

At your pleasure, my good lord.   *[Exit Buckingham.]*
                  Who's within there, ho?
      Enter a Servingman.
Invite my lords of Salisbury and Warwick
To sup with me to-morrow night. Away!   *Exeunt.*

✳

II, i   *Enter the King, Queen, [with her hawk on her fist,]*
    Protector [Gloucester], Cardinal, and Suffolk, [as if
    they came from hawking;] with Falconers halloaing.

QUEEN

1   Believe me, lords, for flying at the brook
2   I saw not better sport these seven years' day.
    Yet, by your leave, the wind was very high,
4   And ten to one old Joan had not gone out.

KING *[to Gloucester]*

5   But what a point, my lord, your falcon made
6   And what a pitch she flew above the rest.

---

69 *hardly . . . hardly* with difficulty . . . barely
II, i St Albans   1 *at the brook* beside the brook, i.e. for water-fowl   2 *these . . . day* for the last seven years   4 *had . . . out* would not have flown at the game (because of the wind)   5 *point* position of vantage to windward about which the hawk flies as she awaits her prey   6 *pitch* altitude; the peak of the hawk's flight, from which she swoops down

To see how God in all his creatures works:
Yea, man and birds are fain of climbing high.

SUFFOLK
No marvel, an it like your majesty,
My Lord Protector's hawks do tower so well;   10
They know their master loves to be aloft
And bears his thoughts above his falcon's pitch.

GLOUCESTER
My lord, 'tis but a base ignoble mind
That mounts no higher than a bird can soar.

CARDINAL
I thought as much. He would be above the clouds.

GLOUCESTER
Ay, my Lord Cardinal, how think you by that?
Were it not good your grace could fly to heaven?

KING
The treasury of everlasting joy.

CARDINAL
Thy heaven is on earth, thine eyes and thoughts
Beat on a crown, the treasure of thy heart;
Pernicious Protector, dangerous peer,
That smooth'st it so with king and commonweal.   22

GLOUCESTER
What, cardinal, is your priesthood grown peremptory?
'Tantaene animis coelestibus irae?'   24
Churchmen so hot? Good uncle, hide such malice;
With such holiness can you do it.   26

SUFFOLK
No malice, sir, no more than well becomes
So good a quarrel and so bad a peer.

GLOUCESTER
As who, my lord?

10 *hawks* (Suffolk and later the cardinal allude not only to the hawks just flown by Gloucester but also to his heraldic badge, a hawk with a maiden's head) 22 *smooth'st it* flatters 24 *Tantaene ... irae?* do heavenly minds nourish such great wrath? (*Aeneid*, I, 11) 26 *can you* i.e. you can (but defective metre suggests that the line is corrupt)

55

SUFFOLK   Why, as you, my lord,
An't like your lordly Lord's Protectorship.

GLOUCESTER
Why, Suffolk, England knows thine insolence.

QUEEN
And thy ambition, Gloucester.

KING   I prithee, peace,
Good queen, and whet not on these furious peers,
For blessed are the peacemakers on earth.

CARDINAL
Let me be blessed for the peace I make
Against this proud Protector with my sword.

GLOUCESTER [aside to Cardinal]
Faith, holy uncle, would 'twere come to that.

CARDINAL [aside to Gloucester]
Marry, when thou dar'st.

GLOUCESTER [aside to Cardinal]
39   Make up no factious numbers for the matter;
In thine own person answer thy abuse.

CARDINAL [aside to Gloucester]
Ay, where thou dar'st not peep; and if thou dar'st,
This evening on the east side of the grove.

KING
How now, my lords?

CARDINAL   Believe me, cousin Gloucester,
44   Had not your man put up the fowl so suddenly,
We had had more sport. – [Aside to Gloucester] Come
with thy two-hand sword.

GLOUCESTER
True uncle –
     [Aside to Cardinal]
47   Are ye advised? The east side of the grove.

CARDINAL [aside to Gloucester]
I am with you.

---

39 Make ... numbers do not make up a war-party 44 put ... fowl startled
the game into flight 47 advised agreed

KING   Why, how now, uncle Gloucester?

GLOUCESTER
   Talking of hawking; nothing else, my lord.
      [Aside to Cardinal]
   Now, by God's Mother, priest, I'll shave your crown for
     this,
   Or all my fence shall fail.   51

CARDINAL *[aside to Gloucester]*
   'Medice, teipsum.'   52
   Protector, see to't well; protect yourself.

KING
   The winds grow high; so do your stomachs, lords.   54
   How irksome is this music to my heart!
   When such strings jar, what hope of harmony?
   I pray, my lords, let me compound this strife.   57
      Enter one [Townsman] crying 'A miracle!'

GLOUCESTER
   What means this noise?
   Fellow, what miracle dost thou proclaim?

TOWNSMAN
   A miracle! a miracle!

SUFFOLK
   Come to the king and tell him what miracle.

TOWNSMAN
   Forsooth, a blind man at Saint Alban's shrine
   Within this half hour hath received his sight –
   A man that ne'er saw in his life before.

KING
   Now God be praised, that to believing souls
   Gives light in darkness, comfort in despair.
      Enter the Mayor of Saint Albans and his Brethren,
      [with music,] bearing the man [Simpcox] between
      two in a chair [, Simpcox's Wife and a crowd of
      Townsmen following].

---

51 *fence* skill in swordsmanship   52 *Medice, teipsum* physician, [cure]
thyself   54 *stomachs* passions   57 *compound* compose

CARDINAL

67   Here comes the townsmen on procession
      To present your highness with the man.

KING

      Great is his comfort in this earthly vale,
      Although by his sight his sin be multiplied.

GLOUCESTER

      Stand by, my masters. Bring him near the king;
      His highness' pleasure is to talk with him.

KING

      Good fellow, tell us here the circumstance,
      That we for thee may glorify the Lord.
      What, hast thou been long blind, and now restored?

SIMPCOX

      Born blind, an't please your grace.

WIFE Ay indeed was he.

SUFFOLK What woman is this?

WIFE His wife, an't like your worship.

GLOUCESTER

80   Hadst thou been his mother, thou couldst have better
      told.

KING

      Where wert thou born?

SIMPCOX

      At Berwick in the North, an't like your grace.

KING

      Poor soul, God's goodness hath been great to thee.
      Let never day nor night unhallowed pass
      But still remember what the Lord hath done.

QUEEN

      Tell me, good fellow, cam'st thou here by chance
      Or of devotion to this holy shrine?

SIMPCOX

      God knows, of pure devotion, being called
      A hundred times and oft'ner in my sleep

67 *on* in

By good Saint Alban, who said, 'Simon, come;   90
Come offer at my shrine and I will help thee.'

WIFE
Most true, forsooth, and many time and oft
Myself have heard a voice to call him so.

CARDINAL
What, art thou lame?

SIMPCOX   Ay, God Almighty help me.

SUFFOLK
How cam'st thou so?

SIMPCOX   A fall off of a tree.

WIFE
A plum tree, master.

GLOUCESTER   How long hast thou been blind?

SIMPCOX
O, born so, master.

GLOUCESTER   What, and wouldst climb a tree?

SIMPCOX
But that in all my life, when I was a youth.   98

WIFE
Too true, and bought his climbing very dear.

GLOUCESTER
Mass, thou lovedst plums well, that wouldst venture so.

SIMPCOX
Alas, good master, my wife desired some damsons   101
And made me climb, with danger of my life.

GLOUCESTER
A subtle knave. But yet it shall not serve.
Let me see thine eyes. Wink now. Now open them.
In my opinion yet thou seest not well.

SIMPCOX Yes, master, clear as day, I thank God and Saint
Alban.

GLOUCESTER
Say'st thou me so? What color is this cloak of?

90 *Simon* (the name of which Simpcox [Simon-boy] is an informal variant)
98 *But ... life* never in all my life except   101 *damsons* a kind of plum

SIMPCOX
Red, master; red as blood.

GLOUCESTER
110 Why, that's well said. What color is my gown of?

SIMPCOX
Black, forsooth; coal-black, as jet.

KING
Why then, thou know'st what color jet is of?

SUFFOLK
And yet, I think, jet did he never see.

GLOUCESTER
But cloaks and gowns before this day a many.

WIFE
Never before this day in all his life.

GLOUCESTER Tell me, sirrah, what's my name?

SIMPCOX Alas, master, I know not.

GLOUCESTER What's his name?

SIMPCOX I know not.

GLOUCESTER Nor his?

SIMPCOX No indeed, master.

GLOUCESTER What's thine own name?

SIMPCOX Saunder Simpcox, an if it please you, master.

GLOUCESTER Then, Saunder, sit there, the lying'st
knave in Christendom. If thou hadst been born blind,
thou mightst as well have known all our names as thus to
name the several colors we do wear. Sight may dis-
128 tinguish of colors; but suddenly to nominate them all, it
is impossible. My lords, Saint Alban here hath done a
miracle; and would ye not think his cunning to be great
that could restore this cripple to his legs again?

SIMPCOX O master, that you could!

GLOUCESTER My masters of Saint Albans, have you not
134 beadles in your town, and things called whips?

MAYOR Yes, my lord, if it please your grace.

128 *nominate* name   134 *beadles* constables

GLOUCESTER Then send for one presently.

MAYOR Sirrah, go fetch the beadle hither straight.
                                    Exit [a Townsman].

GLOUCESTER Now fetch me a stool hither by and by. *[A
stool brought.]* Now, sirrah, if you mean to save yourself
from whipping, leap me over this stool and run away. 140

SIMPCOX
    Alas, master, I am not able to stand alone;
    You go about to torture me in vain.
                Enter a Beadle with whips.

GLOUCESTER Well, sir, we must have you find your legs.
    Sirrah beadle, whip him till he leap over that same stool.

BEADLE I will, my lord. Come on, sirrah, off with your
    doublet quickly.

SIMPCOX Alas, master, what shall I do? I am not able to
    stand.
                *After the Beadle hath hit him once, he leaps over the
                stool and runs away; and they follow and cry
                'A miracle!'*

KING
    O God, seest thou this, and bearest so long?

QUEEN
    It made me laugh to see the villain run.

GLOUCESTER
    Follow the knave, and take this drab away.   151

WIFE
    Alas, sir, we did it for pure need.

GLOUCESTER Let them be whipped through every mar-
    ket town till they come to Berwick, from whence they
    came.   *Exit [Mayor with the Townsmen].*

CARDINAL
    Duke Humphrey has done a miracle to-day.

SUFFOLK
    True; made the lame to leap and fly away.

140 *me* for me (ethical dative)   151 *drab* low woman

GLOUCESTER
But you have done more miracles than I ;
158   You made in a day, my lord, whole towns to fly.
Enter Buckingham.

KING
What tidings with our cousin Buckingham ?

BUCKINGHAM
Such as my heart doth tremble to unfold.
161   A sort of naughty persons, lewdly bent,
Under the countenance and confederacy
Of Lady Eleanor, the Protector's wife,
164   The ringleader and head of all this rout,
Have practiced dangerously against your state,
Dealing with witches and with conjurers,
Whom we have apprehended in the fact,
Raising up wicked spirits from under ground,
169   Demanding of King Henry's life and death
And other of your highness' privy council,
171   As more at large your grace shall understand.

CARDINAL *[aside to Gloucester]*
And so, my Lord Protector, by this means
173   Your lady is forthcoming yet at London.
This news, I think, hath turned your weapon's edge.
'Tis like, my lord, you will not keep your hour.

GLOUCESTER *[aside to Cardinal]*
Ambitious churchman, leave to afflict my heart.
Sorrow and grief have vanquished all my powers ;
And, vanquished as I am, I yield to thee
Or to the meanest groom.

KING
O God, what mischiefs work the wicked ones,
Heaping confusion on their own heads thereby !

---

158 *made . . . fly* i.e. by giving the French provinces away in exchange for
the queen **161** *sort* gang; *naughty* worthless (with implications of
wickedness); *lewdly* wickedly **164** *rout* disorderly crowd **169**
Demanding inquiring **171** *at large* in full **173** *forthcoming* to be tried (see
I, iv, 52)

QUEEN

  Gloucester, see here the taincture of thy nest,   182
  And look thyself be faultless, thou wert best.

GLOUCESTER

  Madam, for myself, to heaven I do appeal,
  How I have loved my king and commonweal ;
  And for my wife, I know not how it stands.
  Sorry I am to hear what I have heard.
  Noble she is ; but if she have forgot
  Honor and virtue and conversed with such
  As, like to pitch, defile nobility,
  I banish her my bed and company
  And give her as a prey to law and shame
  That hath dishonored Gloucester's honest name.

KING

  Well, for this night we will repose us here.
  To-morrow toward London back again
  To look into this business thoroughly
  And call these foul offenders to their answers
  And poise the cause in justice' equal scales,   198
  Whose beam stands sure, whose rightful cause prevails.   199

                        Flourish. Exeunt.

✳

      Enter York, Salisbury, and Warwick.   II, ii

YORK

  Now, my good Lords of Salisbury and Warwick,
  Our simple supper ended, give me leave
  In this close walk to satisfy myself   3
  In craving your opinion of my title,
  Which is infallible, to England's crown.

SALISBURY

  My lord, I long to hear it at full.

---

182 *taincture* fouling (with overtones of 'treason')   **198** *poise* weigh   **199**
stands sure is perfectly level (indicating no bias)
II, ii The Duke of York's garden   **3** *close* private, secluded

WARWICK
    Sweet York, begin ; and if thy claim be good,
    The Nevils are thy subjects to command.
YORK
    Then thus :
10   Edward the Third, my lords, had seven sons :
    The first, Edward the Black Prince, Prince of Wales ;
    The second, William of Hatfield ; and the third,
    Lionel Duke of Clarence ; next to whom
    Was John of Gaunt, the Duke of Lancaster ;
    The fifth was Edmund Langley, Duke of York ;
    The sixth was Thomas of Woodstock, Duke of Gloucester ;
    William of Windsor was the seventh and last.
    Edward the Black Prince died before his father
    And left behind him Richard, his only son,
20   Who after Edward the Third's death reigned as king
    Till Henry Bolingbroke, Duke of Lancaster,
    The eldest son and heir of John of Gaunt,
    Crowned by the name of Henry the Fourth,
    Seized on the realm, deposed the rightful king,
    Sent his poor queen to France from whence she came,
    And him to Pomfret, where, as all you know,
    Harmless Richard was murdered traitorously.
WARWICK
    Father, the duke hath told the truth.
    Thus got the house of Lancaster the crown.
YORK
30   Which now they hold by force, and not by right ;
    For Richard, the first son's heir, being dead,
    The issue of the next son should have reigned.
SALISBURY
    But William of Hatfield died without an heir.
YORK
    The third son, Duke of Clarence, from whose line
    I claim the crown, had issue, Philippe, a daughter,
    Who married Edmund Mortimer, Earl of March.

Edmund had issue, Roger Earl of March;
Roger had issue, Edmund, Anne, and Eleanor.

SALISBURY

This Edmund in the reign of Bolingbroke,   39
As I have read, laid claim unto the crown;
And, but for Owen Glendower, had been king,
Who kept him in captivity till he died.
But to the rest.

YORK   His eldest sister, Anne,
My mother, being heir unto the crown,
Married Richard Earl of Cambridge, who was son
To Edmund Langley, Edward the Third's fifth son.
By her I claim the kingdom. She was heir
To Roger Earl of March, who was the son
Of Edmund Mortimer, who married Philippe,
Sole daughter unto Lionel Duke of Clarence.
So, if the issue of the elder son
Succeed before the younger, I am king.

WARWICK

What plain proceedings is more plain than this?   53
Henry doth claim the crown from John of Gaunt,
The fourth son; York claims it from the third.
Till Lionel's issue fails, his should not reign.   56
It fails not yet, but flourishes in thee

---

39 *Edmund* (Shakespeare here follows the chroniclers in an error and adds some confusion of his own. Edmund Mortimer, 3rd Earl of March, and son-in-law of Lionel, Duke of Clarence, actually had two sons, Roger, 4th Earl of March, and Sir Edmund. Sir Edmund was captured by Glendower and married his daughter [see *1 Henry IV*]. It was Roger Mortimer's son Edmund, 5th Earl of March and nephew of Sir Edmund, who was York's mother's brother and had been named heir to the throne by Richard II. These two are confused in *1 Henry IV* and *1 Henry VI* as well as here. But the further detail, that Edmund was kept by Glendower captive until his death [l. 42], seems to have been derived by Shakespeare incorrectly from Hall, who mentions, in conjunction with his account of Edmund, that Glendower kept Lord Grey of Ruthvin, another son-in-law, 'in captivitee till he died.')   **53** *proceedings* line of descent   **56** *his* i.e. Gaunt's

58   And in thy son, fair slips of such a stock.
        Then, father Salisbury, kneel we together,
        And in this private plot be we the first
        That shall salute our rightful sovereign
        With honor of his birthright to the crown.

BOTH
        Long live our sovereign Richard, England's king.

YORK
        We thank you, lords. But I am not your king
        Till I be crowned and that my sword be stained
        With heart-blood of the house of Lancaster.
        And that's not suddenly to be performed,
68   But with advice and silent secrecy.
        Do you as I do in these dangerous days:
70   Wink at the Duke of Suffolk's insolence,
        At Beaufort's pride, at Somerset's ambition,
        At Buckingham and all the crew of them,
        Till they have snared the shepherd of the flock,
        That virtuous prince, the good Duke Humphrey.
        'Tis that they seek; and they in seeking that
        Shall find their deaths, if York can prophesy.

SALISBURY
        My lord, break we off. We know your mind at full.

WARWICK
        My heart assures me that the Earl of Warwick
        Shall one day make the Duke of York a king.

YORK
        And, Nevil, this I do assure myself,
        Richard shall live to make the Earl of Warwick
        The greatest man in England but the king.   *Exeunt.*

*

---

58 *slips* cuttings   68 *advice* mature reflection   70 *Wink at* ignore

Sound trumpets. Enter the King and State, [i.e. the II, iii
Queen, Gloucester, Suffolk, Buckingham, and the
Cardinal,] with Guard, to banish the Duchess.
[Enter, guarded, the Duchess of Gloucester, Margery
Jourdain, Hume, Southwell, and Bolingbroke. And
then enter to them York, Salisbury, and Warwick.]

KING

Stand forth, Dame Eleanor Cobham, Gloucester's wife.
In sight of God and us your guilt is great.
Receive the sentence of the law for sins
Such as by God's book are adjudged to death.
    [To Jourdain and the others]
You four, from hence to prison back again ;
From thence unto the place of execution.
The witch in Smithfield shall be burned to ashes,
And you three shall be strangled on the gallows.
    [To the Duchess]
You, madam, for you are more nobly born,
Despoilèd of your honor in your life,   *10*
Shall, after three days' open penance done,
Live in your country here in banishment
With Sir John Stanley in the Isle of Man.

ELEANOR

Welcome is banishment. Welcome were my death.

GLOUCESTER

Eleanor, the law, thou seest, hath judgèd thee.
I cannot justify whom the law condemns.
                     [Exeunt the Duchess and the
                           other prisoners, guarded.]
Mine eyes are full of tears, my heart of grief.
Ah, Humphrey, this dishonor in thine age
Will bring thy head with sorrow to the ground.
I beseech your majesty give me leave to go ;
Sorrow would solace, and mine age would ease.   *21*

II, iii The palace in London   21 *would* would have

KING

   Stay, Humphrey Duke of Gloucester, ere thou go,
   Give up thy staff. Henry will to himself
   Protector be ; and God shall be my hope,
   My stay, my guide, and lantern to my feet.
   And go in peace, Humphrey, no less beloved
   Than when thou wert Protector to thy king.

QUEEN

   I see no reason why a king of years
   Should be to be protected like a child.
30   God and King Henry govern England's helm.
31   Give up your staff, sir, and the king his realm.

GLOUCESTER

   My staff ? Here, noble Henry, is my staff.
   As willingly do I the same resign
   As e'er thy father Henry made it mine ;
   And even as willingly at thy feet I leave it
   As others would ambitiously receive it.
   Farewell, good king. When I am dead and gone,
   May honorable peace attend thy throne. *Exit Gloucester.*

QUEEN

   Why, now is Henry king, and Margaret queen,
   And Humphrey Duke of Gloucester scarce himself,
41   That bears so shrewd a maim ; two pulls at once –
   His lady banished, and a limb lopped off.
43   This staff of honor raught, there let it stand
   Where it best fits to be, in Henry's hand.

SUFFOLK

   Thus droops this lofty pine and hangs his sprays ;
46   Thus Eleanor's pride dies in her youngest days.

YORK

   Lords, let him go. Please it your majesty,
   This is the day appointed for the combat,
   And ready are the appellant and defendant,

---

30 *govern* (with the Latin sense of 'steer')   **31** *king his* king's   **41** *bears . . . maim* suffers so severe a loss; *pulls* pluckings   **43** *raught* reached (by us)   **46** *in . . . days* at last (?)

The armorer and his man, to enter the lists;   50
So please your highness to behold the fight.

QUEEN

Ay, good my lord; for purposely therefore
Left I the court, to see this quarrel tried.

KING

A God's name see the lists and all things fit.   54
Here let them end it, and God defend the right.

YORK

I never saw a fellow worse bestead   56
Or more afraid to fight than is the appellant,
The servant of this armorer, my lords.

> *Enter, at one door, the Armorer [Horner] and his*
> *Neighbors, drinking to him so much that he is drunk;*
> *and he enters with a Drum before him, and his staff*
> *with a sandbag fastened to it; and, at the other door,*
> *his Man [Peter], with a Drum and sandbag, and*
> *Prentices drinking to him.*

1. NEIGHBOR Here, neighbor Horner, I drink to you in a
cup of sack; and fear not, neighbor, you shall do well   60
enough.

2. NEIGHBOR And here, neighbor, here's a cup of char-   62
neco.

3. NEIGHBOR And here's a pot of good double-beer,   64
neighbor. Drink, and fear not your man.

ARMORER Let it come, i' faith, and I'll pledge you all;
and a fig for Peter.   67

1. PRENTICE Here, Peter, I drink to thee; and be not
afraid.

2. PRENTICE Be merry, Peter, and fear not thy master.
Fight for credit of the prentices.

PETER I thank you all. Drink, and pray for me, I pray

---

50 *lists* the barriers defining an arena for fighting or tilting; hence, the
arena itself **54** *A* in **56** *bestead* prepared **60** *sack* a stong, dry wine **62**
charneco a sweet wine **64** *double-beer* strong beer **67** *a fig for Peter* I hold
Peter in the utmost contempt (usually accompanied with a gesture made
by putting the thumb between the first and second fingers)

you; for I think I have taken my last draught in this world. Here, Robin, an if I die, I give thee my apron; and, Will, thou shalt have my hammer; and here, Tom, take all the money that I have. O Lord bless me, I pray God, for I am never able to deal with my master, he hath learnt so much fence already.

SALISBURY Come, leave your drinking and fall to blows. Sirrah, what's thy name?

PETER Peter, forsooth.

SALISBURY Peter? What more?

PETER Thump.

SALISBURY Thump? Then see thou thump thy master well.

ARMORER Masters, I am come hither, as it were, upon my man's instigation, to prove him a knave and myself an honest man; and touching the Duke of York, I will take my death I never meant him any ill, nor the king, nor the queen; and therefore, Peter, have at thee with a down-right blow.

86

YORK Dispatch. This knave's tongue begins to double. Sound, trumpets, alarum to the combatants!

[Alarum.] They fight, and Peter strikes him down.

ARMORER Hold, Peter, hold! I confess, I confess treason. *[Dies.]*

YORK Take away his weapon. Fellow, thank God, and the good wine in thy master's way.

PETER O God, have I overcome mine enemies in this presence? O Peter, thou hast prevailed in right.

KING

Go, take hence that traitor from our sight,
For by his death we do perceive his guilt,
And God in justice hath revealed to us
The truth and innocence of this poor fellow,
Which he had thought to have murdered wrongfully.
Come, fellow, follow us for thy reward.

Sound a flourish. Exeunt.

*

86 *downright* straight down

Enter Duke Humphrey [of Gloucester] and his   II, iv
Men in mourning cloaks.

GLOUCESTER

Thus sometimes hath the brightest day a cloud,
And after summer evermore succeeds
Barren winter with his wrathful nipping cold;
So cares and joys abound, as seasons fleet.
Sirs, what's o'clock?

SERVANT   Ten, my lord.

GLOUCESTER

Ten is the hour that was appointed me
To watch the coming of my punished duchess.
Uneath may she endure the flinty streets   8
To tread them with her tender-feeling feet.
Sweet Nell, ill can thy noble mind abrook
The abject people gazing on thy face,   11
With envious looks laughing at thy shame,
That erst did follow thy proud chariot wheels   13
When thou didst ride in triumph through the streets.
But, soft, I think she comes, and I'll prepare
My tear-stained eyes to see her miseries.

> *Enter the Duchess [barefoot] in a white sheet, [with*
> *verses pinned upon her back] and a taper burning in*
> *her hand, with the Sheriff and Officers [and Sir John*
> *Stanley. A crowd following].*

SERVANT

So please your grace, we'll take her from the sheriff.

GLOUCESTER

No, stir not for your lives. Let her pass by.

ELEANOR

Come you, my lord, to see my open shame?
Now thou dost penance too. Look how they gaze.
See how the giddy multitude do point
And nod their heads and throw their eyes on thee.
Ah, Gloucester, hide thee from their hateful looks,

II, iv A street   8 *Uneath* with difficulty, scarcely   11 *abject* common,
low-born   13 *erst* formerly

24 And in thy closet pent up, rue my shame
25 And ban thine enemies, both mine and thine.

GLOUCESTER
Be patient, gentle Nell ; forget this grief.

ELEANOR
Ah, Gloucester, teach me to forget myself.
For, whilst I think I am thy married wife
And thou a prince, Protector of this land,
Methinks I should not thus be led along,
31 Mailed up in shame, with papers on my back,
And followed with a rabble that rejoice
33 To see my tears and hear my deep-fet groans.
The ruthless flint doth cut my tender feet ;
And when I start, the envious people laugh
And bid me be advisèd how I tread.
Ah, Humphrey, can I bear this shameful yoke ?
38 Trowest thou that e'er I'll look upon the world
Or count them happy that enjoys the sun ?
No ; dark shall be my light, and night my day ;
To think upon my pomp shall be my hell.
Sometime I'll say, I am Duke Humphrey's wife,
And he a prince, and ruler of the land ;
Yet so he ruled, and such a prince he was,
As he stood by whilst I, his forlorn duchess,
46 Was made a wonder and a pointing-stock
To every idle rascal follower.
But be thou mild and blush not at my shame,
Nor stir at nothing till the axe of death
Hang over thee, as sure it shortly will.
For Suffolk – he that can do all in all
With her that hateth thee and hates us all –
And York and impious Beaufort, that false priest,
Have all limed bushes to betray thy wings,

---

24 *closet* private room   25 *ban* curse   31 *Mailed up* wrapped up (as a hawk is wrapped up to prevent her struggling)   33 *deep-fet* deeply fetched   38 *Trowest thou* do you believe   46 *pointing-stock* a person pointed at in scorn

And fly thou how thou canst, they'll tangle thee.
But fear not thou until thy foot be snared,
Nor never seek prevention of thy foes.   57

GLOUCESTER
Ah, Nell, forbear ; thou aimest all awry.
I must offend before I be attainted ;   59
And had I twenty times so many foes,
And each of them had twenty times their power,
All these could not procure me any scathe   62
So long as I am loyal, true, and crimeless.
Wouldst have me rescue thee from this reproach ?
Why, yet thy scandal were not wiped away,
But I in danger for the breach of law.
Thy greatest help is quiet, gentle Nell.
I pray thee sort thy heart to patience ;   68
These few days' wonder will be quickly worn.
        Enter a Herald.

HERALD
I summon your grace to his majesty's parliament,
Holden at Bury the first of this next month.   71

GLOUCESTER
And my consent ne'er asked herein before ?
This is close dealing. Well, I will be there.   73
                    [Exit Herald.]
My Nell, I take my leave. And, master sheriff,.
Let not her penance exceed the king's commission.

SHERIFF
An't please your grace, here my commission stays,   76
And Sir John Stanley is appointed now
To take her with him to the Isle of Man.

GLOUCESTER
Must you, Sir John, protect my lady here ?

STANLEY
So am I given in charge, may't please your grace.

57 *prevention of* prior safeguards against   59 *attainted* condemned for
treason   62 *scathe* harm   68 *sort* adapt   71 *Holden* to be held ; *Bury* i.e.
Bury St Edmunds   73 *close* secret   76 *commission stays* authority stops

GLOUCESTER

81   Entreat her not the worse in that I pray
       You use her well. The world may laugh again,
       And I may live to do you kindness if
       You do it her ; and so, Sir John, farewell.

ELEANOR

       What, gone, my lord, and bid me not farewell ?

GLOUCESTER

       Witness my tears, I cannot stay to speak.

                              Exit Gloucester [with his Men].

ELEANOR

       Art thou gone too ? All comfort go with thee !
       For none abides with me. My joy is death –
       Death, at whose name I oft have been afeard,
90   Because I wished this world's eternity.
       Stanley, I prithee go, and take me hence ;
       I care not whither, for I beg no favor.
       Only convey me where thou art commanded.

STANLEY

       Why, madam, that is to the Isle of Man,
95   There to be used according to your state.

ELEANOR

96   That's bad enough, for I am but reproach ;
       And shall I then be used reproachfully ?

STANLEY

       Like to a duchess and Duke Humphrey's lady –
       According to that state you shall be used.

ELEANOR

       Sheriff, farewell, and better than I fare,
101   Although thou hast been conduct of my shame.

SHERIFF

       It is my office ; and, madam, pardon me.

ELEANOR

       Ay, ay, farewell ; thy office is discharged.

---

81 *Entreat* treat   90 *this world's eternity* endless worldly pleasures   95
state social rank (but Eleanor at l. 96 shifts the meaning to 'condition')   96
but reproach entirely a thing to be reproached   101 *conduct* conductor

Come, Stanley, shall we go?

STANLEY
Madam, your penance done, throw off this sheet,
And go we to attire you for our journey.

ELEANOR
My shame will not be shifted with my sheet.   107
No, it will hang upon my richest robes
And show itself, attire me how I can.
Go, lead the way; I long to see my prison.   *Exeunt.*

*

Sound a sennet. Enter [two Heralds before, then]   III, i
Buckingham [and] Suffolk, [then] York [and the]
Cardinal, [then the] King [and the] Queen, [then]
Salisbury and Warwick [with their attendants]
to the Parliament.

KING
I muse my Lord of Gloucester is not come.   1
'Tis not his wont to be the hindmost man,
Whate'er occasion keeps him from us now.

QUEEN
Can you not see? or will ye not observe
The strangeness of his altered countenance?
With what a majesty he bears himself,
How insolent of late he is become,
How proud, how peremptory, and unlike himself?
We know the time since he was mild and affable,   9
And if we did but glance a far-off look,
Immediately he was upon his knee,
That all the court admired him for submission;
But meet him now and, be it in the morn,
When every one will give the time of day,   14

107 *shifted* changed (with a pun on 'shift,' a chemise)
III, i A hall for the session of Parliament (at Bury St Edmunds)   1 *muse*
wonder   9 *We ... since* we remember that once   14 *give ... day* say good
morning

He knits his brow and shows an angry eye
And passeth by with stiff unbowèd knee,
Disdaining duty that to us belongs.
18 Small curs are not regarded when they grin,
19 But great men tremble when the lion roars,
And Humphrey is no little man in England.
First note that he is near you in descent,
And should you fall, he is the next will mount.
23 Me seemeth then it is no policy,
24 Respecting what a rancorous mind he bears
And his advantage following your decease,
That he should come about your royal person
Or be admitted to your highness' council.
By flattery hath he won the commons' hearts;
And when he please to make commotion,
'Tis to be feared they all will follow him.
Now 'tis the spring, and weeds are shallow-rooted.
Suffer them now, and they'll o'ergrow the garden
33 And choke the herbs for want of husbandry.
The reverent care I bear unto my lord
35 Made me collect these dangers in the duke.
36 If it be fond, call it a woman's fear;
Which fear if better reasons can supplant,
38 I will subscribe and say I wronged the duke.
My Lord of Suffolk, Buckingham, and York,
Reprove my allegation if you can,
Or else conclude my words effectual.

SUFFOLK

Well hath your highness seen into this duke,
And had I first been put to speak my mind,
I think I should have told your grace's tale.

---

18 *grin* show their teeth   19 *lion* i.e. Gloucester (who, as the prince, is symbolized by the kingly lion)   23 *Me … policy* it seems to me that it is not wise   24 *Respecting* considering   33 *husbandry* cultivation   35 *collect* infer   36 *fond* foolish   38 *subscribe* acknowledge in writing

The duchess by his subornation,   45
Upon my life, began her devilish practices;   46
Or if he were not privy to those faults,
Yet by reputing of his high descent –   48
As next the king he was successive heir,
And such high vaunts of his nobility –
Did instigate the bedlam brainsick duchess   51
By wicked means to frame our sovereign's fall.
Smooth runs the water where the brook is deep,
And in his simple show he harbors treason.
The fox barks not when he would steal the lamb.
No, no, my sovereign; Gloucester is a man
Unsounded yet and full of deep deceit.   57

CARDINAL
Did he not, contrary to form of law,
Devise strange deaths for small offenses done?   59

YORK
And did he not in his protectorship
Levy great sums of money through the realm
For soldiers' pay in France, and never sent it?
By means whereof the towns each day revolted.

BUCKINGHAM
Tut, these are petty faults to faults unknown
Which time will bring to light in smooth Duke
    Humphrey.

KING
My lords at once, the care you have of us,   66
To mow down thorns that would annoy our foot,
Is worthy praise; but, shall I speak my conscience,
Our kinsman Gloucester is as innocent
From meaning treason to our royal person
As is the sucking lamb or harmless dove.

---

45 *subornation* instigation to crime   **46** *Upon my life* (an oath: Eleanor was accused of practicing upon the king's life, not Suffolk's)   **48** *reputing* thinking repeatedly   **51** *bedlam* crazy   **57** *Unsounded* unrevealed   **59** *strange* exceptionally cruel, illegal   **66** *at once* going to the heart of the matter (?), collectively (?)

72 The duke is virtuous, mild, and too well-given
    To dream on evil or to work my downfall.

QUEEN

74 Ah, what's more dangerous than this fond affiance?
    Seems he a dove? His feathers are but borrowed,
    For he's disposèd as the hateful raven.
    Is he a lamb? His skin is surely lent him,
    For he's inclined as is the ravenous wolves.

79 Who cannot steal a shape that means deceit?
    Take heed, my lord. The welfare of us all
    Hangs on the cutting short that fraudful man.
            Enter Somerset.

SOMERSET

    All health unto my gracious sovereign.

KING

    Welcome, Lord Somerset. What news from France?

SOMERSET

    That all your interest in those territories
    Is utterly bereft you; all is lost

KING

    Cold news, Lord Somerset; but God's will be done.

YORK *[aside]*

    Cold news for me, for I had hope of France
    As firmly as I hope for fertile England.
    Thus are my blossoms blasted in the bud,
    And caterpillars eat my leaves away;

91 But I will remedy this gear ere long
    Or sell my title for a glorious grave.
            Enter Gloucester.

GLOUCESTER

    All happiness unto my lord the king.

94 Pardon, my liege, that I have stayed so long.

SUFFOLK

    Nay, Gloucester, know that thou art come too soon

---

72 *well-given* well-disposed   **74** *fond affiance* foolish confidence   **79** *Who
... deceit* i.e. who that intends to deceive cannot assume a role   **91** *gear*
business   **94** *stayed* delayed

Unless thou wert more loyal than thou art.
I do arrest thee of high treason here.

GLOUCESTER

Well, Suffolk, thou shalt not see me blush
Nor change my countenance for this arrest.
A heart unspotted is not easily daunted.
The purest spring is not so free from mud
As I am clear from treason to my sovereign.
Who can accuse me? Wherein am I guilty?

YORK

'Tis thought, my lord, that you took bribes of France
And, being Protector, stayed the soldiers' pay,   105
By means whereof his highness hath lost France.

GLOUCESTER

Is it but thought so? What are they that think it?
I never robbed the soldiers of their pay
Nor ever had one penny bribe from France.
So help me God as I have watched the night –   110
Ay, night by night – in studying good for England!
That doit that e'er I wrested from the king,   112
Or any groat I hoarded to my use,   113
Be brought against me at my trial day!
No! Many a pound of mine own proper store,   115
Because I would not tax the needy commons,
Have I dispursèd to the garrisons   117
And never asked for restitution.

CARDINAL

It serves you well, my lord, to say so much.

GLOUCESTER

I say no more than truth, so help me God.

YORK

In your protectorship you did devise
Strange tortures for offenders, never heard of,
That England was defamed by tyranny.

105 *stayed* withheld 110 *watched* remained awake throughout 112, 113
doit, groat coins of little value 115 *proper* personal 117 *dispursèd* paid
from the purse

GLOUCESTER

Why, 'tis well known that, whiles I was Protector,
Pity was all the fault that was in me;
For I should melt at an offender's tears
And lowly words were ransom for their fault.
Unless it were a bloody murderer,
Or foul felonious thief that fleeced poor passengers,
130   I never gave them condign punishment.
Murder indeed, that bloody sin, I tortured
132   Above the felon or what trespass else.

SUFFOLK

133   My lord, these faults are easy, quickly answered;
But mightier crimes are laid unto your charge,
Whereof you cannot easily purge yourself.
I do arrest you in his highness' name
And here commit you to my Lord Cardinal
To keep until your further time of trial.

KING

My Lord of Gloucester, 'tis my special hope
140   That you will clear yourself from all suspense.
My conscience tells me you are innocent.

GLOUCESTER

Ah, gracious lord, these days are dangerous.
Virtue is choked with foul ambition
And charity chased hence by rancor's hand;
Foul subornation is predominant
And equity exiled your highness' land.
147   I know their complot is to have my life,
And if my death might make this island happy
149   And prove the period of their tyranny,
I would expend it with all willingness.
But mine is made the prologue to their play,
For thousands more, that yet suspect no peril,
Will not conclude their plotted tragedy.

130 *condign* well-deserved   132 *Above ... else* beyond felony or any other
crime   133 *easy* unimportant   140 *suspense* doubt as to your character
147 *complot* conspiracy   149 *period* end

Beaufort's red sparkling eyes blab his heart's malice
And Suffolk's cloudy brow his stormy hate;
Sharp Buckingham unburdens with his tongue
The envious load that lies upon his heart;
And dogged York, that reaches at the moon,
Whose overweening arm I have plucked back,
By false accuse doth level at my life;   160
And you, my sovereign lady, with the rest,
Causeless have laid disgraces on my head
And with your best endeavor have stirred up
My liefest liege to be mine enemy.   164
Ay, all of you have laid your heads together –
Myself had notice of your conventicles –   166
And all to make away my guiltless life.
I shall not want false witness to condemn me
Nor store of treasons to augment my guilt.
The ancient proverb will be well effected:
'A staff is quickly found to beat a dog.'

CARDINAL
My liege, his railing is intolerable.
If those that care to keep your royal person
From treason's secret knife and traitor's rage
Be thus upbraided, chid, and rated at,   175
And the offender granted scope of speech,
'Twill make them cool in zeal unto your grace.

SUFFOLK
Hath he not twit our sovereign lady here   178
With ignominious words, though clerkly couched,   179
As if she had subornèd some to swear
False allegations to o'erthrow his state?

QUEEN
But I can give the loser leave to chide.

GLOUCESTER
Far truer spoke than meant; I lose indeed.

160 *accuse* accusation; *level* aim   164 *liefest liege* dearest sovereign   166
conventicles secret gatherings   175 *rated at* complained against   178 *twit*
twitted   179 *clerkly couched* artfully, learnedly phrased

184   Beshrew the winners, for they played me false;
     And well such losers may have leave to speak.

BUCKINGHAM

186   He'll wrest the sense and hold us here all day.
     Lord Cardinal, he is your prisoner.

CARDINAL

     Sirs, take away the duke and guard him sure.

GLOUCESTER

     Ah, thus King Henry throws away his crutch
     Before his legs be firm to bear his body.
     Thus is the shepherd beaten from thy side,
192   And wolves are gnarling who shall gnaw thee first.
     Ah that my fear were false, ah that it were!
     For, good King Henry, thy decay I fear.

                Exit Gloucester [with the Cardinal's men].

KING

     My lords, what to your wisdoms seemeth best
     Do or undo, as if ourself were here.

QUEEN

     What, will your highness leave the parliament?

KING

     Ay, Margaret. My heart is drowned with grief,
     Whose flood begins to flow within mine eyes:
200   My body round engirt with misery –
     For what's more miserable than discontent?
     Ah, uncle Humphrey, in thy face I see
     The map of honor, truth, and loyalty;
     And yet, good Humphrey, is the hour to come
     That e'er I proved thee false or feared thy faith.
     What low'ring star now envies thy estate
     That these great lords and Margaret our queen
     Do seek subversion of thy harmless life?
     Thou never didst them wrong nor no man wrong.
     And as the butcher takes away the calf
     And binds the wretch and beats it when it strains,

---

184 *Beshrew* bad luck to   186 *wrest the sense* distort the meaning   192
gnarling snarling

Bearing it to the bloody slaughterhouse,
Even so remorseless have they borne him hence;
And as the dam runs lowing up and down, 214
Looking the way her harmless young one went,
And can do naught but wail her darling's loss,
Even so myself bewails good Gloucester's case
With sad unhelpful tears, and with dimmed eyes
Look after him and cannot do him good,
So mighty are his vowèd enemies.
His fortunes I will weep, and 'twixt each groan
Say 'Who's a traitor? Gloucester he is none.'
                    [Exit King with Buckingham, Salisbury,
                                        and Warwick.]

QUEEN
Free lords, cold snow melts with the sun's hot beams. 223
Henry my lord is cold in great affairs,
Too full of foolish pity; and Gloucester's show
Beguiles him as the mournful crocodile
With sorrow snares relenting passengers,
Or as the snake, rolled in a flow'ring bank,
With shining checkered slough, doth sting a child 229
That for the beauty thinks it excellent.
Believe me, lords, were none more wise than I—
And yet herein I judge mine own wit good—
This Gloucester should be quickly rid the world,
To rid us from the fear we have of him.

CARDINAL
That he should die is worthy policy;
But yet we want a color for his death. 236
'Tis meet he be condemned by course of law.

SUFFOLK
But, in my mind, that were no policy.
The king will labor still to save his life,
The commons haply rise to save his life; 240

214 *dam* mother   223 *Free* noble, generous   229 *slough* skin   236 *color*
legal pretext (with a quibble arising from *die*/dye in l. 235)   240 *haply*
perhaps

241 And yet we have but trivial argument,
      More than mistrust, that shows him worthy death.

YORK

243 So that, by this, you would not have him die.

SUFFOLK

244 Ah, York, no man alive so fain as I.

YORK *[aside]*

      'Tis York that hath more reason for his death. –
      But, my Lord Cardinal, and you, my Lord of Suffolk,
      Say as you think and speak it from your souls:
248 Were't not all one an empty eagle were set
      To guard the chicken from a hungry kite
      As place Duke Humphrey for the king's Protector?

QUEEN

      So the poor chicken should be sure of death.

SUFFOLK

      Madam, 'tis true; and were't not madness then
253 To make the fox surveyor of the fold?
      Who being accused a crafty murderer,
255 His guilt should be but idly posted over
      Because his purpose is not executed.
      No, let him die in that he is a fox,
      By nature proved an enemy to the flock,
259 Before his chaps be stained with crimson blood,
      As Humphrey, proved by treasons, to my liege.
261 And do not stand on quillets how to slay him;
262 Be it by gins, by snares, by subtlety,
      Sleeping or waking, 'tis no matter how,
      So he be dead; for that is good deceit
265 Which mates him first that first intends deceit.

QUEEN

      Thrice-noble Suffolk, 'tis resolutely spoke.

---

241 *argument* proof   243 *by this* i.e. by your reasoning   244 *fain*
eager   248 *empty* i.e. hungry   253 *surveyor* overseer   255 *posted over*
disregarded   259 *chaps* i.e. chops, jaws   261 *stand on quillets* be scrupulous about details   262 *gins* engines, i.e. traps   265 *mates* checkmates

SUFFOLK

Not resolute, except so much were done,
For things are often spoke and seldom meant;
But that my heart accordeth with my tongue,
Seeing the deed is meritorious,
And to preserve my sovereign from his foe,
Say but the word, and I will be his priest.   272

CARDINAL

But I would have him dead, my Lord of Suffolk,
Ere you can take due orders for a priest.   274
Say you consent and censure well the deed,   275
And I'll provide his executioner,
I tender so the safety of my liege.

SUFFOLK

Here is my hand, the deed is worthy doing.

QUEEN

And so say I.

YORK

And I. And now we three have spoke it,
It skills not greatly who impugns our doom.   281
            Enter a Post.

POST

Great lords, from Ireland am I come amain   282
To signify that rebels there are up   283
And put the Englishmen unto the sword.
Send succors, lords, and stop the rage betime,   285
Before the wound do grow uncurable;
For, being green, there is great hope of help.   287

CARDINAL

A breach that craves a quick expedient stop.
What counsel give you in this weighty cause?

YORK

That Somerset be sent as regent thither.

---

272 *be his priest* i.e. give him the last rites (with obvious irony)   **274** *take
... priest* prepare yourself for the priesthood   **275** *censure well* approve
281 *doom* judgment   **282** *amain* hastily   **283** *signify* announce   **285**
betime soon   **287** *green* fresh

291   'Tis meet that lucky ruler be employed;
      Witness the fortune he hath had in France.

SOMERSET

293   If York with all his far-fet policy
      Had been the regent there instead of me,
      He never would have stayed in France so long.

YORK

      No, not to lose it all, as thou hast done.

297   I rather would have lost my life betimes
      Than bring a burden of dishonor home
      By staying there so long till all were lost.

300   Show me one scar charactered on thy skin.
      Men's flesh preserved so whole do seldom win.

QUEEN

      Nay then, this spark will prove a raging fire
      If wind and fuel be brought to feed it with.
      No more, good York; sweet Somerset, be still.
      Thy fortune, York, hadst thou been regent there,

306   Might happily have proved far worse than his.

YORK

      What, worse than naught? Nay, then a shame take all!

SOMERSET

      And, in the number, thee that wishest shame!

CARDINAL

      My Lord of York, try what your fortune is.

310   Th' uncivil kerns of Ireland are in arms

311   And temper clay with blood of Englishmen.
      To Ireland will you lead a band of men,
      Collected choicely, from each county some,
      And try your hap against the Irishmen?

YORK

      I will, my lord, so please his majesty.

SUFFOLK

      Why, our authority is his consent,

---

291 *meet* fitting   293 *far-fet* far-fetched, artfully contrived   297 *betimes* forthwith   300 *charactered* inscribed   306 *happily* haply, perhaps   310 *uncivil kerns* wild and irregular foot-soldiers   311 *temper* soften

And what we do establish he confirms.
Then, noble York, take thou this task in hand.

YORK
I am content. Provide me soldiers, lords,
Whiles I take order for mine own affairs.   320

SUFFOLK
A charge, Lord York, that I will see performed.
But now return we to the false Duke Humphrey.

CARDINAL
No more of him ; for I will deal with him
That henceforth he shall trouble us no more.
And so break off ; the day is almost spent.   325
Lord Suffolk, you and I must talk of that event.   326

YORK
My Lord of Suffolk, within fourteen days
At Bristow I expect my soldiers,   328
For there I'll ship them all for Ireland.

SUFFOLK
I'll see it truly done, my Lord of York.

                              Exeunt. Manet York.

YORK
Now, York, or never, steel thy fearful thoughts
And change misdoubt to resolution.   332
Be that thou hop'st to be ; or what thou art
Resign to death : it is not worth th' enjoying.
Let pale-faced fear keep with the mean-born man   335
And find no harbor in a royal heart.
Faster than springtime show'rs comes thought on
     thought,
And not a thought but thinks on dignity.   338
My brain, more busy than the laboring spider,
Weaves tedious snares to trap mine enemies.   340
Well, nobles, well, 'tis politicly done
To send me packing with an host of men.

320 *take order for* arrange 325 *break off* talk no more 326 *event*
outcome 328 *Bristow* Bristol 332 *misdoubt* fear 335 *keep* live 338
dignity high position 340 *tedious* complicated

343   I fear me you but warm the starvèd snake,
Who, cherished in your breasts, will sting your hearts.
'Twas men I lacked, and you will give them me;
I take it kindly. Yet be well assured
You put sharp weapons in a madman's hands.
Whiles I in Ireland nourish a mighty band,
I will stir up in England some black storm
Shall blow ten thousand souls to heaven – or hell;
And this fell tempest shall not cease to rage
Until the golden circuit on my head,
Like to the glorious sun's transparent beams,
354   Do calm the fury of this mad-bred flaw.
355   And for a minister of my intent
I have seduced a headstrong Kentishman,
John Cade of Ashford,
To make commotion, as full well he can,
359   Under the title of John Mortimer.
In Ireland have I seen this stubborn Cade
Oppose himself against a troop of kerns,
362   And fought so long till that his thighs with darts
363   Were almost like a sharp-quilled porpentine;
And in the end being rescued, I have seen
365   Him caper upright like a wild Morisco,
Shaking the bloody darts as he his bells.
Full often, like a shag-haired crafty kern,
Hath he conversèd with the enemy
And undiscovered come to me again
And given me notice of their villainies.
This devil here shall be my substitute;
For that John Mortimer which now is dead
In face, in gait, in speech, he doth resemble.
By this I shall perceive the commons' mind,

---

343 *starvèd* frozen   **354** *flaw* squall   **355** *minister* agent   **359** *Mortimer* (the family name of the descendants of Philippe, daughter of Lionel, Duke of Clarence, third son of Edward III. Cade would thus claim the crown through the same line as York himself, cf. II, ii, 10 ff.)   **362** *darts* light spears (with which kerns were usually armed)   **363** *porpentine* porcupine   **365** *Morisco* morris-dancer

How they affect the house and claim of York.   375
Say he be taken, racked, and torturèd;
I know no pain they can inflict upon him
Will make him say I moved him to those arms.
Say that he thrive, as 'tis great like he will;   379
Why, then from Ireland come I with my strength
And reap the harvest which that rascal sowed;
For, Humphrey being dead, as he shall be,
And Henry put apart, the next for me.   *Exit.*

*

*Enter two or three running over the stage, from the   III, ii
murder of Duke Humphrey.*

1. MURDERER
Run to my Lord of Suffolk; let him know
We have dispatched the duke, as he commanded.

2. MURDERER
O that it were to do! What have we done?   3
Didst ever hear a man so penitent?
          Enter Suffolk.

1. MURDERER
Here comes my lord.

SUFFOLK
Now, sirs, have you dispatched this thing?

1. MURDERER
Ay, my good lord; he's dead.

SUFFOLK
Why, that's well said. Go, get you to my house;
I will reward you for this venturous deed.
The king and all the peers are here at hand.
Have you laid fair the bed? Is all things well,
According as I gave directions?

1. MURDERER
'Tis, my good lord.

375 *affect* like   379 *great like* very likely
III, ii A room adjoining Gloucester's bedchamber   3 *O ... do* i.e. would
that it had not been done yet

SUFFOLK

Away! be gone!   *Exeunt [Murderers].*
> *Sound trumpets. Enter the King, the Queen,*
> *Cardinal, Somerset, with Attendants.*

KING

Go call our uncle to our presence straight.
Say we intend to try his grace to-day,
17   If he be guilty, as 'tis publishèd.

SUFFOLK

I'll call him presently, my noble lord.   *Exit.*

KING

Lords, take your places; and I pray you all
20   Proceed no straiter 'gainst our uncle Gloucester
Than from true evidence, of good esteem,
22   He be approved in practice culpable.

QUEEN

God forbid any malice should prevail
24   That faultless may condemn a nobleman;
Pray God he may acquit him of suspicion.

KING

I thank thee, Meg. These words content me much.
> *Enter Suffolk.*

How now? Why look'st thou pale? Why tremblest thou?
Where is our uncle? What's the matter, Suffolk?

SUFFOLK

Dead in his bed, my lord; Gloucester is dead.

QUEEN

30   Marry, God forfend!

CARDINAL

God's secret judgment. I did dream to-night
32   The duke was dumb and could not speak a word.
> *King sounds.*

QUEEN

How fares my lord? Help, lords! The king is dead.

---

17 *If* whether   20 *straiter* stricter   22 *approved* proved   24 *That ...*
nobleman i.e. that may condemn a nobleman who is faultless   30 *forfend*
forbid   32 s.d. *sounds* swoons

SOMERSET
    Rear up his body ; wring him by the nose.   34
QUEEN
    Run, go ! help, help ! O Henry, ope thine eyes.
SUFFOLK
    He doth revive again. Madam, be patient.
KING
    O heavenly God.
QUEEN   How fares my gracious lord ?
SUFFOLK
    Comfort, my sovereign. Gracious Henry, comfort.
KING
    What, doth my Lord of Suffolk comfort me ?
    Came he right now to sing a raven's note   40
    Whose dismal tune bereft my vital pow'rs,
    And thinks he that the chirping of a wren
    By crying comfort from a hollow breast
    Can chase away the first-conceivèd sound ?
    Hide not thy poison with such sugared words.
    Lay not thy hands on me. Forbear, I say !
    Their touch affrights me as a serpent's sting.
    Thou baleful messenger, out of my sight !
    Upon thy eyeballs murderous tyranny
    Sits in grim majesty to fright the world.
    Look not upon me, for thine eyes are wounding.
    Yet do not go away. Come, basilisk,   52
    And kill the innocent gazer with thy sight ;
    For in the shade of death I shall find joy –
    In life but double death, now Gloucester's dead.
QUEEN
    Why do you rate my Lord of Suffolk thus ?   56
    Although the duke was enemy to him,
    Yet he most Christianlike laments his death ;
    And for myself, foe as he was to me,

---

34 *Rear up* raise; *wring ... nose* (supposed to aid in restoring consciousness)   40 *raven's note* (a bad omen)   52 *basilisk* a fabulous serpent,
said to kill by its look   56 *rate* complain against, berate

Might liquid tears or heart-offending groans
61 Or blood-consuming sighs recall his life,
I would be blind with weeping, sick with groans,
Look pale as primrose with blood-drinking sighs,
And all to have the noble duke alive.
What know I how the world may deem of me?
66 For it is known we were but hollow friends.
It may be judged I made the duke away;
So shall my name with slander's tongue be wounded
And princes' courts be filled with my reproach.
This get I by his death. Ay me unhappy,
To be a queen, and crowned with infamy!

KING

Ah, woe is me for Gloucester, wretched man.

QUEEN

Be woe for me, more wretched than he is.
What, dost thou turn away, and hide thy face?
I am no loathsome leper. Look on me.
76 What? Art thou like the adder waxen deaf?
Be poisonous too, and kill thy forlorn queen.
Is all thy comfort shut in Gloucester's tomb?
Why, then Dame Margaret was ne'er thy joy.
80 Erect his statue and worship it,
And make my image but an alehouse sign.
Was I for this nigh wracked upon the sea
83 And twice by awkward wind from England's bank
Drove back again unto my native clime?
What boded this but well-forewarning wind
Did seem to say, 'Seek not a scorpion's nest
Nor set no footing on this unkind shore'?
What did I then but cursed the gentle gusts
89 And he that loosed them forth their brazen caves,
And bid them blow toward England's blessèd shore
Or turn our stern upon a dreadful rock?

61 *blood-consuming* (because each sigh was thought to cost the heart a drop of blood) 66 *hollow friends* i.e. enemies 76 *waxen* grown 80 *statue* (trisyllabic: 'statuë') 83 *awkward* adverse 89 *he* i.e. Aeolus, god of the winds

Yet Aeolus would not be a murderer,
But left that hateful office unto thee.
The pretty vaulting sea refused to drown me,
Knowing that thou wouldst have me drowned on shore
With tears as salt as sea through thy unkindness.
The splitting rocks cowered in the sinking sands
And would not dash me with their ragged sides,
Because thy flinty heart, more hard than they,   99
Might in thy palace perish Margaret.
As far as I could ken thy chalky cliffs,   101
When from thy shore the tempest beat us back,
I stood upon the hatches in the storm,
And when the dusky sky began to rob
My earnest-gaping sight of thy land's view,
I took a costly jewel from my neck,
A heart it was, bound in with diamonds,
And threw it toward thy land. The sea received it,
And so I wished thy body might my heart;
And even with this I lost fair England's view,
And bid mine eyes be packing with my heart,   111
And called them blind and dusky spectacles   112
For losing ken of Albion's wishèd coast.   113
How often have I tempted Suffolk's tongue
(The agent of thy foul inconstancy)
To sit and witch me as Ascanius did   116
When he to madding Dido would unfold   117
His father's acts commenced in burning Troy!
Am I not witched like her? or thou not false like him?
Ay me, I can no more. Die, Margaret!
For Henry weeps that thou dost live so long.
         Noise within. Enter Warwick, [Salisbury,] and
         many Commons.

99 *Because* so that 101 *ken* discern 111 *be packing* be gone 112
spectacles viewers (specifically telescopes) 113 *Albion's* England's 116
witch bewitch; *Ascanius* son of the Trojan hero Aeneas (in the *Aeneid* it is
Cupid disguised as Ascanius who is on hand when Aeneas himself tells
Dido, queen of Carthage, of his adventures) 117 *madding* going mad (in
this case, with love)

WARWICK

It is reported, mighty sovereign,
That good Duke Humphrey traitorously is murdered
By Suffolk and the Cardinal Beaufort's means.
The commons, like an angry hive of bees
That want their leader, scatter up and down
And care not who they sting in his revenge.
128 Myself have calmed their spleenful mutiny
129 Until they hear the order of his death.

KING

That he is dead, good Warwick, 'tis too true;
But how he died God knows, not Henry.
Enter his chamber, view his breathless corpse,
133 And comment then upon his sudden death.

WARWICK

That shall I do, my liege. Stay, Salisbury,
With the rude multitude till I return.   *[Exit.]*
           [Exit Salisbury with the Commons.]

KING

O thou that judgest all things, stay my thoughts –
My thoughts, that labor to persuade my soul
Some violent hands were laid on Humphrey's life.
139 If my suspect be false, forgive me, God;
For judgment only doth belong to thee.
141 Fain would I go to chafe his paly lips
With twenty thousand kisses and to drain
Upon his face an ocean of salt tears,
To tell my love unto his dumb deaf trunk,
And with my fingers feel his hand unfeeling.
146 But all in vain are these mean obsequies;
      Bed put forth [with the body. Enter Warwick].
And to survey his dead and earthy image,
What were it but to make my sorrow greater?

WARWICK

Come hither, gracious sovereign, view this body.

---

128 *spleenful* angry   129 *order* manner   133 *comment ... upon* explain   139
suspect suspicion   141 *chafe* warm; *paly* pale   146 *obsequies* funeral rites

KING
>   That is to see how deep my grave is made;
>   For with his soul fled all my worldly solace,
>   For seeing him, I see my life in death.

WARWICK
>   As surely as my soul intends to live
>   With that dread King that took our state upon him
>   To free us from his Father's wrathful curse,
>   I do believe that violent hands were laid
>   Upon the life of this thrice-famèd duke.

SUFFOLK
>   A dreadful oath, sworn with a solemn tongue.
>   What instance gives Lord Warwick for his vow?   159

WARWICK
>   See how the blood is settled in his face.
>   Oft have I seen a timely-parted ghost,   161
>   Of ashy semblance, meagre, pale, and bloodless,
>   Being all descended to the laboring heart,
>   Who, in the conflict that it holds with death,
>   Attracts the same for aidance 'gainst the enemy,
>   Which with the heart there cools, and ne'er returneth
>   To blush and beautify the cheek again.
>   But see, his face is black and full of blood;
>   His eyeballs further out than when he lived,
>   Staring full ghastly, like a strangled man;
>   His hair upreared, his nostrils stretched with struggling;
>   His hands abroad displayed, as one that grasped
>   And tugged for life and was by strength subdued.
>   Look, on the sheets his hair, you see, is sticking;
>   His well-proportioned beard made rough and rugged,
>   Like to the summer's corn by tempest lodged.   176
>   It cannot be but he was murdered here.
>   The least of all these signs were probable.

SUFFOLK
>   Why, Warwick, who should do the duke to death?

159 *instance* proof   161 *timely-parted* departed at a fitting time   176
lodged levelled

Myself and Beaufort had him in protection,
And we, I hope, sir, are no murderers.

WARWICK

But both of you were vowed Duke Humphrey's foes,
And you (forsooth) had the good duke to keep.
'Tis like you would not feast him like a friend,
And 'tis well seen he found an enemy.

QUEEN

Then you belike suspect these noblemen
187 As guilty of Duke Humphrey's timeless death.

WARWICK

Who finds the heifer dead and bleeding fresh
And sees fast-by a butcher with an axe,
But will suspect 'twas he that made the slaughter?
191 Who finds the partridge in the puttock's nest
But may imagine how the bird was dead,
Although the kite soar with unbloodied beak?
Even so suspicious is this tragedy.

QUEEN

Are you the butcher, Suffolk? Where's your knife?
Is Beaufort termed a kite? Where are his talons?

SUFFOLK

I wear no knife to slaughter sleeping men;
But here's a vengeful sword, rusted with ease,
That shall be scourèd in his rancorous heart
That slanders me with murder's crimson badge.
Say, if thou dar'st, proud Lord of Warwickshire,
That I am faulty in Duke Humphrey's death.
                    [Exeunt Cardinal, Somerset, and Attendants.
                                    Bed drawn in.]

WARWICK

What dares not Warwick, if false Suffolk dare him?

QUEEN

204 He dares not calm his contumelious spirit,

---

187 *timeless* untimely   191 *puttock's* kite's (cf. l. 196)   204 *contumelious*
contentious

Nor cease to be an arrogant controller, 205
Though Suffolk dare him twenty thousand times.

WARWICK
Madam, be still – with reverence may I say,
For every word you speak in his behalf
Is slander to your royal dignity.

SUFFOLK
Blunt-witted lord, ignoble in demeanor!
If ever lady wronged her lord so much,
Thy mother took into her blameful bed
Some stern untutored churl, and noble stock
Was graft with crab-tree slip, whose fruit thou art, 214
And never of the Nevils' noble race.

WARWICK
But that the guilt of murder bucklers thee, 216
And I should rob the deathsman of his fee,
Quitting thee thereby of ten thousand shames, 218
And that my sovereign's presence makes me mild,
I would, false murd'rous coward, on thy knee
Make thee beg pardon for thy passèd speech 221
And say it was thy mother that thou meant'st,
That thou thyself wast born in bastardy;
And after all this fearful homage done, 224
Give thee thy hire, and send thy soul to hell,
Pernicious bloodsucker of sleeping men!

SUFFOLK
Thou shalt be waking while I shed thy blood,
If from this presence thou dar'st go with me.

WARWICK
Away even now, or I will drag thee hence!
Unworthy though thou art, I'll cope with thee
And do some service to Duke Humphrey's ghost.
　　　　　Exeunt [Suffolk and Warwick, pulling him out].

---

205 *controller* critic　**214** *slip* cutting (probably with punning reference to the sense 'moral lapse')　**216** *bucklers* shields　**218** *Quitting* ridding　**221** *passèd* just spoken　**224** *fearful homage* cowardly submission

KING

What stronger breastplate than a heart untainted?
Thrice is he armed that hath his quarrel just,
And he but naked, though locked up in steel,
Whose conscience with injustice is corrupted.

   A noise within [of Commons crying 'Down with
   Suffolk'].

QUEEN

What noise is this?

   Enter Suffolk and Warwick, with their weapons
   drawn.

KING

Why, how now, lords? your wrathful weapons drawn
Here in our presence? Dare you be so bold?
Why, what tumultuous clamor have we here?

SUFFOLK

The trait'rous Warwick, with the men of Bury,
Set all upon me, mighty sovereign.

   Enter Salisbury [from the Commons within, again
   crying 'Down with Suffolk'].

SALISBURY *[to the Commons within]*

242   Sirs, stand apart. The king shall know your mind. –
Dread lord, the commons send you word by me,
Unless Lord Suffolk straight be done to death
Or banishèd fair England's territories,
They will by violence tear him from your palace
And torture him with grievous ling'ring death.
They say, by him the good Duke Humphrey died;
They say, in him they fear your highness' death;
And mere instinct of love and loyalty –
251   Free from a stubborn opposite intent,
As being thought to contradict your liking –
253   Makes them thus forward in his banishment.

---

242 *stand apart* separate, fall back   251–52 *Free ... liking* i.e. innocent of
any stubbornness in crossing your desire   253 *forward in* insistent upon

They say, in care of your most royal person,
That if your highness should intend to sleep
And charge that no man should disturb your rest
In pain of your dislike or pain of death,
Yet, notwithstanding such a strait edict,
Were there a serpent seen with forkèd tongue
That slily glided towards your majesty,
It were but necessary you were waked,
Lest, being suffered in that harmful slumber,
The mortal worm might make the sleep eternal.   263
And therefore do they cry, though you forbid,
That they will guard you, whe'r you will or no,
From such fell serpents as false Suffolk is;   266
With whose envenomèd and fatal sting
Your loving uncle, twenty times his worth,
They say is shamefully bereft of life.

COMMONS [within]
  An answer from the king, my Lord of Salisbury!

SUFFOLK
  'Tis like the commons, rude unpolished hinds,   271
Could send such message to their sovereign!
But you, my lord, were glad to be employed,
To show how quaint an orator you are.   274
But all the honor Salisbury hath won
Is that he was the lord ambassador
Sent from a sort of tinkers to the king.   277

COMMONS [within]
  An answer from the king, or we will all break in!

KING
  Go, Salisbury, and tell them all from me
I thank them for their tender loving care;
And had I not been cited so by them,   281
Yet did I purpose as they do entreat.

---

263 *mortal worm* deadly snake 266 *fell* savage, cruel 271 *'Tis like* it is
likely (ironic); *hinds* boors 274 *quaint* clever 277 *sort* gang 281 *cited*
incited

For sure my thoughts do hourly prophesy
Mischance unto my state by Suffolk's means;
And therefore by His Majesty I swear
Whose far unworthy deputy I am,
287   He shall not breathe infection in this air
But three days longer, on the pain of death.

[Exit Salisbury.]

QUEEN
O Henry, let me plead for gentle Suffolk.

KING
Ungentle queen, to call him gentle Suffolk.
No more, I say. If thou dost plead for him,
Thou wilt but add increase unto my wrath.
Had I but said, I would have kept my word;
But when I swear, it is irrevocable. —
If after three days' space thou here be'st found
On any ground that I am ruler of,
The world shall not be ransom for thy life. —
Come, Warwick, come, good Warwick, go with me;
I have great matters to impart to thee.

Exit [King with Warwick].

QUEEN
Mischance and sorrow go along with you;
Heart's discontent and sour affliction
Be playfellows to keep you company.
There's two of you; the devil make a third,
And threefold vengeance tend upon your steps.

SUFFOLK
Cease, gentle queen, these execrations
306   And let thy Suffolk take his heavy leave.

QUEEN
Fie, coward woman and soft-hearted wretch.
Hast thou not spirit to curse thine enemy?

SUFFOLK
A plague upon them! Wherefore should I curse them?

287 *breathe infection in* infect by breathing into   306 *heavy* mournful

Would curses kill as doth the mandrake's groan,   310
I would invent as bitter searching terms,
As curst, as harsh, and horrible to hear,   312
Delivered strongly through my fixèd teeth,
With full as many signs of deadly hate,
As lean-faced Envy in her loathsome cave.
My tongue should stumble in mine earnest words,
Mine eyes should sparkle like the beaten flint,
Mine hair be fixed an end, as one distract;   318
Ay, every joint should seem to curse and ban;   319
And even now my burdened heart would break
Should I not curse them. Poison be their drink!
Gall, worse than gall, the daintiest that they taste;
Their sweetest shade a grove of cypress trees;   323
Their chiefest prospect murd'ring basilisks;   324
Their softest touch as smart as lizards' stings;   325
Their music frightful as the serpent's hiss,
And boding screech owls make the consort full!   327
All the foul terrors in dark-seated hell —

QUEEN
Enough, sweet Suffolk. Thou torment'st thyself;
And these dread curses, like the sun 'gainst glass,
Or like an overchargèd gun, recoil
And turn the force of them upon thyself.

SUFFOLK
You bade me ban, and will you bid me leave?   333
Now by the ground that I am banished from,
Well could I curse away a winter's night,
Though standing naked on a mountain top
Where biting cold would never let grass grow,
And think it but a minute spent in sport.

310 *mandrake's groan* (the mandrake, a poisonous plant with a forked root that gave it a vague similarity to the human form, was supposed, when pulled from the ground, to utter a cry or groan which could kill the hearer or drive him mad) 312 *curst* full of damnation 318 *an* on; *distract* distracted 319 *ban* chide bitterly 323 *cypress trees* (because often planted near cemeteries) 324 *basilisks* (see III, ii, 52n.) 325 *lizards'* serpents' 327 *consort* band of musicians 333 *leave* stop

QUEEN

O, let me entreat thee cease ! Give me thy hand,
That I may dew it with my mournful tears ;
Nor let the rain of heaven wet this place
342 To wash away my woeful monuments.
O, could this kiss be printed in thy hand,
    [Kisses his hand.]
344 That thou mightst think upon these by the seal
Through whom a thousand sighs are breathed for thee !
346 So get thee gone, that I may know my grief.
347 'Tis but surmised whiles thou art standing by,
As one that surfeits, thinking on a want.
349 I will repeal thee or, be well assured,
350 Adventure to be banishèd myself ;
And banishèd I am, if but from thee.
Go, speak not to me. Even now be gone.
O, go not yet ! Even thus two friends condemned
Embrace, and kiss, and take ten thousand leaves,
Loather a hundred times to part than die.
Yet now farewell, and farewell life with thee.

SUFFOLK

Thus is poor Suffolk ten times banishèd,
Once by the king and three times thrice by thee.
'Tis not the land I care for, wert thou thence.
A wilderness is populous enough,
So Suffolk had thy heavenly company ;
For where thou art, there is the world itself
363 With every several pleasure in the world ;
And where thou art not, desolation.
I can no more. Live thou to joy thy life ;
Myself no joy in naught, but that thou liv'st.
    Enter Vaux.

342 *monuments* remembrances (i.e. the marks of my tears)   344 *That ... seal* i.e. that by the impression (seal) my lips make upon your hand, you may think of them (*these* [lips] is the antecedent of *whom*)   346 *know* fully realize   347–48 *'Tis ... want* i.e. while you remain here, I can only guess at the experience of hunger   349 *repeal thee* have your banishment repealed   350 *Adventure* risk   363 *several* different, distinct

QUEEN
Whither goes Vaux so fast? What news, I prithee?

VAUX
To signify unto his majesty
That Cardinal Beaufort is at point of death,
For suddenly a grievous sickness took him
That makes him gasp and stare and catch the air,
Blaspheming God and cursing men on earth.
Sometime he talks as if Duke Humphrey's ghost
Were by his side; sometime he calls the king
And whispers to his pillow, as to him,
The secrets of his overchargèd soul;
And I am sent to tell his majesty
That even now he cries aloud for him.

QUEEN
Go tell this heavy message to the king.   *Exit [Vaux].* 379
Ay me! What is this world? What news are these?
But wherefore grieve I at an hour's poor loss,   381
Omitting Suffolk's exile, my soul's treasure?
Why only, Suffolk, mourn I not for thee,
And with the southern clouds contend in tears –   384
Theirs for the earth's increase, mine for my sorrow's?
Now get thee hence. The king thou know'st is coming.
If thou be found by me, thou art but dead.

SUFFOLK
If I depart from thee, I cannot live;
And in thy sight to die, what were it else
But like a pleasant slumber in thy lap?
Here could I breathe my soul into the air,
As mild and gentle as the cradle-babe
Dying with mother's dug between its lips;
Where, from thy sight, I should be raging mad
And cry out for thee to close up mine eyes,
To have thee with thy lips to stop my mouth.

---

379 *heavy* serious, sad   381 *hour's poor loss* (the cardinal, an old man, had only a short time to live; the loss of this 'hour' is not worth great grief)   384 *southern clouds* (conventional source of rain)

So shouldst thou either turn my flying soul,
Or I should breathe it so into thy body,
399   And then it lived in sweet Elysium.
To die by thee were but to die in jest;
From thee to die were torture more than death.
O, let me stay, befall what may befall!

QUEEN
403   Away! Though parting be a fretful corrosive,
404   It is applièd to a deathful wound.
To France, sweet Suffolk. Let me hear from thee;
For wheresoe'er thou art in this world's globe,
407   I'll have an Iris that shall find thee out.

SUFFOLK
I go.

QUEEN   And take my heart with thee.
[She kisses him.]

SUFFOLK
409   A jewel, locked into the woefull'st cask
That ever did contain a thing of worth.
Even as a splitted bark, so sunder we.
This way fall I to death.

QUEEN   This way for me.
Exeunt [severally].

*

III, iii   *Enter the King, Salisbury, and Warwick, to the*
            Cardinal in bed [raving and staring as if mad].

KING
How fares my lord? Speak, Beaufort, to thy sovereign.

CARDINAL
If thou be'st Death, I'll give thee England's treasure,
Enough to purchase such another island,
So thou wilt let me live and feel no pain.

---

399 *Elysium* classical Paradise   403 *corrosive* painful medicine   404
deathful deadly   407 *Iris* messenger of Juno, queen of the gods   409 *cask*
casket
III, iii The Cardinal's bedchamber

KING
Ah, what a sign it is of evil life
Where death's approach is seen so terrible.

WARWICK
Beaufort, it is thy sovereign speaks to thee.

CARDINAL
Bring me unto my trial when you will.
Died he not in his bed? Where should he die? 9
Can I make men live, whe'r they will or no?
O, torture me no more! I will confess.
Alive again? Then show me where he is.
I'll give a thousand pound to look upon him.
He hath no eyes; the dust hath blinded them.
Comb down his hair. Look, look! it stands upright,
Like lime-twigs set to catch my wingèd soul. 16
Give me some drink, and bid the apothecary
Bring the strong poison that I bought of him.

KING
O thou eternal Mover of the heavens,
Look with a gentle eye upon this wretch.
O, beat away the busy meddling fiend
That lays strong siege unto this wretch's soul,
And from his bosom purge this black despair.

WARWICK
See how the pangs of death do make him grin.

SALISBURY
Disturb him not; let him pass peaceably.

KING
Peace to his soul, if God's good pleasure be.
Lord Cardinal, if thou think'st on heaven's bliss,
Hold up thy hand, make signal of thy hope.
He dies and makes no sign. O God, forgive him.

WARWICK
So bad a death argues a monstrous life. 30

9 *he* i.e. Duke Humphrey   16 *lime-twigs* (see I, iii, 86n.)   30 *argues* gives proof of

KING

    Forbear to judge, for we are sinners all.
32 Close up his eyes and draw the curtain close,
    And let us all to meditation.   *Exeunt.*

*

IV, i   *Alarum. Fight at sea. Ordnance goes off. Enter*
          Lieutenant, [Master, Mate, Walter Whitmore, and
          Soldiers, guarding] Suffolk [disguised, and
          Gentlemen].

LIEUTENANT

1   The gaudy, blabbing, and remorseful day
    Is crept into the bosom of the sea,
3   And now loud-howling wolves arouse the jades
    That drag the tragic melancholy night,
    Who with their drowsy, slow, and flagging wings
6   Clip dead men's graves, and from their misty jaws
    Breathe foul contagious darkness in the air.
8   Therefore bring forth the soldiers of our prize;
9   For, whilst our pinnace anchors in the Downs,
    Here shall they make their ransom on the sand
    Or with their blood stain this discolored shore.
    Master, this prisoner freely give I thee;
13 And thou that art his Mate, make boot of this;
    The other, Walter Whitmore, is thy share.

1. GENTLEMAN

    What is my ransom, Master? Let me know.

MASTER

    A thousand crowns, or else lay down your head.

MATE

    And so much shall you give, or off goes yours.

32 *curtain* i.e. of the bed
IV, i The coast of Kent, near the Downs   **1** *gaudy* bright; *blabbing*
garrulous, telltale; *remorseful* full of pitiable events   **3** *jades* horses, i.e. the
dragons of Hecate, which draw the night across the sky   **6** *Clip* embrace
8 *soldiers … prize* i.e. the soldiers we have captured   **9** *Downs* anchorage
off Kent   **13** *boot* profit

LIEUTENANT
> What, think you much to pay two thousand crowns,
> And bear the name and port of gentlemen?   19
> Cut both the villains' throats, for die you shall.
> The lives of those which we have lost in fight
> Be counterpoised with such a petty sum?

1. GENTLEMAN
> I'll give it, sir, and therefore spare my life.

2. GENTLEMAN
> And so will I, and write home for it straight.

WHITMORE
> I lost mine eye in laying the prize aboard,   25
>   [To Suffolk]
> And therefore to revenge it shalt thou die;
> And so should these, if I might have my will.

LIEUTENANT
> Be not so rash; take ransom, let him live.

SUFFOLK
> Look on my George; I am a gentleman.   29
> Rate me at what thou wilt, thou shalt be paid.   30

WHITMORE
> And so am I. My name is Walter Whitmore.
> How now? Why starts thou? What, doth death affright?

SUFFOLK
> Thy name affrights me, in whose sound is death.   33
> A cunning man did calculate my birth   34
> And told me that by water I should die.
> Yet let not this make thee be bloody-minded;
> Thy name is Gaultier, being rightly sounded.   37

WHITMORE
> Gaultier or Walter, which it is I care not.
> Never yet did base dishonor blur our name

19 *port* demeanor   25 *laying ... aboard* boarding the captured ship   29 *George* badge representing Saint George and the dragon, an insigne of the Order of the Garter   30 *Rate* value   33 *sound* (*Walter* was pronounced 'Wa'ter')   34 *cunning man* fortune-teller; *calculate my birth* (astrologers required the moment of one's birth in order to cast a horoscope)   37 *Gaultier* (*Walter* in French)

But with our sword we wiped away the blot;
Therefore, when merchantlike I sell revenge,
42 Broke be my sword, my arms torn and defaced,
And I proclaimed a coward through the world.

SUFFOLK
Stay, Whitmore, for thy prisoner is a prince,
The Duke of Suffolk, William de la Pole.

WHITMORE
The Duke of Suffolk muffled up in rags?

SUFFOLK
Ay, but these rags are no part of the duke.
[Jove sometime went disguised, and why not I?]

LIEUTENANT
But Jove was never slain, as thou shalt be.

SUFFOLK
50 Obscure and lousy swain, King Henry's blood,
The honorable blood of Lancaster,
52 Must not be shed by such a jaded groom.
Hast thou not kissed thy hand and held my stirrup?
54 Bare-headed plodded by my footcloth mule,
And thought thee happy when I shook my head?
How often hast thou waited at my cup,
57 Fed from my trencher, kneeled down at the board,
When I have feasted with Queen Margaret?
59 Remember it, and let it make thee crestfall'n,
60 Ay, and allay this thy abortive pride.
61 How in our voiding lobby hast thou stood
And duly waited for my coming forth!
This hand of mine hath writ in thy behalf,
And therefore shall it charm thy riotous tongue.

---

42 *arms* coat of arms   50 *King Henry's blood* (Suffolk falsely claimed that his mother was a distant cousin of Henry VI)   52 *jaded* (1) lowly-bred, (2) having to do with horses   54 *footcloth mule* mule covered with an ornamented caparison   57 *trencher* platter   59 *crestfall'n* humble (with punning allusion to Whitmore's claim to gentility, the 'crest' being a part of the armorial bearings)   60 *abortive* monstrous   61 *voiding lobby* waiting room

WHITMORE
Speak, captain, shall I stab the forlorn swain? 65

LIEUTENANT
First let my words stab him, as he hath me.

SUFFOLK
Base slave, thy words are blunt, and so art thou.

LIEUTENANT
Convey him hence, and on our long-boat's side
Strike off his head.

SUFFOLK   Thou dar'st not, for thy own.

LIEUTENANT Pole – 70
SUFFOLK Pole?

LIEUTENANT
Ay, kennel, puddle, sink! whose filth and dirt 72
Troubles the silver spring where England drinks.
Now will I dam up this thy yawning mouth
For swallowing the treasure of the realm.
Thy lips that kissed the queen shall sweep the ground,
And thou that smiledst at good Duke Humphrey's death
Against the senseless winds shall grin in vain, 78
Who in contempt shall hiss at thee again.
And wedded be thou to the hags of hell
For daring to affy a mighty lord 81
Unto the daughter of a worthless king,
Having neither subject, wealth, nor diadem.
By devilish policy art thou grown great,
And, like ambitious Sulla, overgorged 85
With gobbets of thy mother's bleeding heart. 86
By thee Anjou and Maine were sold to France;
The false revolting Normans thorough thee 88
Disdain to call us lord, and Picardy

---

65 *captain* (a courtesy title given – as customarily – to the lieutenant because he is the commander of a ship) 70–72 *Pole … kennel* (wordplay on 'poll' [head], 'Pole' [Suffolk's family name, pronounced 'pool'], and 'pool' [of water]; a kennel is an open gutter) 72 *sink* cesspool 78 *senseless* unfeeling 81 *affy* affiance 85 *Sulla* Lucius Cornelius Sulla (138–78 B.C.), the first Roman dictator to issue proscriptions 86 *gobbets* chunks of flesh 88 *thorough* through

Hath slain their governors, surprised our forts,
And sent the ragged soldiers wounded home.
The princely Warwick and the Nevils all,
Whose dreadful swords were never drawn in vain,
As hating thee, are rising up in arms;
And now the house of York, thrust from the crown
By shameful murder of a guiltless king
And lofty, proud, encroaching tyranny,
Burns with revenging fire, whose hopeful colors
99   Advance our half-faced sun, striving to shine,
100   Under the which is writ 'Invitis nubibus.'
The commons here in Kent are up in arms,
And to conclude, reproach and beggary
Is crept into the palace of our king,
And all by thee. Away! convey him hence.

SUFFOLK
O that I were a god, to shoot forth thunder
Upon these paltry, servile, abject drudges.
Small things make base men proud. This villain here,
Being captain of a pinnace, threatens more
109   Than Bargulus, the strong Illyrian pirate.
Drones suck not eagles' blood but rob beehives.
It is impossible that I should die
By such a lowly vassal as thyself.
Thy words move rage and not remorse in me.
I go of message from the queen to France.
115   I charge thee waft me safely 'cross the Channel.

LIEUTENANT Walter!

WHITMORE
Come, Suffolk, I must waft thee to thy death.
118 SUFFOLK Paene gelidus timor occupat artus. It is thee
    I fear.

---

99 *half-faced sun* (a sun bursting through clouds was the device of Edward
III and Richard II, the *guiltless king* of l. 96)   100 *Invitis nubibus* in spite
of clouds (source unidentified)   109 *Bargulus* i.e. Bardylis (fl. 383 B.C.) a
Balkan chieftain (Shakespeare's 'Bargulus' comes from Cicero, *De Officiis*,
II, 11)   115 *waft* transport by water   118 *Paene ... artus* cold fear seizes
my limbs almost entirely

WHITMORE
> Thou shalt have cause to fear before I leave thee.
> What, are ye daunted now ? Now will ye stoop ?

1. GENTLEMAN
> My gracious lord, entreat him, speak him fair.

SUFFOLK
> Suffolk's imperial tongue is stern and rough,
> Used to command, untaught to plead for favor.
> Far be it we should honor such as these
> With humble suit. No, rather let my head
> Stoop to the block than these knees bow to any
> Save to the God of heaven and to my king ;
> And sooner dance upon a bloody pole
> Than stand uncovered to the vulgar groom.   129
> True nobility is exempt from fear.
> More can I bear than you dare execute.

LIEUTENANT
> Hale him away and let him talk no more.

SUFFOLK
> Come, soldiers, show what cruelty ye can,
> That this my death may never be forgot.
> Great men oft die by vile bezonians.   135
> A Roman sworder and banditto slave
> Murdered sweet Tully ; Brutus' bastard hand   137
> Stabbed Julius Caesar ; savage islanders   138
> Pompey the Great ; and Suffolk dies by pirates.
> > *Exit Walter [Whitmore] with Suffolk.*

LIEUTENANT
> And as for these whose ransom we have set,
> It is our pleasure one of them depart.
> Therefore come you with us, and let him go.
> > *Exeunt Lieutenant and the rest.*

---

129 *uncovered* bareheaded   **135** *bezonians* beggars   **137** *Tully* i.e. Marcus
Tullius Cicero ; *Brutus' bastard hand* (Brutus was reputed to be the bastard
son of Julius Caesar)   **138** *savage islanders* i.e. of Lesbos (according to one
version of the story ; according to Plutarch, Pompey was killed in Egypt by
his former officers in Ptolemy's hire)

Manet the First Gentleman.
Enter Walter [Whitmore] with the body [of Suffolk].

WHITMORE
There let his head and lifeless body lie
Until the queen his mistress bury it.   *Exit Walter.*

1. GENTLEMAN
O barbarous and bloody spectacle!
His body will I bear unto the king.
If he revenge it not, yet will his friends;
148 So will the queen, that living held him dear.
                               [Exit with the body.]

*

IV, ii   *Enter two Rebels [with long staves].*

1. REBEL Come and get thee a sword, though made of a
2 lath. They have been up these two days.

2. REBEL They have the more need to sleep now then.

1. REBEL I tell thee Jack Cade the clothier means to dress
5 the commonwealth and turn it and set a new nap upon it.

2. REBEL So he had need, for 'tis threadbare. Well, I say
it was never merry world in England since gentlemen
8 came up.

1. REBEL O miserable age! Virtue is not regarded in
handicraftsmen.

11 2. REBEL The nobility think scorn to go in leather aprons.

1. REBEL Nay, more, the king's council are no good
workmen.

2. REBEL True; and yet it is said, 'Labor in thy voca-
tion'; which is as much to say as 'Let the magistrates be
laboring men'; and therefore should we be magistrates.

1. REBEL Thou hast hit it; for there's no better sign of a
brave mind than a hard hand.

---

148 s.d. *body* (and the head, with which the queen enters at IV, iv)
IV, ii A heath in Kent near London (Blackheath)   2 *lath* slight piece of
wood   5 *nap* the fuzz or down on the surface of a piece of cloth (with
allusion to Cade's occupation of shearman, mentioned at l. 121)   8 *came
up* rose into fashion   11 *leather aprons* (worn by workmen)

2 . REBEL I see them, I see them! There's Best's son, the tanner of Wingham –   20

1 . REBEL He shall have the skins of our enemies to make dog's leather of.   22

2 . REBEL And Dick the butcher –

1 . REBEL Then is sin struck down like an ox and iniquity's throat cut like a calf.

2 . REBEL And Smith the weaver.

1 . REBEL Argo, their thread of life is spun.   27

2 . REBEL Come, come, let's fall in with them.

> *Drum. Enter Cade, Dick [the] Butcher, Smith the Weaver, and a Sawyer, with infinite numbers [bearing long staves].*

CADE We, John Cade, so termed of our supposed father –

BUTCHER *[aside]* Or rather, of stealing a cade of herrings.   30

CADE For our enemies shall fall before us, inspired with the spirit of putting down kings and princes – Command silence!   31

BUTCHER Silence!

CADE My father was a Mortimer –   35

BUTCHER *[aside]* He was an honest man and a good bricklayer.   36

CADE My mother a Plantagenet –

BUTCHER *[aside]* I knew her well. She was a midwife.

CADE My wife descended of the Lacies.   39

BUTCHER *[aside]* She was indeed a pedlar's daughter and sold many laces.

WEAVER *[aside]* But now of late, not able to travel with her furred pack, she washes bucks here at home.   43

---

20 *Wingham* a village near Canterbury 22 *dog's leather* (used for gloves) 27 *Argo* ergo, therefore (mispronounced) 30 *cade* barrel 31 *fall* (punning on 'cado,' I fall) 35 *Mortimer* (who could, like York, claim the crown through Lionel, Duke of Clarence; see III, i, 359n.) 36 *bricklayer* (invited by a pun on 'Mortimer' / 'mortarer') 39 *Lacies* (Lacy was the surname of the Earls of Lincoln) 43 *furred pack* pedlar's pack, made of skin with the hair outward; *washes bucks* does laundry ('buck' is lye; 'bucks' are the clothes treated with it. There is also a punning reference to 'furred pack' as a herd of deer.)

CADE Therefore am I of an honorable house.

45 BUTCHER [aside] Ay, by my faith, the field is honorable
and there was he born, under a hedge; for his father had
47 never a house but the cage.

CADE Valiant I am.

49 WEAVER [aside] 'A must needs, for beggary is valiant.

CADE I am able to endure much.

BUTCHER [aside] No question of that, for I have seen him
whipped three market days together.

CADE I fear neither sword nor fire.

WEAVER [aside] He need not fear the sword, for his coat
55 is of proof.

BUTCHER [aside] But methinks he should stand in fear of
57 fire, being burnt i' th' hand for stealing of sheep.

CADE Be brave then, for your captain is brave and vows
reformation. There shall be in England seven halfpenny
60 loaves sold for a penny; the three-hooped pot shall have
61 ten hoops, and I will make it felony to drink small beer.
62 All the realm shall be in common, and in Cheapside
63 shall my palfrey go to grass; and when I am king, as
king I will be –

ALL God save your majesty!

CADE I thank you, good people – there shall be no money;
67 all shall eat and drink on my score; and I will apparel
them all in one livery, that they may agree like brothers
and worship me their lord.

BUTCHER The first thing we do, let's kill all the lawyers.

CADE Nay, that I mean to do. Is not this a lamentable
thing, that of the skin of an innocent lamb should be

45 *field* (with punning allusion to a heraldic 'field,' the surface of an
escutcheon)   47 *cage* a small portable prison for the exposure of minor
criminals in public places   49 *valiant* sturdy (the giving of alms to 'valiant
beggars,' those able to work, was illegal)   55 *proof* (1) of good quality,
reliable (of a coat of mail), (2) well-worn   57 *burnt i' th' hand* branded   60
three-hooped pot (Wooden drinking pots were banded with metal, a quart
pot having three bands or hoops. Cade means that for the price of a quart
one will be able to buy more than three quarts.)   61 *small beer* weak beer
(everyone will drink stronger double-beer)   62 *Cheapside* the location of
many of the London markets   63 *palfrey* saddle horse   67 *score* account

made parchment? that parchment, being scribbled o'er,
should undo a man? Some say the bee stings, but I say
'tis the bee's wax; for I did but seal once to a thing, and I
was never mine own man since. How now? Who's
there?

    Enter a Clerk [as prisoner].

WEAVER The clerk of Chartham. He can write and read   77
  and cast account.   78

CADE O monstrous!

WEAVER We took him setting of boys' copies.   80

CADE Here's a villain.

WEAVER Has a book in his pocket with red letters in't.   82

CADE Nay, then he is a conjurer.

BUTCHER Nay, he can make obligations and write court-   84
  hand.

CADE I am sorry for't. The man is a proper man, of mine   85
  honor. Unless I find him guilty, he shall not die. Come
  hither, sirrah, I must examine thee. What is thy name?

CLERK Emmanuel.

BUTCHER They use to write it on the top of letters. 'Twill   89
  go hard with you.

CADE Let me alone. Dost thou use to write thy name? or
  hast thou a mark to thyself, like an honest plain-dealing
  man?

CLERK Sir, I thank God, I have been so well brought up
  that I can write my name.

ALL He hath confessed. Away with him! He's a villain
  and a traitor.

CADE Away with him, I say. Hang him with his pen and
  inkhorn about his neck.   *Exit one with the Clerk.*

    Enter Messenger.

MESSENGER Where's our general?

77 *Chartham* a village near Canterbury   78 *cast account* do arithmetic   80
setting . . . copies preparing handwriting exercises for boys   82 *book . . . in't*
(probably a primer)   84 *obligations* bonds; *court-hand* varieties of handwriting, used for legal documents   85 *proper* decent looking   89 *They . . .*
letters (*Emmanuel*, 'God with us,' was sometimes prefixed to letters and
documents)

100 CADE Here I am, thou particular fellow.

MESSENGER Fly, fly, fly! Sir Humphrey Stafford and his
brother are hard by, with the king's forces.

CADE Stand, villain, stand, or I'll fell thee down. He shall
be encount'red with a man as good as himself. He is but
a knight, is 'a?

106 MESSENGER No.

CADE To equal him, I will make myself a knight presently.
[Kneels.] Rise up Sir John Mortimer. *[Rises.]* Now have
at him!

*Enter Sir Humphrey Stafford and his brother
[William], with Drum and Soldiers.*

STAFFORD

110 Rebellious hinds, the filth and scum of Kent,
Marked for the gallows, lay your weapons down;
Home to your cottages, forsake this groom.

113 The king is merciful, if you revolt.

WILLIAM

But angry, wrathful, and inclined to blood,
If you go forward. Therefore yield or die.

CADE

116 As for these silken-coated slaves, I pass not.
It is to you, good people, that I speak,
Over whom (in time to come) I hope to reign,
For I am rightful heir unto the crown.

STAFFORD

Villain, thy father was a plasterer,

121 And thou thyself a shearman, art thou not?

CADE

And Adam was a gardener.

WILLIAM And what of that?

CADE

Marry, this: Edmund Mortimer, Earl of March,
Married the Duke of Clarence' daughter, did he not?

---

100 *particular* (in answer to 'general')   106 *No* i.e. yes, he is only a knight
110 *hinds* peasants   113 *revolt* turn back   116 *pass* care   121 *shearman*
workman who cuts the nap from cloth during its manufacture (cf. l. 5)

STAFFORD Ay, sir.

CADE

By her he had two children at one birth.

WILLIAM That's false.

CADE

Ay, there's the question. But I say 'tis true.
The elder of them, being put to nurse,
Was by a beggar woman stol'n away
And, ignorant of his birth and parentage,
Became a bricklayer when he came to age.
His son am I. Deny it if you can.

BUTCHER

Nay, 'tis too true. Therefore he shall be king.   135

WEAVER Sir, he made a chimney in my father's house,
and the bricks are alive at this day to testify it. Therefore
deny it not.

STAFFORD

And will you credit this base drudge's words   139
That speaks he knows not what?

ALL

Ay, marry, will we. Therefore get ye gone.

WILLIAM

Jack Cade, the Duke of York hath taught you this.

CADE [aside]

He lies, for I invented it myself. –
Go to, sirrah, tell the king from me that, for his father's
sake, Henry the Fifth (in whose time boys went to span- 145
counter for French crowns), I am content he shall reign, 146
but I'll be Protector over him.

BUTCHER And furthermore we'll have the Lord Say's 148
head for selling the dukedom of Maine.

135 *too* very   139 *drudge's* workman's   145 *span-counter* a game in which
one player attempts to toss a counter to land less than a span's distance
from another's counter   146 *crowns* (1) coins stamped with a crown, (2)
kings or kingdoms, by synecdoche   148 *Lord Say* (James Fiennes, Lord
Say and Sele and Treasurer of England at the time of Cade's rebellion, had
been associated with Suffolk in the loss of Anjou and Maine. He was hated
for his harshness.)

150 CADE And good reason; for thereby is England mained
and fain to go with a staff, but that my puissance holds it
up. Fellow kings, I tell you that that Lord Say hath
gelded the commonwealth and made it an eunuch; and
more than that, he can speak French, and therefore he is
a traitor.

STAFFORD
O gross and miserable ignorance.

CADE Nay, answer, if you can. The Frenchmen are our
enemies. Go to then, I ask but this: Can he that speaks
with the tongue of an enemy be a good counsellor, or
no?

ALL No, no! and therefore we'll have his head.

WILLIAM
160   Well, seeing gentle words will not prevail,
Assail them with the army of the king.

STAFFORD
Herald, away; and throughout every town
Proclaim them traitors that are up with Cade,
That those which fly before the battle ends
May, even in their wives' and children's sight,
Be hanged up for example at their doors;
And you that be the king's friends, follow me.
                              Exit [Stafford with his men].

CADE
And you that love the commons, follow me.
Now show yourself men; 'tis for liberty!
We will not leave one lord, one gentleman;
171   Spare none but such as go in clouted shoon,
For they are thrifty honest men and such
As would (but that they dare not) take our parts.

BUTCHER They are all in order and march toward us.

CADE But then are we in order when we are most out of
order. Come, march forward!   *Exeunt.*

---

150 *mained* maimed   171 *clouted shoon* hobnailed shoes

Alarums to the fight, wherein both the Staffords are IV, iii
slain. Enter Cade and the rest.

CADE Where's Dick, the butcher of Ashford?

BUTCHER Here, sir.

CADE They fell before thee like sheep and oxen, and thou
behavedst thyself as if thou hadst been in thine own
slaughterhouse. Therefore thus will I reward thee: the
Lent shall be as long again as it is, and thou shalt have a 6
license to kill for a hundred lacking one.

BUTCHER I desire no more.

CADE And, to speak truth, thou deserv'st no less. This
monument of the victory will I bear *[puts on Sir Humphrey's helmet]*; and the bodies shall be dragged at my
horse heels till I do come to London, where we will have
the mayor's sword borne before us.

BUTCHER If we mean to thrive and do good, break open
the jails and let out the prisoners.

CADE Fear not that, I warrant thee. Come, let's march to- 16
wards London. *Exeunt.*

*

Enter the King, with a supplication, and the Queen IV, iv
*with Suffolk's head; the Duke of Buckingham and
the Lord Say.*

QUEEN *[apart]*
Oft have I heard that grief softens the mind
And makes it fearful and degenerate.
Think therefore on revenge and cease to weep.
But who can cease to weep, and look on this?
Here may his head lie on my throbbing breast,
But where's the body that I should embrace?

IV, iii 6–7 *Lent ... one* (In Queen Elizabeth's reign the slaughtering of
meat was forbidden during Lent except for the provision of the sick. For
Dick's benefit Cade will double the length of Lent and allow him to supply
meat to ninety-nine people a week or, possibly, to slaughter ninety-nine
animals a week.) 16 *Fear* doubt
IV, iv The royal palace in London s.d. *Lord Say* (see IV, ii, 148n.)

BUCKINGHAM What answer makes your grace to the
rebels' supplication?

KING

I'll send some holy bishop to entreat,
10 For God forbid so many simple souls
Should perish by the sword. And I myself,
Rather than bloody war shall cut them short,
Will parley with Jack Cade their general.
But stay, I'll read it over once again.

QUEEN [apart]

Ah, barbarous villains; hath this lovely face
Ruled like a wandering planet over me,
And could it not enforce them to relent
That were unworthy to behold the same?

KING

Lord Say, Jack Cade hath sworn to have thy head.

SAY

20 Ay, but I hope your highness shall have his.

KING

How now, madam?
Still lamenting and mourning for Suffolk's death?
I fear me, love, if that I had been dead,
Thou wouldest not have mourned so much for me.

QUEEN

No, my love, I should not mourn, but die for thee.
                  Enter a Messenger.

KING

How now, what news? Why com'st thou in such haste?

MESSENGER

27 The rebels are in Southwark. Fly, my lord!
Jack Cade proclaims himself Lord Mortimer,
Descended from the Duke of Clarence' house,
And calls your grace usurper openly
And vows to crown himself in Westminster.
His army is a ragged multitude

27 *Southwark* a suburb south of London, in Surrey

Of hinds and peasants, rude and merciless. 33
Sir Humphrey Stafford and his brother's death
Hath given them heart and courage to proceed.
All scholars, lawyers, courtiers, gentlemen,
They call false caterpillars and intend their death.

KING
O graceless men! they know not what they do.

BUCKINGHAM
My gracious lord, retire to Killingworth 39
Until a power be raised to put them down.

QUEEN
Ah, were the Duke of Suffolk now alive,
These Kentish rebels would be soon appeased.

KING
Lord Say, the traitors hate thee;
Therefore away with us to Killingworth.

SAY
So might your grace's person be in danger.
The sight of me is odious in their eyes;
And therefore in this city will I stay
And live alone as secret as I may.
        Enter another Messenger.

MESSENGER
Jack Cade hath gotten London Bridge;
The citizens fly and forsake their houses;
The rascal people, thirsting after prey,
Join with the traitor, and they jointly swear
To spoil the city and your royal court. 53

BUCKINGHAM
Then linger not, my lord. Away, take horse!

KING
Come, Margaret. God, our hope, will succor us.

QUEEN *[aside]*
My hope is gone now Suffolk is deceased.

33 *hinds* workers, peasants 39 *Killingworth* i.e. Kenilworth Castle in
Warwickshire 53 *spoil* despoil

KING [*to Lord Say*]
    Farewell, my lord. Trust not the Kentish rebels.
BUCKINGHAM
    Trust nobody, for fear you be betrayed.
SAY
    The trust I have is in mine innocence,
    And therefore am I bold and resolute.   *Exeunt.*

*

IV, v   *Enter [aloft] Lord Scales upon the Tower, walking.*
               Then enters two or three Citizens below.

SCALES
    How now? Is Jack Cade slain?
1. CITIZEN No, my lord, nor likely to be slain; for they
    have won the Bridge, killing all those that withstand
    them. The Lord Mayor craves aid of your honor from
    the Tower to defend the city from the rebels.
SCALES
    Such aid as I can spare you shall command,
    But I am troubled here with them myself;
    The rebels have assayed to win the Tower.
9   But get you to Smithfield and gather head,
    And thither I will send you Matthew Goffe.
    Fight for your king, your country, and your lives;
    And so farewell, for I must hence again.   *Exeunt.*

*

IV, vi   *Enter Jack Cade and the rest, and strikes his staff on*
               London Stone.

CADE Now is Mortimer lord of this city. And here, sitting
    upon London Stone, I charge and command that, of the

IV, v Before the Tower of London   s.d. *Lord Scales* (Lord Thomas
Scales, who had fought with Talbot in France, was charged by the king
with the defense of the Tower)   9 *Smithfield* a section of London, in
which there were open fields
IV, vi The streets of London·   s.d. *London Stone* an ancient landmark, in
Cannon Street

city's cost, the pissing conduit run nothing but claret 3
wine this first year of our reign. And now henceforward
it shall be treason for any that calls me other than Lord
Mortimer.

    Enter a Soldier, running.

SOLDIER Jack Cade! Jack Cade!

CADE Knock him down there.

    They kill him.

BUTCHER If this fellow be wise, he'll never call ye Jack
Cade more. I think he hath a very fair warning.

    [Enter Messenger.]

MESSENGER My lord, there's an army gathered together
in Smithfield.

CADE Come then, let's go fight with them. But first go and
set London Bridge on fire, and, if you can, burn down
the Tower too. Come, let's away.   *Exeunt omnes.*

    Alarums. Matthew Goffe is slain, and all the rest   IV, vii
    [of the loyal forces]. Then enter Jack Cade with his
    company.

CADE So, sirs. Now go some and pull down the Savoy; 1
others to th' Inns of Court. Down with them all!   2

BUTCHER I have a suit unto your lordship.

CADE Be it a lordship, thou shalt have it for that word.

BUTCHER Only that the laws of England may come out of
your mouth.

2. REBEL *[aside]* Mass, 'twill be sore law then, for he was 7
thrust in the mouth with a spear, and 'tis not whole yet.

WEAVER *[aside]* Nay, John, it will be stinking law, for his
breath stinks with eating toasted cheese.

CADE I have thought upon it; it shall be so. Away, burn
all the records of the realm! My mouth shall be the
parliament of England.

---

3 *pissing conduit* a fountain from which the poor drew water
IV, vii 1 *Savoy* the London residence of the Duke of Lancaster (an
anachronism, as the building was burned during Wat Tyler's rebellion and
not rebuilt until 1505)   2 *Inns of Court* the centre of legal training and
practice   7 *sore* (1) poor, (2) painful

2. REBEL [*aside*] Then we are like to have biting statutes, unless his teeth be pulled out.

CADE And henceforward all things shall be in common.
Enter a Messenger.

MESSENGER My lord, a prize, a prize! Here's the Lord Say, which sold the towns in France; he that made us
19 pay one-and-twenty fifteens, and one shilling to the
20 pound, the last subsidy.
Enter First Rebel, with the Lord Say.

CADE Well, he shall be beheaded for it ten times. Ah, thou
22 say, thou serge, nay, thou buckram lord: now art thou
23 within point-blank of our jurisdiction regal. What canst thou answer to my majesty for giving up of Normandy
25 unto Mounsieur Basimecu, the Dauphin of France? Be it known unto thee by these presence, even the presence
27 of Lord Mortimer, that I am the besom that must sweep the court clean of such filth as thou art. Thou hast most traitorously corrupted the youth of the realm in erecting a grammar school; and whereas, before, our forefathers
31 had no other books but the score and the tally, thou hast
32 caused printing to be used, and, contrary to the king his crown and dignity, thou hast built a paper mill. It will be proved to thy face that thou hast men about thee that usually talk of a noun and a verb and such abominable words as no Christian ear can endure to hear. Thou hast appointed justices of peace, to call poor men before them about matters they were not able to answer. Moreover,

---

19–20 *one-and-twenty ... pound* i.e. very high personal property taxes ('fifteens' were a levy of one-fifteenth the value; 'one-and-twenty fifteens' is a deliberate exaggeration) 20 *the last subsidy* at the time of the last general tax 22 *serge* (from 'say,' a silk resembling serge); *buckram* a stiff, coarse linen (used in making props and artificial figures for the stage; thus, 'false') 23 *within point-blank of* i.e. directly before 25 *Basimecu* i.e. '*baise-mon-cul*,' kiss-my-arse 27 *besom* broom 31 *score ... tally* (To furnish a record of a debt, a stick would be scored or marked transversely and then split lengthwise, one half being retained by the debtor and one by the creditor. The two halves were called tallies.) 32 *king his* king's

thou hast put them in prison, and because they could 39
not read, thou hast hanged them, when, indeed, only for
that cause they have been most worthy to live. Thou
dost ride in a footcloth, dost thou not? 42

SAY What of that?

CADE Marry, thou ought'st not to let thy horse wear a
cloak when honester men than thou go in their hose and
doublets.

BUTCHER And work in their shirt too; as myself, for
example, that am a butcher.

SAY You men of Kent —

BUTCHER What say you of Kent?

SAY Nothing but this — 'tis 'bona terra, mala gens.' 51

CADE Away with him, away with him! He speaks Latin.

SAY
Hear me but speak, and bear me where'er you will.
Kent, in the Commentaries Caesar writ,
Is termed the civil'st place of all this isle.
Sweet is the country, because full of riches;
The people liberal, valiant, active, wealthy,
Which makes me hope you are not void of pity.
I sold not Maine, I lost not Normandy;
Yet to recover them would lose my life.
Justice with favor have I always done; 61
Prayers and tears have moved me, gifts could never.
When have I aught exacted at your hands,
But to maintain the king, the realm, and you?
Large gifts have I bestowed on learnèd clerks,
Because my book preferred me to the king. 66
And, seeing ignorance is the curse of God,
Knowledge the wing wherewith we fly to heaven,
Unless you be possessed with devilish spirits,

39–40 *could not read* i.e. could not read Latin and thus claim exemption from civil trial through 'benefit of clergy'   **42** *footcloth* (see IV, i, 54n.)   **51** *bona ... gens* a good country, a wicked people   **61** *favor* lenience   **66** *book* learning

You cannot but forbear to murder me.
This tongue hath parleyed unto foreign kings
72   For your behoof.

CADE Tut! when struck'st thou one blow in the field?

SAY

Great men have reaching hands. Oft have I struck
Those that I never saw, and struck them dead.

I. REBEL O monstrous coward! What, to come behind
folks?

SAY

These cheeks are pale for watching for your good.

CADE Give him a box o' th' ear, and that will make 'em
red again.

SAY

80   Long sitting to determine poor men's causes
Hath made me full of sickness and diseases.

82 CADE Ye shall have a hempen caudle then and pap with a
hatchet.

BUTCHER Why dost thou quiver, man?

SAY

The palsy, and not fear, provokes me.

CADE Nay, he nods at us, as who should say, 'I'll be even
with you.' I'll see if his head will stand steadier on a pole
or no. Take him away and behead him.

SAY

Tell me: wherein have I offended most?
Have I affected wealth or honor? Speak.
Are my chests filled up with extorted gold?
Is my apparel sumptuous to behold?
Whom have I injured, that ye seek my death?
These hands are free from guiltless blood-shedding,
This breast from harboring foul deceitful thoughts.
O, let me live!

---

72 *behoof* behalf   80 *sitting* i.e. as a judge   82 *caudle* warm gruel ('hempen
caudle' was a euphemism for the hangman's rope)   82–83 *pap . . . hatchet*
(proverbial, meaning to punish – children, usually – under the guise of
kindness)

CADE *[aside]* I feel remorse in myself with his words, but
I'll bridle it. He shall die, an it be but for pleading so
well for his life. – Away with him! he has a familiar under   99
his tongue; he speaks not a God's name. Go, take him   100
away, I say, and strike off his head presently; and then
break into his son-in-law's house, Sir James Cromer,   102
and strike off his head, and bring them both upon two
poles hither.

ALL It shall be done.

SAY

Ah, countrymen! If when you make your prayers,
God should be so obdurate as yourselves,
How would it fare with your departed souls?
And therefore yet relent, and save my life.

CADE Away with him, and do as I command ye.
                    [Exeunt some with the Lord Say.]
The proudest peer in the realm shall not wear a head on
his shoulders unless he pay me tribute. There shall not a
maid be married but she shall pay to me her maidenhead
ere they have it. Men shall hold of me in capite; and we   113
charge and command that their wives be as free as heart
can wish or tongue can tell.

BUTCHER My lord, when shall we go to Cheapside and
take up commodities upon our bills?   117

CADE Marry, presently.   118

ALL O brave!   119

        *Enter two with the heads [of the Lord Say and
        Sir James Cromer upon two poles].*

CADE But is not this braver? Let them kiss one another,   120
for they loved well when they were alive. Now part them

---

99 *familiar* attendant evil spirit, for whose services one sold his soul to the
Devil   **100** *a* in   **102** *Sir James Cromer* (actually Sir William Cromer,
who was sheriff of Kent in 1445 and perhaps in 1450. His widow, Lord
Say's daughter, was later to marry Sir Alexander Iden, who killed
Cade.)   **113** *in capite* by grant directly from the king ('capite': head,
permitting a punning allusion to *maidenhead* l. 112)   **117** *take ... bills* buy
goods on credit (with pun on 'bills': halberds)   **118** *presently* immediately   **119** *brave* splendid   **120** *braver* worthier, better

again, lest they consult about the giving up of some
more towns in France. Soldiers, defer the spoil of the
city until night; for with these borne before us instead
125 of maces will we ride through the streets, and at every
corner have them kiss. Away!

                              Exit [Cade with his Company].

IV, viii   *Alarum and retreat. Enter again Cade and all his
rabblement.*

1 CADE Up Fish Street! down Saint Magnus Corner! Kill
2 and knock down! Throw them into Thames!

      Sound a parley.

What noise is this I hear? Dare any be so bold to sound
retreat or parley when I command them kill?

      Enter Buckingham and Old Clifford.

BUCKINGHAM

Ay, here they be that dare and will disturb thee.
Know, Cade, we come ambassadors from the king
Unto the commons, whom thou hast misled,
And here pronounce free pardon to them all
That will forsake thee and go home in peace.

CLIFFORD

What say ye, countrymen? Will ye relent
And yield to mercy whilst 'tis offered you,
Or let a rebel lead you to your deaths?
Who loves the king, and will embrace his pardon,
Fling up his cap and say 'God save his majesty!'
Who hateth him and honors not his father,
Henry the Fifth, that made all France to quake,
Shake he his weapon at us and pass by.

ALL God save the king! God save the king!

CADE What, Buckingham and Clifford, are ye so brave?
And you, base peasants, do ye believe him? Will you

---

125 *maces* staffs of office
IV, viii 1 *Fish Street* (just across London Bridge from Southwark); *Saint
Magnus Corner* (St Magnus' Church was at the end of Fish Street, near
London Bridge)   **2** s.d. *parley* trumpet call indicating a temporary truce

needs be hanged with your pardons about your necks?   21
Hath my sword therefore broke through London gates,
that you should leave me at the White Hart in South-   23
wark? I thought ye would never have given out these   24
arms till you had recovered your ancient freedom. But
you are all recreants and dastards and delight to live in
slavery to the nobility. Let them break your backs with
burdens, take your houses over your heads, ravish your
wives and daughters before your faces. For me, I will
make shift for one; and so God's curse light upon you
all!

ALL We'll follow Cade! We'll follow Cade!

CLIFFORD
  Is Cade the son of Henry the Fifth
  That thus you do exclaim you'll go with him?
  Will he conduct you through the heart of France
  And make the meanest of you earls and dukes?
  Alas, he hath no home, no place to fly to;
  Nor knows he how to live but by the spoil,
  Unless by robbing of your friends and us.
  Were't not a shame that whilst you live at jar   39
  The fearful French, whom you late vanquishèd,
  Should make a start o'er seas and vanquish you?   41
  Methinks already in this civil broil
  I see them lording it in London streets,
  Crying 'Villiago!' unto all they meet.   44
  Better ten thousand base-born Cades miscarry
  Than you should stoop unto a Frenchman's mercy.
  To France, to France, and get what you have lost;
  Spare England, for it is your native coast.
  Henry hath money, you are strong and manly;
  God on our side, doubt not of victory.

ALL A Clifford! a Clifford! We'll follow the king and
  Clifford.

---

21 *hanged ... necks* i.e. pardons will be worthless   23 *White Hart* an inn,
next to Chaucer's Tabard   24 *given out* abandoned   39 *jar* discord   41
start sudden attack   44 *Villiago* villain

CADE *[aside]* Was ever feather so lightly blown to and fro
as this multitude? The name of Henry the Fifth hales
them to an hundred mischiefs and makes them leave me
56   desolate. I see them lay their heads together to surprise
57   me. My sword make way for me, for here is no staying.
In despite of the devils and hell, have through the very
middest of you! and heavens and honor be witness that
no want of resolution in me, but only my followers' base
and ignominious treason, makes me betake me to my
heels.   *Exit [Cade, running through them with his*
                        sword, and flies away].

BUCKINGHAM
What, is he fled? Go some, and follow him;
And he that brings his head unto the king
Shall have a thousand crowns for his reward.
                                    Exeunt some of them.
Follow me, soldiers. We'll devise a mean
To reconcile you all unto the king.   *Exeunt omnes.*

*

IV, ix   *Sound trumpets. Enter King, Queen, and [Edmund,*
                  Duke of] Somerset, on the terrace [aloft].

KING
1   Was ever king that joyed an earthly throne
And could command no more content than I?
No sooner was I crept out of my cradle
But I was made a king, at nine months old.
Was never subject longed to be a king
As I do long and wish to be a subject.
          Enter [below] Buckingham and [Old] Clifford.

BUCKINGHAM
Health and glad tidings to your majesty!

KING
8   Why, Buckingham, is the traitor Cade surprised?
Or is he but retired to make him strong?

56 *surprise* capture   57 *staying* hesitating
IV, ix A royal palace (Kenilworth)   1 *joyed* enjoyed   8 *surprised* taken

Enter [below] Multitudes with halters about their necks.

CLIFFORD

He is fled, my lord, and all his powers do yield,
And humbly thus, with halters on their necks,
Expect your highness' doom of life or death.   12

KING

Then, heaven, set ope thy everlasting gates
To entertain my vows of thanks and praise.   14
Soldiers, this day have you redeemed your lives
And showed how well you love your prince and country.
Continue still in this so good a mind,
And Henry, though he be infortunate,
Assure yourselves, will never be unkind.
And so, with thanks, and pardon to you all,
I do dismiss you to your several countries.   21

ALL

God save the king! God save the king!
    Enter a Messenger.

MESSENGER

Please it your grace to be advertisèd   23
The Duke of York is newly come from Ireland
And with a puissant and a mighty power
Of gallowglasses and stout kerns   26
Is marching hitherward in proud array,
And still proclaimeth, as he comes along,
His arms are only to remove from thee
The Duke of Somerset, whom he terms a traitor.

KING

Thus stands my state, 'twixt Cade and York distressed;
Like to a ship that, having 'scaped a tempest,
Is straightway calmed, and boarded with a pirate.   33
But now is Cade driven back, his men dispersed,   34

---

12 *Expect* await, *doom* judgment   14 *entertain* receive   21 *countries*
regions   23 *advertisèd* informed   26 *gallowglasses ... kerns* Irish clans-
men, foot soldiers usually armed with axe and sword or darts respectively
33 *calmed* becalmed   34 *But now* just now

35 And now is York in arms to second him.
  I pray thee, Buckingham, go and meet him,
  And ask him what's the reason of these arms;
  Tell him I'll send Duke Edmund to the Tower.
  And, Somerset, we will commit thee thither
  Until his army be dismissed from him.

SOMERSET
  My lord,
  I'll yield myself to prison willingly,
  Or unto death, to do my country good.

KING
  In any case, be not too rough in terms,
45 For he is fierce and cannot brook hard language.

BUCKINGHAM
  I will, my lord, and doubt not so to deal
  As all things shall redound unto your good.

KING
  Come, wife, let's in, and learn to govern better;
49 For yet may England curse my wretched reign.

          Flourish. Exeunt.

*

IV, x   *Enter Cade.*

 CADE Fie on ambitions! Fie on myself, that have a sword
  and yet am ready to famish. These five days have I hid me
  in these woods and durst not peep out, for all the country
4 is laid for me; but now am I so hungry that, if I might
5 have a lease of my life for a thousand years, I could stay
  no longer. Wherefore, on a brick wall have I climbed
7 into this garden, to see if I can eat grass, or pick a sallet
8 another while, which is not amiss to cool a man's stom-
  ach this hot weather. And I think this word 'sallet' was
10 born to do me good; for many a time, but for a sallet, my

___

35 *second* follow 45 *brook* endure 49 *yet* up to now
IV, x Iden's garden (Kent) 4 *is laid for* is watching for (cf. 'They are
laying for him') 5 *stay* wait 7 *a sallet* salad greens 8 *while* time 10
sallet helmet (cf. IV, iii, 9–11)

brainpan had been cleft with a brown bill; and many a 11
time, when I have been dry, and bravely marching, it
hath served me instead of a quart pot to drink in; and
now the word 'sallet' must serve me to feed on.

Enter Iden [and his men].

IDEN

Lord, who would live turmoilèd in the court
And may enjoy such quiet walks as these?
This small inheritance my father left me
Contenteth me, and worth a monarchy.
I seek not to wax great by others' waning,
Or gather wealth, I care not with what envy.
Sufficeth that I have maintains my state   21
And send the poor well pleasèd from my gate.

CADE Here's the lord of the soil come to seize me for a
stray, for entering his fee simple without leave. – Ah, 24
villain, thou wilt betray me and get a thousand crowns of
the king by carrying my head to him; but I'll make thee
eat iron like an ostrich and swallow my sword like a 27
great pin ere thou and I part.

IDEN

Why, rude companion, whatsoe'er thou be,   29
I know thee not. Why then should I betray thee?
Is't not enough to break into my garden
And like a thief to come to rob my grounds,
Climbing my walls in spite of me the owner,
But thou wilt brave me with these saucy terms?   34

CADE Brave thee? Ay, by the best blood that ever was
broached, and beard thee too. Look on me well. I have 36
eat no meat these five days; yet, come thou and thy five 37
men, and if I do not leave you all as dead as a doornail, I
pray God I may never eat grass more.

11 *brown bill* halberd, varnished to prevent rust   21 *that* that which   24
fee simple land held in unencumbered legal possession (the holder of which
had the right to seize stray animals found on his property)   27 *eat …
ostrich* (according to Elizabethan natural history, the ostrich ate iron for his
health)   29 *rude companion* base fellow   34 *brave* confront boldly; *saucy*
insolent   36 *beard* defy   37 *eat* (pronounced 'et')

IDEN

    Nay, it shall ne'er be said, while England stands,
    That Alexander Iden, an esquire of Kent,
42   Took odds to combat a poor famished man.
    Oppose thy steadfast-gazing eyes to mine;
    See if thou canst outface me with thy looks.
    Set limb to limb, and thou art far the lesser;
    Thy hand is but a finger to my fist,
47   Thy leg a stick comparèd with this truncheon;
    My foot shall fight with all the strength thou hast;
    And if mine arm be heavèd in the air,
    Thy grave is digged already in the earth.
    As for words, whose greatness answers words,
    Let this my sword report what speech forbears.

CADE By my valor, the most complete champion that ever
    I heard. Steel, if thou turn the edge, or cut not out the
    burly-boned clown in chines of beef ere thou sleep in
    thy sheath, I beseech God on my knees thou mayst
    be turned to hobnails.

          Here they fight. [Cade falls.]

    O, I am slain! Famine and no other hath slain me. Let
    ten thousand devils come against me, and give me but
60   the ten meals I have lost, and I'd defy them all. Wither,
    garden, and be henceforth a burying place to all that do
    dwell in this house, because the unconquered soul of
    Cade is fled.

IDEN

    Is't Cade that I have slain, that monstrous traitor?
    Sword, I will hallow thee for this thy deed
    And hang thee o'er my tomb when I am dead.
    Ne'er shall this blood be wipèd from thy point,
    But thou shalt wear it as a herald's coat,
69   To emblaze the honor that thy master got.

CADE Iden, farewell, and be proud of thy victory. Tell

---

42 *odds* advantage   47 *truncheon* stout staff (i.e. Iden's leg)   69 *emblaze*
signify, set forth publicly

Kent from me, she hath lost her best man, and exhort
all the world to be cowards ; for I, that never feared any,
am vanquished by famine, not by valor.
> *Dies.*

IDEN
How much thou wrong'st me, heaven be my judge.
Die, damnèd wretch, the curse of her that bare thee !
And as I thrust thy body in with my sword,   76
So wish I, I might thrust thy soul to hell !
Hence will I drag thee headlong by the heels   78
Unto a dunghill, which shall be thy grave,
And there cut off thy most ungracious head,
Which I will bear in triumph to the king,
Leaving thy trunk for crows to feed upon.
> *Exit [with his men and Cade's body].*

*

> *Enter York and his army of Irish, with Drum and*   V, i
> *Colors.*

YORK
From Ireland thus comes York to claim his right
And pluck the crown from feeble Henry's head.
Ring bells aloud, burn bonfires clear and bright,
To entertain great England's lawful king.
Ah, Sancta Majestas ! who would not buy thee dear ;   5
Let them obey that knows not how to rule.
This hand was made to handle naught but gold ;
I cannot give due action to my words
Except a sword or sceptre balance it.
A sceptre shall it have, have I a soul,   10
On which I'll toss the fleur-de-luce of France.   11

---

76 *thrust . . . sword* thrust my sword into thy body   78 *headlong* at full
length
V, i Fields (between London and St Albans)   s.d. *Drum* i.e. drummer;
Colors flags   5 *Sancta Majestas* sacred majesty   10 *have I* as sure as I have
11 *toss* impale, as on a pike; *fleur-de-luce* (device on the arms of France)

135

Enter Buckingham.
[*Aside*]
    Whom have we here? Buckingham, to disturb me?
    The king hath sent him sure. I must dissemble.

BUCKINGHAM
    York, if thou meanest well, I greet thee well.

YORK
    Humphrey of Buckingham, I accept thy greeting.
    Art thou a messenger or come of pleasure?

BUCKINGHAM
    A messenger from Henry, our dread liege,
    To know the reason of these arms in peace;
    Or why thou, being a subject as I am,
    Against thy oath and true allegiance sworn
    Should raise so great a power without his leave,
    Or dare to bring thy force so near the court.

YORK [*aside*]
    Scarce can I speak, my choler is so great.
    O, I could hew up rocks and fight with flint,
    I am so angry at these abject terms;
26   And now, like Ajax Telamonius,
    On sheep or oxen could I spend my fury.
    I am far better born than is the king,
    More like a king, more kingly in my thoughts.
30   But I must make fair weather yet a while,
    Till Henry be more weak, and I more strong. –
    Buckingham, I prithee pardon me
    That I have given no answer all this while.
    My mind was troubled with deep melancholy.
    The cause why I have brought this army hither
    Is to remove proud Somerset from the king,
    Seditious to his grace and to the state.

BUCKINGHAM
    That is too much presumption on thy part.
    But if thy arms be to no other end,

---

26 *Ajax Telamonius* (Ajax, son of Telamon, in a mad rage attacked a flock of
sheep, believing them to be his enemies)   30 *make fair weather* dissemble

The king hath yielded unto thy demand.
The Duke of Somerset is in the Tower.

YORK
Upon thine honor, is he prisoner?

BUCKINGHAM
Upon mine honor, he is prisoner.

YORK
Then, Buckingham, I do dismiss my powers.
Soldiers, I thank you all. Disperse yourselves;
Meet me to-morrow in Saint George's Field,   46
You shall have pay and everything you wish.

                              [Exeunt Soldiers.]

And let my sovereign, virtuous Henry,
Command my eldest son, nay, all my sons,   49
As pledges of my fealty and love.
I'll send them all as willing as I live.
Land, goods, horse, armor, anything I have
Is his to use, so Somerset may die.

BUCKINGHAM
York, I commend this kind submission.
We twain will go into his highness' tent.
          Enter King and Attendants.

KING
Buckingham, doth York intend no harm to us
That thus he marcheth with thee arm in arm?

YORK
In all submission and humility
York doth present himself unto your highness.

KING
Then what intends these forces thou dost bring?

YORK
To heave the traitor Somerset from hence
And fight against that monstrous rebel Cade,
Who since I heard to be discomfited.   63
          Enter Iden, with Cade's head.

46 *Saint George's Field* an open field between Southwark and Lambeth,
used as a parade ground   49 *Command* demand   63 *discomfited* routed

IDEN

64   If one so rude and of so mean condition
May pass into the presence of a king,
Lo, I present your grace a traitor's head,
The head of Cade, whom I in combat slew.

KING

The head of Cade ? Great God, how just art thou !
O, let me view his visage, being dead,
That living wrought me such exceeding trouble.
Tell me my friend, art thou the man that slew him ?

IDEN

I was, an't like your majesty.

KING

73   How art thou called, and what is thy degree ?

IDEN

Alexander Iden, that's my name ;
A poor esquire of Kent that loves his king.

BUCKINGHAM

So please it you, my lord, 'twere not amiss
He were created knight for his good service.

KING

Iden, kneel down. *[He kneels.]* Rise up a knight.
    [He rises.]
We give thee for reward a thousand marks,
And will that thou henceforth attend on us.

IDEN

May Iden live to merit such a bounty,
And never live but true unto his liege.
    Enter Queen and Somerset.

KING

See, Buckingham, Somerset comes with th' queen.
Go bid her hide him quickly from the duke.

QUEEN

For thousand Yorks he shall not hide his head,
86   But boldly stand and front him to his face.

---

64 *rude* simple, uncultivated   73 *degree* social rank   86 *front* confront

YORK

> How now ? Is Somerset at liberty ?
> Then, York, unloose thy long-imprisoned thoughts
> And let thy tongue be equal with thy heart.
> Shall I endure the sight of Somerset ?
> False king, why hast thou broken faith with me,
> Knowing how hardly I can brook abuse ?   92
> King did I call thee ? No ! thou art not king,
> Not fit to govern and rule multitudes,
> Which dar'st not, no, nor canst not rule a traitor.
> That head of thine doth not become a crown ;
> Thy hand is made to grasp a palmer's staff   97
> And not to grace an awful princely sceptre.
> That gold must round engirt these brows of mine,
> Whose smile and frown, like to Achilles' spear,   100
> Is able with the change to kill and cure.
> Here is a hand to hold a sceptre up
> And with the same to act controlling laws.   103
> Give place. By heaven, thou shalt rule no more
> O'er him whom heaven created for thy ruler.

SOMERSET

> O monstrous traitor ! I arrest thee, York,
> Of capital treason 'gainst the king and crown.
> Obey, audacious traitor ; kneel for grace.

YORK

> Wouldst have me kneel ? First let me ask of these
> If they can brook I bow a knee to man.   110
> Sirrah, call in my sons to be my bail. *[Exit an Attendant.]*
> I know, ere they will have me go to ward,   112
> They'll pawn their swords for my enfranchisement.   113

QUEEN

> Call hither Clifford. Bid him come amain   114

92 *brook* endure (with pun on *broken*, l. 91) 97 *palmer's* pilgrim's 100
Achilles' spear (Telephus was cured by rust from the spear of Achilles, by
which he had been wounded) 103 *act* enact 110 *they* i.e. his hands (cf. l.
102) (?), his weapons (?) (perhaps a line has been lost) 112 *to ward* into
custody 113 *pawn . . . enfranchisement* pledge (used ironically) their
swords for my freedom 114 *amain* speedily

To say if that the bastard boys of York
Shall be the surety for their traitor father.

[Exit an Attendant.]

YORK

117 O blood-bespotted Neapolitan,
Outcast of Naples, England's bloody scourge,
The sons of York, thy betters in their birth,
120 Shall be their father's bail; and bane to those
That for my surety will refuse the boys!

*Enter Edward and Richard [with Drum and Soldiers
at one door].*

See where they come. I'll warrant they'll make it good.

*Enter Clifford [and his Son with Drum and Soldiers
at the other door. Clifford kneels to King Henry].*

QUEEN

And here comes Clifford to deny their bail.

CLIFFORD

Health and all happiness to my lord the king.

YORK

I thank thee, Clifford. Say, what news with thee?
Nay, do not fright us with an angry look.
We are thy sovereign, Clifford; kneel again.
For thy mistaking so, we pardon thee.

CLIFFORD

This is my king, York, I do not mistake;
But thou mistakes me much to think I do.
131 To Bedlam with him! Is the man grown mad?

KING

132 Ay, Clifford. A bedlam and ambitious humor
Makes him oppose himself against his king.

CLIFFORD

He is a traitor; let him to the Tower,
And chop away that factious pate of his.

---

117 *Neapolitan* (because Margaret's father claimed the kingdom of
Naples) 120 *bane* destruction 131 *Bedlam* Bethlehem Hospital, for the
insane 132 *bedlam . . . humor* mad . . . disposition

QUEEN

> He is arrested, but will not obey.
> His sons, he says, shall give their words for him.

YORK

> Will you not, sons?

EDWARD

> Ay, noble father, if our words will serve.

RICHARD

> And if words will not, then our weapons shall.

CLIFFORD

> Why, what a brood of traitors have we here.

YORK

> Look in a glass and call thy image so.
> I am thy king, and thou a false-heart traitor.
> Call hither to the stake my two brave bears,   144
> That with the very shaking of their chains
> They may astonish these fell-lurking curs.   146
> Bid Salisbury and Warwick come to me.

> *[Exit an Attendant.]*
> *Enter the Earls of Warwick and Salisbury [with*
> *Drum and Soldiers].*

CLIFFORD

> Are these thy bears? We'll bait thy bears to death
> And manacle the berard in their chains   149
> If thou dar'st bring them to the baiting place.

RICHARD

> Oft have I seen a hot o'erweening cur
> Run back and bite because he was withheld,
> Who, being suffered with the bear's fell paw,   153
> Hath clapped his tail between his legs and cried;
> And such a piece of service will you do
> If you oppose yourselves to match Lord Warwick.

144–46 *stake, bears, chains, curs* (allusions to bearbaiting, at which chained bears were attacked by dogs. Warwick's badge was a bear and a ragged staff.)   146 *fell-lurking* treacherous   149 *berard* i.e. bear-herd, keeper of the bears   153 *suffered* hurt; *fell* ruthless, dangerous

CLIFFORD

157   Hence, heap of wrath, foul indigested lump,
      As crooked in thy manners as thy shape.

YORK

      Nay, we shall heat you thoroughly anon.

CLIFFORD

      Take heed lest by your heat you burn yourselves.

KING

      Why Warwick, hath thy knee forgot to bow?
      Old Salisbury, shame to thy silver hair,
      Thou mad misleader of thy brainsick son.
      What, wilt thou on thy deathbed play the ruffian

165   And seek for sorrow with thy spectacles?
      O, where is faith? O, where is loyalty?
      If it be banished from the frosty head,
      Where shall it find a harbor in the earth?
      Wilt thou go dig a grave to find our war,
      And shame thine honorable age with blood?
      Why art thou old, and want'st experience?
      Or wherefore dost abuse it if thou hast it?
      For shame! In duty bend thy knee to me,

174   That bows unto the grave with mickle age.

SALISBURY

      My lord, I have considered with myself
      The title of this most renownèd duke

177   And, in my conscience, do repute his grace
      The rightful heir to England's royal seat.

KING

      Hast thou not sworn allegiance unto me?

SALISBURY I have.

KING

181   Canst thou dispense with heaven for such an oath?

157–58 *heap … shape* (in reference to Richard's premature birth and his
deformities. Bear cubs too were supposed to be born as lumps of matter
which were licked into shape by their dam.)   165 *spectacles* eyes   174
mickle much   177 *repute* consider   181 *dispense* make terms

SALISBURY
    It is great sin to swear unto a sin,
    But greater sin to keep a sinful oath.
    Who can be bound by any solemn vow
    To do a murd'rous deed, to rob a man,
    To force a spotless virgin's chastity,
    To reave the orphan of his patrimony,   187
    To wring the widow from her customed right,   188
    And have no other reason for this wrong
    But that he was bound by a solemn oath?

QUEEN
    A subtle traitor needs no sophister.   191

KING
    Call Buckingham and bid him arm himself.

YORK
    Call Buckingham and all the friends thou hast,
    I am resolved for death or dignity.

CLIFFORD
    The first I warrant thee, if dreams prove true.

WARWICK
    Thou were best to go to bed and dream again
    To keep thee from the tempest of the field.

CLIFFORD
    I am resolved to bear a greater storm
    Than any thou canst conjure up to-day;
    And that I'll write upon thy burgonet,   200
    Might I but know thee by thy house's badge.

WARWICK
    Now, by my father's badge, old Nevil's crest,   202
    The rampant bear chained to the ragged staff,
    This day I'll wear aloft my burgonet,

---

187 *reave* bereave 188 *customed right* traditional right to a portion of her husband's estate 191 *sophister* clever disputer 200 *burgonet* light helmet, upon which the wearer's device was usually mounted 202 *old Nevil's crest* (Warwick actually inherited his earldom and the bear device from his wife's family, the Beauchamps; the Nevils' device was a bull)

205   As on a mountain top the cedar shows,
That keeps his leaves in spite of any storm,
Even to affright thee with the view thereof.

CLIFFORD

And from thy burgonet I'll rend thy bear
And tread it under foot with all contempt,
Despite the berard that protects the bear.

YOUNG CLIFFORD

And so to arms, victorious father,
To quell the rebels and their complices.

RICHARD

Fie! charity, for shame! Speak not in spite,
For you shall sup with Jesu Christ to-night.

YOUNG CLIFFORD

215   Foul stigmatic, that's more than thou canst tell.

RICHARD

If not in heaven, you'll surely sup in hell.

Exeunt [severally].

V, ii   *[Alarums to the battle.] Enter Warwick.*

WARWICK

Clifford of Cumberland, 'tis Warwick calls!
And if thou dost not hide thee from the bear,
Now, when the angry trumpet sounds alarum
And dead men's cries do fill the empty air,
Clifford, I say, come forth and fight with me!
Proud Northern lord, Clifford of Cumberland,
Warwick is hoarse with calling thee to arms.

Enter York.

How now, my noble lord? What, all afoot?

YORK

The deadly-handed Clifford slew my steed;
But match to match I have encount'red him
And made a prey for carrion kites and crows
Even of the bonny beast he loved so well.

Enter Clifford.

---

205 *cedar* (symbol of royalty)   **215** *stigmatic* a criminal branded with the mark of his crime (as Richard is 'branded' by his deformities)

WARWICK
Of one or both of us the time is come.

YORK
Hold, Warwick, seek thee out some other chase,   14
For I myself must hunt this deer to death.

WARWICK
Then nobly, York! 'Tis for a crown thou fight'st.
As I intend, Clifford, to thrive to-day,
It grieves my soul to leave thee unassailed. *Exit Warwick.*

CLIFFORD
What seest thou in me, York? Why dost thou pause?

YORK
With thy brave bearing should I be in love   20
But that thou art so fast mine enemy.   21

CLIFFORD
Nor should thy prowess want praise and esteem
But that 'tis shown ignobly and in treason.

YORK
So let it help me now against thy sword
As I in justice and true right express it.

CLIFFORD
My soul and body on the action both.

YORK
A dreadful lay! Address thee instantly.   27
    [Alarums. They fight, and York kills Clifford.]

CLIFFORD La fin couronne les oeuvres.   28
    [Dies.]

YORK
Thus war hath given thee peace, for thou art still.
Peace with his soul, heaven, if it be thy will.   *[Exit.]*
    Enter Young Clifford.

YOUNG CLIFFORD
Shame and confusion! All is on the rout.
Fear frames disorder, and disorder wounds   32

V, ii   14 *chase* game   20 *bearing* demeanor   21 *fast* firmly   27 *lay*
wager; *Address thee* prepare yourself   28 *La fin … oeuvres* the end crowns
every work   32 *frames* fashions

Where it should guard. O war, thou son of hell,
Whom angry heavens do make their minister,
35 Throw in the frozen bosoms of our part
Hot coals of vengeance. Let no soldier fly.
37 He that is truly dedicate to war
38 Hath no self-love ; nor he that loves himself
Hath not essentially, but by circumstance,
The name of valor. *[Sees his father's body.]* O, let the vile
   world end
41 And the premisèd flames of the last day
Knit earth and heaven together.
Now let the general trumpet blow his blast,
44 Particularities and petty sounds
To cease. Wast thou ordained, dear father,
To lose thy youth in peace and to achieve
The silver livery of advisèd age,
48 And in thy reverence and thy chair-days thus
To die in ruffian battle ? Even at this sight
My heart is turned to stone ; and while 'tis mine,
It shall be stony. York not our old men spares ;
No more will I their babes. Tears virginal
53 Shall be to me even as the dew to fire ;
And beauty, that the tyrant oft reclaims,
Shall to my flaming wrath be oil and flax.
Henceforth I will not have to do with pity.
Meet I an infant of the house of York,
58 Into as many gobbets will I cut it
59 As wild Medea young Absyrtus did.

---

35 *part* party   37 *dedicate* dedicated   38–40 *nor he . . . valor* i.e. the man who loves himself may have the outward trappings of valor (*circumstance*: accident), but he lacks the essence of valor   41 *premisèd* foretold (?), being sent before their time (?)   44 *Particularities* details   48 *chair-days* days of comfort and ease enjoyed in old age   53 *dew to fire* (there was a common notion that fine droplets of water sprayed on fire would make it burn hotter by reducing the flames to coals)   58 *gobbets* lumps of flesh   59 *Medea . . . Absyrtus* (as she fled by ship with Jason, Medea murdered her brother Absyrtus and threw pieces of his body into the sea, so that her father, stopping to collect them, would be delayed in his pursuit)

In cruelty will I seek out my fame.
Come, thou new ruin of old Clifford's house :   61
As did Aeneas old Anchises bear,   62
So bear I thee upon my manly shoulders ;
But then Aeneas bare a living load,
Nothing so heavy as these woes of mine.   65
                [Exit with the body.]
    [Alarums.] Enter Richard and Somerset to fight.
    [Somerset is killed.]

RICHARD
So lie thou there.
For underneath an alehouse' paltry sign,
The Castle in Saint Albans, Somerset
Hath made the wizard famous in his death.   69
Sword, hold thy temper ; heart, be wrathful still.
Priests pray for enemies, but princes kill.   *[Exit.]*   71
    [Alarums again.] Fight. Excursions. [And then
    enter some bearing the Duke of Buckingham wounded
    to his tent ; they pass over and go off.] Enter King,
    Queen, and others.

QUEEN
Away, my lord ! You are slow. For shame, away !
KING
Can we outrun the heavens ? Good Margaret, stay.   73
QUEEN
What are you made of ? You'll nor fight nor fly.   74
Now is it manhood, wisdom, and defense
To give the enemy way, and to secure us   76
By what we can, which can no more but fly.
    Alarum afar off.
If you be ta'en, we then should see the bottom

---

61 *new ... house* i.e. old Clifford's body   **62** *Aeneas ... Anchises* (as they
escaped from fallen Troy, Aeneas carried his aged father, Anchises, on his
shoulders)   **65** *heavy* (1) weighty, (2) sorrowful   **69** *Hath ... death* (the
spirit raised by Margery Jourdain had said that Somerset should shun
castles; see I, iv, 34)   **71** s.d. *Excursions* attacks and counter-attacks   **73**
outrun the heavens escape the decision of God   **74** *nor ... nor* neither ...
nor   **76** *secure us* make us safe

79 Of all our fortunes ; but if we haply 'scape
(As well we may, if not through your neglect),
We shall to London get, where you are loved,
And where this breach now in our fortunes made
May readily be stopped.
    Enter [Young] Clifford.

YOUNG CLIFFORD
But that my heart's on future mischief set,
I would speak blasphemy ere bid you fly,
86 But fly you must. Uncurable discomfit
Reigns in the hearts of all our present parts.
Away, for your relief ! and we will live
89 To see their day and then our fortune give.
Away, my lord, away !   *Exeunt.*

V, iii   *Alarum. Retreat. [Flourish.] Enter York, Richard,*
     Warwick, and Soldiers, with Drum and Colors.

YORK
Old Salisbury, who can report of him,
2 That winter lion, who in rage forgets
3 Agèd contusions and all brush of time
4 And, like a gallant in the brow of youth,
5 Repairs him with occasion ? This happy day
Is not itself, nor have we won one foot,
If Salisbury be lost.

RICHARD   My noble father,
8 Three times to-day I holp him to his horse,
9 Three times bestrid him ; thrice I led him off,
Persuaded him from any further act ;
11 But still where danger was, still there I met him ;
12 And like rich hangings in a homely house,
So was his will in his old feeble body.
But, noble as he is, look where he comes.

---

79 *haply* perhaps   **86** *Uncurable discomfit* hopeless defeat   **89** *To see . . .
give* i.e. to see their day of defeat and give them the bad luck we now suffer
V, iii s.d. *Drum* i.e. drummer   **2** *winter* i.e. ancient   **3** *brush* collision
4 *gallant* young lover; *brow* front, top   **5** *Repairs . . . occasion* revives
himself with action   **8** *holp* helped   **9** *bestrid him* stood over him to
protect him   **11** *still . . . still* always . . . always   **12** *homely* modest

Enter Salisbury.

SALISBURY

  Now, by my sword, well hast thou fought to-day.
  By th' mass, so did we all. I thank you, Richard;
  God knows how long it is I have to live,
  And it hath pleased Him that three times to-day
  You have defended me from imminent death.
  Well, lords, we have not got that which we have.   20
  'Tis not enough our foes are this time fled,
  Being opposites of such repairing nature.   22

YORK

  I know our safety is to follow them;
  For, as I hear, the king is fled to London
  To call a present court of parliament.
  Let us pursue him ere the writs go forth.   26
  What says Lord Warwick? Shall we after them?

WARWICK

  After them? Nay, before them, if we can.
  Now, by my faith, lords, 'twas a glorious day.
  Saint Albans battle, won by famous York,
  Shall be eternized in all age to come.   31
  Sound drum and trumpets, and to London all;
  And more such days as these to us befall!   *Exeunt.*

---

20 *got ... have* i.e. secured what we have won   **22** *opposites ... nature*
enemies who can so quickly recover   **26** *writs* (calling the parliament)   **31**
eternized immortalized

THE THIRD PART
OF KING HENRY
THE SIXTH

King Henry the Sixth
Edward, Prince of Wales, his son
Lewis XI, King of France
Henry and Edmund Beaufort, Dukes of Somerset
Thomas Beaufort, Duke of Exeter
John de Vere, Earl of Oxford
Henry Percy, Earl of Northumberland
Ralph Nevil, Earl of Westmoreland
John, Lord Clifford
Richard Plantagenet, Duke of York
Edward, Earl of March, afterwards Duke of York
    and King Edward IV
Edmund, Earl of Rutland
George, afterwards Duke of Clarence
Richard, afterwards Duke of Gloucester
} his sons
John Mowbray, Duke of Norfolk
John Nevil, Marquess of Montague
Richard Nevil, Earl of Warwick
Sir William Herbert, Earl of Pembroke
William, Lord Hastings
Humphrey, Lord Stafford
Sir John and Sir Hugh Mortimer, uncles to Richard,
    Duke of York
Henry, young Earl of Richmond
Anthony Woodville, Lord Rivers, brother to Lady Grey
Sir William Stanley
Sir John Montgomery
Somervile
Tutor to Rutland
Mayor of York and Aldermen
Mayor of Coventry
Lieutenant of the Tower
A Nobleman
Two Keepers

A Son that has killed his father
A Father that has killed his son
The French Admiral
Queen Margaret
Lady Grey, a widow, afterwards Queen Elizabeth
Bona, sister to the French Queen
Soldiers, Attendants, Messengers, Watchmen,
   a Huntsman

Scene : *England and France*]

THE THIRD PART
OF KING HENRY
THE SIXTH

*Alarum. Enter [wearing white roses in their hats,
Richard] Plantagenet, [Duke of York,] Edward,
Richard, Norfolk, Montague, Warwick, [with
Drum] and Soldiers.*

WARWICK

  I wonder how the king escaped our hands?

YORK

  While we pursued the horsemen of the North,
  He slily stole away and left his men;
  Whereat the great Lord of Northumberland,
  Whose warlike ears could never brook retreat,   5
  Cheered up the drooping army; and himself,
  Lord Clifford, and Lord Stafford, all abreast,
  Charged our main battle's front and, breaking in,
  Were by the swords of common soldiers slain.   9

EDWARD

  Lord Stafford's father, Duke of Buckingham,
  Is either slain or wounded dangerous;
  I cleft his beaver with a downright blow.   12
  That this is true, father, behold his blood.
    [Shows his bloody sword.]

MONTAGUE

  And, cousin, here's the Earl of Wiltshire's blood,

I, i Parliament House in London   **s.d.** *Alarum* a trumpet call   **5** *brook*
endure; *retreat* i.e. the trumpet call signalling retreat   **9** *Were ... slain* (in
2 Henry VI, V, ii, Clifford is killed by York)   **12** *beaver* helmet (actually
the face-piece)

Whom I encount'red as the battles joined.

RICHARD

Speak thou for me and tell them what I did.
    [Throws down Somerset's head.]

YORK

Richard hath best deserved of all my sons.
But is your grace dead, my Lord of Somerset?

NORFOLK

19 Such hope have all the line of John of Gaunt.

RICHARD

Thus do I hope to shake King Henry's head.

WARWICK

And so do I. Victorious Prince of York,
Before I see thee seated in that throne
Which now the house of Lancaster usurps,
I vow by heaven these eyes shall never close.
This is the palace of the fearful king
And this the regal seat. Possess it, York;
For this is thine, and not King Henry's heirs'.

YORK

Assist me then, sweet Warwick, and I will;
For hither we have broken in by force.

NORFOLK

We'll all assist you. He that flies shall die.

YORK

Thanks, gentle Norfolk. Stay by me, my lords;
32 And, soldiers, stay, and lodge by me this night.
    They go up.

WARWICK

And when the king comes, offer him no violence
34 Unless he seek to thrust you out perforce.
    [The Soldiers conceal themselves.]

---

19 *Such ... Gaunt* i.e. may all the descendants of John of Gaunt look for
the same fate (Edmund, 2nd Duke of Somerset, was a grandson of John of
Gaunt, Duke of Lancaster; Henry VI was a great-grandson) 32 s.d.
They go up (the chair of state, which York occupies, is probably placed on a
raised platform) 34 *perforce* by force

YORK

  The queen this day here holds her parliament,
  But little thinks we shall be of her council.
  By words or blows here let us win our right.

RICHARD

  Armed as we are, let's stay within this house.

WARWICK

  The bloody parliament shall this be called
  Unless Plantagenet, Duke of York, be king
  And bashful Henry deposed, whose cowardice
  Hath made us bywords to our enemies.

YORK

  Then leave me not, my lords. Be resolute.
  I mean to take possession of my right.

WARWICK

  Neither the king, nor he that loves him best,
  The proudest he that holds up Lancaster,
  Dares stir a wing if Warwick shake his bells.   47
  I'll plant Plantagenet, root him up who dares.
  Resolve thee, Richard; claim the English crown.   49

     [York sits in the throne.] Flourish. Enter King
     Hanry, Clifford, Northumberland, Westmoreland,
     Exeter, and the rest [with red roses in their hats].

KING HENRY

  My lords, look where the sturdy rebel sits,
  Even in the chair of state! Belike he means,   51
  Backed by the power of Warwick, that false peer,
  To aspire unto the crown and reign as king.
  Earl of Northumberland, he slew thy father,
  And thine, Lord Clifford, and you both have vowed
    revenge
  On him, his sons, his favorites, and his friends.

NORTHUMBERLAND

  If I be not, heavens be revenged on me.

---

47 *if ... bells* i.e. when his blood is up (bells were fastened to the legs of hawks; their ringing supposedly increased the falcons' ferocity in attacking their prey)   49 *Resolve thee* decide firmly   51 *Belike* it is likely that

CLIFFORD
The hope thereof makes Clifford mourn in steel.

WESTMORELAND
What, shall we suffer this? Let's pluck him down.
My heart for anger burns. I cannot brook it.

KING HENRY
Be patient, gentle Earl of Westmoreland.

CLIFFORD
62 Patience is for poltroons, such as he.
He durst not sit there, had your father lived.
My gracious lord, here in the parliament
Let us assail the family of York.

NORTHUMBERLAND
Well hast thou spoken, cousin. Be it so.

KING HENRY
67 Ah, know you not the city favors them
And they have troops of soldiers at their beck?

EXETER
But when the duke is slain, they'll quickly fly.

KING HENRY
Far be the thought of this from Henry's heart,
71 To make a shambles of the parliament house.
Cousin of Exeter, frowns, words, and threats
Shall be the war that Henry means to use.
Thou factious Duke of York, descend my throne
And kneel for grace and mercy at my feet.
I am thy sovereign.

YORK   I am thine.

EXETER
For shame, come down. He made thee Duke of York.

YORK
78 It was my inheritance, as the earldom was.

---

62 *poltroons* cowards **67** *the city* i.e. London (as distinct from the court) **71** *shambles* slaughterhouse **78** *earldom* i.e. the Earldom of March (a title inherited by York from his mother, Anne Mortimer; it was through the Mortimers that he also claimed the crown – cf. II, i, 179)

EXETER
Thy father was a traitor to the crown.   79

WARWICK
Exeter, thou art a traitor to the crown
In following this usurping Henry.

CLIFFORD
Whom should he follow but his natural king?

WARWICK
True, Clifford; and that's Richard Duke of York.

KING HENRY
And shall I stand, and thou sit in my throne?

YORK
It must and shall be so. Content thyself.

WARWICK
Be Duke of Lancaster; let him be king.

WESTMORELAND
He is both king and Duke of Lancaster,
And that the Lord of Westmoreland shall maintain.

WARWICK
And Warwick shall disprove it. You forget
That we are those which chased you from the field
And slew your fathers and with colors spread   91
Marched through the city to the palace gates.

NORTHUMBERLAND
Yes, Warwick, I remember it to my grief;
And, by his soul, thou and thy house shall rue it.

WESTMORELAND
Plantagenet, of thee and these thy sons,
Thy kinsmen, and thy friends, I'll have more lives
Than drops of blood were in my father's veins.

CLIFFORD
Urge it no more; lest that instead of words
I send thee, Warwick, such a messenger
As shall revenge his death before I stir.

79 *Thy father ... crown* (York's father, Richard, Earl of Cambridge, was
executed during the reign of Henry V)   91 *colors* flags

WARWICK

Poor Clifford, how I scorn his worthless threats.

YORK

Will you we show our title to the crown?
If not, our swords shall plead it in the field.

KING HENRY

What title hast thou, traitor, to the crown?

105   Thy father was, as thou art, Duke of York;
Thy grandfather, Roger Mortimer, Earl of March.
I am the son of Henry the Fifth,
Who made the Dauphin and the French to stoop
And seized upon their towns and provinces.

WARWICK

110   Talk not of France, sith thou hast lost it all.

KING HENRY

111   The Lord Protector lost it, and not I.
When I was crowned I was but nine months old.

RICHARD

You are old enough now, and yet methinks you lose.
Father, tear the crown from the usurper's head.

EDWARD

Sweet father, do so. Set it on your head.

MONTAGUE *[to York]*

Good brother, as thou lov'st and honorest arms,
Let's fight it out and not stand cavilling thus.

RICHARD

Sound drums and trumpets, and the king will fly.

YORK

Sons, peace!

KING HENRY

Peace thou! and give King Henry leave to speak.

WARWICK

Plantagenet shall speak first. Hear him, lords,

---

105 *Thy father ... York* (York actually inherited his title from his uncle; cf. ll. 77–79)   **110** *sith* since   **111** *Lord Protector* i.e. Humphrey, Duke of Gloucester

And be you silent and attentive too,
For he that interrupts him shall not live.

KING HENRY
Think'st thou that I will leave my kingly throne,
Wherein my grandsire and my father sat?
No! First shall war unpeople this my realm;
Ay, and their colors, often borne in France,
And now in England to our heart's great sorrow,
Shall be my winding sheet. Why faint you, lords?   129
My title's good, and better far than his.

WARWICK
Prove it, Henry, and thou shalt be king.

KING HENRY
Henry the Fourth by conquest got the crown.

YORK
'Twas by rebellion against his king.

KING HENRY [aside]
I know not what to say; my title's weak. –
Tell me, may not a king adopt an heir?

YORK
What then?

KING HENRY
An if he may, then am I lawful king,   137
For Richard, in the view of many lords,
Resigned the crown to Henry the Fourth,
Whose heir my father was, and I am his.

YORK
He rose against him, being his sovereign,
And make him to resign his crown perforce.

WARWICK
Suppose, my lords, he did it unconstrained,
Think you 'twere prejudicial to his crown?

EXETER
No; for he could not so resign his crown
But that the next heir should succeed and reign.

---

129 *winding sheet* shroud; *faint* lose heart   **137** *An if* if

KING HENRY
Art thou against us, Duke of Exeter?

EXETER
His is the right, and therefore pardon me.

YORK
Why whisper you, my lords, and answer not?

EXETER
150   My conscience tells me he is lawful king.

KING HENRY [aside]
All will revolt from me and turn to him.

NORTHUMBERLAND
Plantagenet, for all the claim thou lay'st,
Think not that Henry shall be so deposed.

WARWICK
Deposed he shall be, in despite of all.

NORTHUMBERLAND
Thou art deceived. 'Tis not thy Southern power
Of Essex, Norfolk, Suffolk, nor of Kent,
Which makes thee thus presumptuous and proud,
Can set the Duke up in despite of me.

CLIFFORD
King Henry, be thy title right or wrong,
160   Lord Clifford vows to fight in thy defense.
May that ground gape and swallow me alive
Where I shall kneel to him that slew my father.

KING HENRY
O Clifford, how thy words revive my heart.

YORK
Henry of Lancaster, resign thy crown.
What mutter you or what conspire you, lords?

WARWICK
Do right unto this princely Duke of York,
Or I will fill the house with armèd men
And over the chair of state, where now he sits,
169   Write up his title with usurping blood.

169 *usurping blood* i.e. King Henry's

*He stamps with his foot, and the Soldiers show
themselves.*

KING HENRY

My Lord of Warwick, hear but one word.
Let me for this my lifetime reign as king.

YORK

Confirm the crown to me and to mine heirs
And thou shalt reign in quiet while thou liv'st.

KING HENRY

I am content. Richard Plantagenet,
Enjoy the kingdom after my decease.

CLIFFORD

What wrong is this unto the prince your son!

WARWICK

What good is this to England and himself!

WESTMORELAND

Base, fearful, and despairing Henry.

CLIFFORD

How hast thou injured both thyself and us!

WESTMORELAND

I cannot stay to hear these articles.   180

NORTHUMBERLAND

Nor I.

CLIFFORD

Come, cousin, let us tell the queen these news.

WESTMORELAND

Farewell, faint-hearted and degenerate king,
In whose cold blood no spark of honor bides.
                    [Exit Westmoreland with his men.]

NORTHUMBERLAND

Be thou a prey unto the house of York
And die in bands for this unmanly deed.   186
                    [Exit Northumberland with his men.]

CLIFFORD

In dreadful war mayst thou be overcome

---

180 *articles* clauses in a legal document (i.e. further details of the
agreement)   186 *bands* bonds

Or live in peace abandoned and despised!

[Exit Clifford with his men.]

WARWICK

Turn this way, Henry, and regard them not.

EXETER

They seek revenge and therefore will not yield.

KING HENRY

Ah, Exeter.

WARWICK   Why should you sigh, my lord?

KING HENRY

Not for myself, Lord Warwick, but my son,
Whom I unnaturally shall disinherit.

194   But be it as it may. *[To York.]* I here entail
The crown to thee and to thine heirs forever,
Conditionally that here thou take an oath
To cease this civil war, and whilst I live
To honor me as thy king and sovereign,
And neither by treason nor hostility
To seek to put me down and reign thyself.

YORK

This oath I willingly take, and will perform.

Here they come down.

WARWICK

Long live King Henry! Plantagenet, embrace him.

KING HENRY

203   And long live thou, and these thy forward sons.

YORK

Now York and Lancaster are reconciled.

EXETER

205   Accursed be he that seeks to make them foes!   *Sennet.*

YORK

206   Farewell, my gracious lord. I'll to my castle.

[Exit York with his sons.]

---

194 *entail* bequeath inalienably   **203** *forward* spirited   **205** s.d. *Sennet* a trumpet call indicating a ceremonial entrance or exit   **206** *castle* i.e. Sandal, near Wakefield, Yorkshire

WARWICK
    And I'll keep London with my soldiers.
                        [Exit Warwick with his men.]

NORFOLK
    And I to Norfolk with my followers.
                        [Exit Norfolk with his men.]

MONTAGUE
    And I unto the sea, from whence I came.   209
                        [Exit Montague with his men.]

KING HENRY
    And I with grief and sorrow to the court.
        Enter the Queen [Margaret and Edward, Prince of
        Wales].

EXETER
    Here comes the queen, whose looks bewray her anger.   211
    I'll steal away.
KING HENRY   Exeter, so will I.
QUEEN MARGARET
    Nay, go not from me. I will follow thee.
KING HENRY
    Be patient, gentle queen, and I will stay.
QUEEN MARGARET
    Who can be patient in such extremes?
    Ah, wretched man! Would I had died a maid
    And never seen thee, never borne thee son,
    Seeing thou hast proved so unnatural a father.
    Hath he deserved to lose his birthright thus?
    Hadst thou but loved him half so well as I,   220
    Or felt that pain which I did for him once,
    Or nourished him as I did with my blood,
    Thou wouldst have left thy dearest heart-blood there
    Rather than have made that savage duke thine heir
    And disinherited thine only son.

209 I . . . came (John Nevil, Marquess of Montague, did not come from the
sea, and in I, ii is at Sandal Castle. It is possible that he has been confused
with his uncle, William Nevil. See l. 239n.)   211 bewray expose

PRINCE
>Father, you cannot disinherit me.
>If you be king, why should not I succeed?

KING HENRY
>Pardon me, Margaret. Pardon me, sweet son.
>The Earl of Warwick and the duke enforced me.

QUEEN MARGARET
>Enforced thee? Art thou king, and wilt be forced?
>I shame to hear thee speak. Ah, timorous wretch,
>Thou hast undone thyself, thy son, and me,
>And giv'n unto the house of York such head
>As thou shalt reign but by their sufferance.
>To entail him and his heirs unto the crown,
>What is it but to make thy sepulchre
>And creep into it far before thy time?
>Warwick is chancellor and the lord of Calais;
>Stern Falconbridge commands the narrow seas;
>The duke is made Protector of the realm;
>And yet shalt thou be safe? Such safety finds
>The trembling lamb environèd with wolves.
>Had I been there, which am a silly woman,
>The soldiers should have tossed me on their pikes
>Before I would have granted to that act.
>But thou preferr'st thy life before thine honor;
>And seeing thou dost, I here divorce myself
>Both from thy table, Henry, and thy bed
>Until that act of parliament be repealed
>Whereby my son is disinherited.
>The Northern lords, that have forsworn thy colors,
>Will follow mine, if once they see them spread;

233 *giv'n . . . head* i.e. slackened the horse's reins so as to allow him to move his head more freely and, hence, to run more rapidly   239 *Stern . . . seas* (William Nevil, Baron Fauconberg and Warwick's uncle, served as Warwick's deputy at Calais in 1459–60, whence he would have commanded the Straits of Dover – the 'narrow seas')   242 *environèd* surrounded   243 *silly* helpless   244 *pikes* halberds   245 *granted* conceded

And spread they shall be, to thy foul disgrace
And utter ruin of the house of York.
Thus do I leave thee. Come, son, let's away.
Our army is ready. Come, we'll after them.

KING HENRY
Stay, gentle Margaret, and hear me speak.

QUEEN MARGARET
Thou hast spoke too much already. Get thee gone.

KING HENRY
Gentle son Edward, thou wilt stay with me?

QUEEN MARGARET
Ay, to be murdered by his enemies!   260

PRINCE
When I return with victory from the field
I'll see your grace. Till then I'll follow her.

QUEEN MARGARET
Come, son, away. We may not linger thus.
                    [Exeunt Queen Margaret and the Prince.]

KING HENRY
Poor queen! How love to me and to her son
Hath made her break out into terms of rage.
Revenged may she be on that hateful duke,
Whose haughty spirit, wingèd with desire,
Will cost my crown and like an empty eagle   268
Tire on the flesh of me and of my son.   269
The loss of those three lords torments my heart.
I'll write unto them and entreat them fair.
Come, cousin, you shall be the messenger.

EXETER
And I hope, shall reconcile them all.   273
                    Exit [King Henry with Exeter]. Flourish.

*

268 *cost* accost, assail   269 *Tire* feed greedily   273 s.d. *Flourish* a trumpet
fanfare

I, ii   *Enter Richard, Edward, and Montague.*

RICHARD

1   Brother, though I be youngest, give me leave.

EDWARD

No, I can better play the orator.

MONTAGUE

But I have reasons strong and forcible.
          Enter the Duke of York.

YORK

Why, how now, sons and cousin ? at a strife ?
What is your quarrel ? How began it first ?

EDWARD

No quarrel, but a slight contention.

YORK

About what ?

RICHARD

About that which concerns your grace and us –
The crown of England, father, which is yours.

YORK

Mine, boy ? Not till King Henry be dead.

RICHARD

Your right depends not on his life or death.

EDWARD

Now you are heir ; therefore enjoy it now.

13   By giving the house of Lancaster leave to breathe,
It will outrun you, father, in the end.

YORK

I took an oath that he should quietly reign.

EDWARD

But for a kingdom any oath may be broken.
I would break a thousand oaths to reign one year.

RICHARD

No. God forbid your grace should be forsworn.

YORK

I shall be, if I claim by open war.

I, ii The Duke of York's castle, Sandal (Wakefield)   **1** *give me leave* allow
me (to speak)   **13** *leave to breathe* i.e. a respite

RICHARD
>I'll prove the contrary if you'll hear me speak.

YORK
>Thou canst not, son. It is impossible.

RICHARD
>An oath is of no moment, being not took   22
>Before a true and lawful magistrate
>That hath authority over him that swears.
>Henry had none, but did usurp the place.
>Then, seeing 'twas he that made you to depose,   26
>Your oath, my lord, is vain and frivolous.
>Therefore, to arms! And, father, do but think
>How sweet a thing it is to wear a crown,
>Within whose circuit is Elysium   30
>And all that poets feign of bliss and joy.
>Why do we linger thus? I cannot rest
>Until the white rose that I wear be dyed
>Even in the lukewarm blood of Henry's heart.

YORK
>Richard, enough. I will be king or die.
>Cousin, thou shalt to London presently   36
>And whet on Warwick to this enterprise.
>Thou, Richard, shalt to the Duke of Norfolk
>And tell him privily of our intent.   39
>You, Edward, shall unto my Lord Cobham,
>With whom the Kentishmen will willingly rise.
>In them I trust; for they are soldiers,
>Witty, courteous, liberal, full of spirit.
>While you are thus employed, what resteth more   44
>But that I seek occasion how to rise,
>And yet the king not privy to my drift,   46
>Nor any of the house of Lancaster?
>>*Enter a Messenger.*
>But stay, what news? Why com'st thou in such post?   48

22 *moment* importance 26 *depose* swear 30 *Elysium* classical Paradise
36 *presently* immediately 39 *privily* secretly 44 *what resteth more* what
else remains 46 *privy to* aware of 48 *post* haste

MESSENGER
>The queen with all the Northern earls and lords
>Intend here to besiege you in your castle.
>She is hard by with twenty thousand men;
52 >And therefore fortify your hold, my lord.

YORK
>Ay, with my sword. What, think'st thou that we fear
>   them?
>Edward and Richard, you shall stay with me;
>My cousin Montague shall post to London.
>Let noble Warwick, Cobham, and the rest,
>Whom we have left protectors of the king,
58 >With pow'rful policy strengthen themselves
>And trust not simple Henry nor his oaths.

MONTAGUE
>Cousin, I go. I'll win them; fear it not.
>And thus most humbly I do take my leave.

>   *Exit Montague.*
>*Enter [Sir John] Mortimer, and [Sir Hugh,] his*
>*brother.*

YORK
>Sir John and Sir Hugh Mortimer, mine uncles,
>You are come to Sandal in a happy hour.
>The army of the queen mean to besiege us.

JOHN
>She shall not need; we'll meet her in the field.

YORK
>What, with five thousand men?

RICHARD
>Ay, with five hundred, father, for a need.
68 >A woman's general. What should we fear?
>   *A march afar off.*

EDWARD
>I hear their drums. Let's set our men in order
70 >And issue forth and bid them battle straight.

---

52 *hold* stronghold   **58** *policy* stratagem   **68 s.d.** *A march* drum-beats   **70** *straight* immediately

YORK

    Five men to twenty! Though the odds be great,
    I doubt not, uncle, of our victory.
    Many a battle have I won in France
    When as the enemy hath been ten to one.   74
    Why should I not now have the like success?
                Alarum. Exit [York with the rest].

*

    Enter Rutland and his Tutor.   I, iii

RUTLAND

    Ah, whither shall I fly to scape their hands?
    Ah, tutor, look where bloody Clifford comes.
        Enter Clifford [and Soldiers].

CLIFFORD

    Chaplain, away! Thy priesthood saves thy life.
    As for the brat of this accursèd duke,
    Whose father slew my father, he shall die.

TUTOR

    And I, my lord, will bear him company.

CLIFFORD

    Soldiers, away with him!

TUTOR

    Ah, Clifford, murder not this innocent child,
    Lest thou be hated both of God and man.
                Exit [dragged off by Soldiers].

CLIFFORD

    How now? Is he dead already? Or is it fear
    That makes him close his eyes? I'll open them.

RUTLAND

    So looks the pent-up lion o'er the wretch   12
    That trembles under his devouring paws;
    And so he walks, insulting o'er his prey,   14

74 *When as* when
I, iii Fields near York's castle   12 *pent-up* caged, hence fierce   14 *insulting* exulting

And so he comes, to rend his limbs asunder.
Ah, gentle Clifford, kill me with thy sword
And not with such a cruel threat'ning look.
Sweet Clifford, hear me speak before I die.
I am too mean a subject for thy wrath.
20   Be thou revenged on men and let me live.

CLIFFORD

In vain thou speak'st, poor boy. My father's blood
Hath stopped the passage where thy words should enter .

RUTLAND

Then let my father's blood open it again.
He is a man, and, Clifford, cope with him.

CLIFFORD

Had I thy brethren here, their lives and thine
Were not revenge sufficient for me.
No, if I digged up thy forefathers' graves
And hung their rotten coffins up in chains,
It could not slake mine ire nor ease my heart.
30   The sight of any of the house of York
Is as a Fury to torment my soul ;
And till I root out their accursèd line
And leave not one alive, I live in hell.
Therefore –

RUTLAND

O, let me pray before I take my death !
To thee I pray. Sweet Clifford, pity me.

CLIFFORD

Such pity as my rapier's point affords.

RUTLAND

I never did thee harm. Why wilt thou slay me ?

CLIFFORD

Thy father hath.

RUTLAND   But 'twas ere I was born.
Thou hast one son. For his sake pity me.
41   Lest in revenge thereof, sith God is just,

41 *sith* since

He be as miserably slain as I.
Ah, let me live in prison all my days ;
And when I give occasion of offense,
Then let me die, for now thou hast no cause.

CLIFFORD
No cause ?
Thy father slew my father. Therefore die.
    [Stabs him.]

RUTLAND
Di faciant laudis summa sit ista tuae !   48
    [Dies.]

CLIFFORD
Plantagenet, I come, Plantagenet !
And this thy son's blood cleaving to my blade
Shall rust upon my weapon till thy blood,
Congealed with this, do make me wipe off both.   *Exit.*
    Alarum. Enter Richard Duke of York.   I, iv

YORK
The army of the queen hath got the field.
My uncles both are slain in rescuing me,
And all my followers to the eager foe
Turn back and fly, like ships before the wind   4
Or lambs pursued by hunger-starvèd wolves.
My sons – God knows what hath bechancèd them ;
But this I know, they have demeaned themselves   7
Like men born to renown by life or death.
Three times did Richard make a lane to me
And thrice cried 'Courage, father ! fight it out !'
And full as oft came Edward to my side
With purple falchion, painted to the hilt   12
In blood of those that had encount'red him.
And when the hardiest warriors did retire,
Richard cried 'Charge ! and give no foot of ground !'

---

48 *Di ... tuae* may the gods grant that this be the height of your fame
(Ovid, *Heroides*, II, 66)
I, iv   4 *Turn back* i.e. turn their backs   7 *demeaned* behaved   12 *falchion*
curved broadsword

And cried 'A crown, or else a glorious tomb!
A sceptre, or an earthly sepulchre!'
With this we charged again; but out alas!
19 We bodged again, as I have seen a swan
20 With bootless labor swim against the tide
21 And spend her strength with overmatching waves.
        A short alarum within.
Ah, hark! The fatal followers do pursue,
And I am faint and cannot fly their fury;
And were I strong, I would not shun their fury.
25 The sands are numb'red that makes up my life.
Here must I stay and here my life must end.
        *Enter the Queen [Margaret], Clifford, Northumber-
        land, the young Prince, and Soldiers.*
Come, bloody Clifford, rough Northumberland,
I dare your quenchless fury to more rage.
29 I am your butt and I abide your shot.

NORTHUMBERLAND
Yield to our mercy, proud Plantagenet.

CLIFFFORD
Ay, to such mercy as his ruthless arm
With downright payment showed unto my father.
33 Now Phaeton hath tumbled from his car
34 And made an evening at the noontide prick.

YORK
35 My ashes, as the phoenix, may bring forth
A bird that will revenge upon you all;
And in that hope I throw mine eyes to heaven,
Scorning whate'er you can afflict me with.
Why come you not? What? multitudes, and fear?

---

19 *bodged* botched   20 *bootless* fruitless   21 *with* against   25 *sands* i.e. in
the hourglass   29 *butt* target for archery   33 *Phaeton* the son of Apollo,
who took his father's sun-chariot and, unable to manage it, was dashed to
pieces (a conventional symbol of presumption, appropriate here because
the sun was a Yorkist device)   34 *noontide prick* mark on sundial indicating noon   35 *phoenix* a miraculous bird that died through spontaneous
combustion and rose again from its own ashes

CLIFFORD

So cowards fight when they can fly no further;
So doves do peck the falcon's piercing talons;
So desperate thieves, all hopeless of their lives,
Breathe out invectives 'gainst the officers.

YORK

O Clifford, but bethink thee once again,
And in thy thought o'errun my former time;   45
And, if thou canst for blushing, view this face,
And bite thy tongue that slanders him with cowardice
Whose frown hath made thee faint and fly ere this.

CLIFFORD

I will not bandy with thee word for word,   49
But buckle with thee blows, twice two for one.   50

QUEEN MARGARET

Hold, valiant Clifford! For a thousand causes
I would prolong awhile the traitor's life.
Wrath makes him deaf. Speak thou, Northumberland.

NORTHUMBERLAND

Hold, Clifford! Do not honor him so much
To prick thy finger, though to wound his heart.
What valor were it, when a cur doth grin,   56
For one to thrust his hand between his teeth
When he might spurn him with his foot away?
It is war's prize to take all vantages;   59
And ten to one is no impeach of valor.   60
    [Fight and take him.]

CLIFFORD

Ay, ay, so strives the woodcock with the gin.   61

NORTHUMBERLAND

So doth the cony struggle in the net.   62

YORK

So triumph thieves upon their conquered booty;

---

45 *o'errun* review   49 *bandy* exchange   50 *buckle* grapple, engage
56 *grin* show his teeth   59 *prize* reward   60 *impeach* calling in question
61 *woodcock* (proverbially stupid, as was the *cony*, l. 62); *gin* engine, trap
62 cony rabbit

64   So true men yield, with robbers so o'ermatched.
NORTHUMBERLAND
        What would your grace have done unto him now?
QUEEN MARGARET
        Brave warriors, Clifford and Northumberland,
67   Come, make him stand upon this molehill here
68   That raught at mountains with outstretchèd arms,
69   Yet parted but the shadow with his hand.
        What, was it you that would be England's king?
71   Was't you that revelled in our parliament
        And made a preachment of your high descent?
73   Where are your mess of sons to back you now?
        The wanton Edward, and the lusty George?
75   And where's that valiant crookback prodigy,
        Dicky your boy, that with his grumbling voice
77   Was wont to cheer his dad in mutinies?
        Or, with the rest, where is your darling Rutland?
79   Look, York! I stained this napkin with the blood
        That valiant Clifford with his rapier's point
        Made issue from the bosom of the boy;
        And if thine eyes can water for his death,
        I give thee this to dry thy cheeks withal.
        Alas, poor York! but that I hate thee deadly,
        I should lament thy miserable state.
        I prithee grieve, to make me merry, York.
        What? hath thy fiery heart so parched thine entrails
        That not a tear can fall for Rutland's death?
        Why art thou patient, man? Thou shouldst be mad;
        And I to make thee mad do mock thee thus.
        Stamp, rave, and fret, that I may sing and dance.
92   Thou wouldst be fee'd, I see, to make me sport.
        York cannot speak unless he wear a crown.
        A crown for York! and, lords, bow low to him.

---

64 *true* honest   67 *stand . . . here* (with allusion to the 'king of the molehill,'
a term of contempt)   68 *raught* reached   69 *but* only   71 *revelled* enjoyed
yourself   73 *mess* a group of four   75 *prodigy* monster   77 *mutinies*
rebellions   79 *napkin* handkerchief   92 *fee'd* paid

Hold you his hands whilst I do set it on.
    [Puts a paper crown on his head.]
Ay, marry, sir, now looks he like a king.   96
Ay, this is he that took King Henry's chair
And this is he was his adopted heir.
But how is it that great Plantagenet
Is crowned so soon, and broke his solemn oath?
As I bethink me, you should not be king
Till our King Henry had shook hands with death.
And will you pale your head in Henry's glory   103
And rob his temples of the diadem
Now in his life, against your holy oath?
O, 'tis a fault too too unpardonable.
Off with the crown, and with the crown his head.
And whilst we breathe, take time to do him dead.   108

CLIFFORD
That is my office, for my father's sake.

QUEEN MARGARET
Nay, stay. Let's hear the orisons he makes.   110

YORK
She-wolf of France, but worse than wolves of France,
Whose tongue more poisons than the adder's tooth,
How ill-beseeming is it in thy sex
To triumph like an Amazonian trull   114
Upon their woes whom fortune captivates.
But that thy face is vizard-like, unchanging,   116
Made impudent with use of evil deeds,
I would assay, proud queen, to make thee blush.   118
To tell thee whence thou cam'st, of whom derived,
Were shame enough to shame thee, wert thou not
    shameless.
Thy father bears the type of King of Naples,   121
Of both the Sicils and Jerusalem,   122

96 *marry* by the Virgin Mary (with weakened force) **103** *pale* encircle
108 *breathe* rest **110** *orisons* prayers **114** *Amazonian* (the Amazons, who
figure in classical story, were a legendary race of female warriors) **116**
vizard-like mask-like **118** *assay* try **121** *type* title **122** *both the Sicils*
i.e. Sicily and Naples

123   Yet not so wealthy as an English yeoman.
       Hath that poor monarch taught thee to insult?
125   It needs not nor it boots thee not, proud queen,
126   Unless the adage must be verified,
       That beggars mounted run their horse to death.
       'Tis beauty that doth oft make women proud;
       But God he knows thy share thereof is small.
       'Tis virtue that doth make them most admired;
       The contrary doth make thee wond'red at.
132   'Tis government that makes them seem divine;
       The want thereof makes thee abominable.
       Thou art as opposite to every good
135   As the Antipodes are unto us
136   Or as the South to the Septentrion.
       O tiger's heart wrapped in a woman's hide!
       How couldst thou drain the lifeblood of the child,
       To bid the father wipe his eyes withal,
       And yet be seen to bear a woman's face?
       Women are soft, mild, pitiful, and flexible;
       Thou stern, obdurate, flinty, rough, remorseless.
       Bid'st thou me rage? Why, now thou hast thy wish.
       Wouldst have me weep? Why, now thou hast thy will.
       For raging wind blows up incessant showers,
       And when the rage allays the rain begins.
147   These tears are my sweet Rutland's obsequies,
       And every drop cries vengeance for his death
149   'Gainst thee, fell Clifford, and thee, false Frenchwoman.

NORTHUMBERLAND
150   Beshrew me but his passions moves me so
       That hardly can I check my eyes from tears.

YORK
       That face of his the hungry cannibals

---

123 *yeoman* landowner (below the rank of gentleman)   125 *boots* profits
126 *adage* proverb   132 *government* self-control   135 *Antipodes* the other
side of the world   136 *Septentrion* the Big Dipper, i.e. the North   147
obsequies funeral rites   149 *fell* cruel   150 *Beshrew* curse

Would not have touched, would not have stained with
    blood;
But you are more inhuman, more inexorable –
O, ten times more! – than tigers of Hyrcania.   155
See, ruthless queen, a hapless father's tears.   156
This cloth thou dipp'dst in blood of my sweet boy,
And I with tears do wash the blood away.
Keep thou the napkin and go boast of this;
And if thou tell'st the heavy story right,   160
Upon my soul, the hearers will shed tears.
Yea, even my foes will shed fast-falling tears
And say, 'Alas, it was a piteous deed!'
There, take the crown, and with the crown my curse;
And in thy need such comfort come to thee
As now I reap at thy too cruel hand.
Hard-hearted Clifford, take me from the world.
My soul to heaven, my blood upon your heads.

NORTHUMBERLAND
Had he been slaughterman to all my kin,
I should not for my life but weep with him
To see how inly sorrow gripes his soul.   171

QUEEN MARGARET
What, weeping-ripe, my Lord Northumberland?   172
Think but upon the wrong he did us all
And that will quickly dry thy melting tears.   174

CLIFFORD
Here's for my oath, here's for my father's death.
    [Stabs him.]

QUEEN MARGARET
And here's to right our gentle-hearted king.
    [Stabs him.]

YORK
Open thy gate of mercy, gracious God,

---

155 *Hyrcania* a region of ancient Persia (the reference to the fierceness of Hyrcanian tigers is ultimately from the *Aeneid*, IV, 366–67)   **156** *hapless* luckless   **160** *heavy* sorrowful   **171** *inly* heartfelt   **172** *weeping-ripe* ready for weeping   **174** *melting tears* tears arising from a softened heart

My soul flies through these wounds to seek out thee.
        [Dies.]
QUEEN MARGARET
    Off with his head and set it on York gates,
    So York may overlook the town of York.
            Flourish. Exit [Queen Margaret with her followers].

*

II, i   *A march. Enter Edward, Richard, and their Power.*
    EDWARD
        I wonder how our princely father scaped,
        Or whether he be 'scaped away or no
        From Clifford's and Northumberland's pursuit.
        Had he been ta'en, we should have heard the news;
        Had he been slain, we should have heard the news;
        Or had he scaped, methinks we should have heard
        The happy tidings of his good escape.
        How fares my brother? Why is he so sad?
    RICHARD
        I cannot joy until I be resolved
10   Where our right valiant father is become.
        I saw him in the battle range about
12   And watched him how he singled Clifford forth.
        Methought he bore him in the thickest troop
14   As doth a lion in a herd of neat,
        Or as a bear encompassed round with dogs,
16   Who having pinched a few and made them cry,
        The rest stand all aloof and bark at him.
        So fared our father with his enemies;
        So fled his enemies my warlike father.
20   Methinks 'tis prize enough to be his son.
        See how the morning opes her golden gates
        And takes her farewell of the glorious sun.

II, i *Fields near the Welsh border (Marches)*   10 *Where ... is become* what
has happened to ...   12 *forth* out   14 *neat* cattle   16 *pinched* bitten   20
prize privilege

How well resembles it the prime of youth
Trimmed like a younker prancing to his love.   24

EDWARD
Dazzle mine eyes, or do I see three suns?   25

RICHARD
Three glorious suns, each one a perfect sun,
Not separated with the racking clouds,   27
But severed in a pale clear-shining sky.
See, see! They join, embrace, and seem to kiss,
As if they vowed some league inviolable.
Now are they but one lamp, one light, one sun.
In this the heaven figures some event.   32

EDWARD
'Tis wondrous strange, the like yet never heard of.
I think it cites us, brother, to the field,   34
That we, the sons of brave Plantagenet,
Each one already blazing by our meeds,   36
Should notwithstanding join our lights together
And overshine the earth, as this the world.   38
Whate'er it bodes, henceforward will I bear
Upon my target three fair-shining suns.

RICHARD
Nay, bear three daughters. By your leave I speak it,   41
You love the breeder better than the male.   42
Enter one [Messenger] blowing [a horn].
But what art thou whose heavy looks foretell
Some dreadful story hanging on thy tongue?

MESSENGER
Ah, one that was a woeful looker-on
When as the noble Duke of York was slain,   46
Your princely father and my loving lord.

---

24 *Trimmed* dressed up; *younker* young man   25 *Dazzle mine eyes* do my eyes blur   27 *racking* passing   32 *figures* prefigures, foretells   34 *cites* incites   36 *meeds* merits   38 *overshine* light up; *this* i.e. this phenomenon   41 *daughters* (with obvious pun on *suns*, l. 40)   42 *breeder* female; s.d. *blowing [a horn]* (indicating that the Messenger is a post-rider)   46 *When as* when

EDWARD
O speak no more, for I have heard too much.

RICHARD
Say how he died, for I will hear it all.

MESSENGER
50 Environèd he was with many foes,
51 And stood against them as the hope of Troy
Against the Greeks that would have ent'red Troy.
But Hercules himself must yield to odds;
And many strokes, though with a little axe,
Hews down and fells the hardest-timbered oak.
By many hands your father was subdued,
But only slaught'red by the ireful arm
Of unrelenting Clifford and the queen,
59 Who crowned the gracious duke in high despite,
Laughed in his face, and when with grief he wept,
The ruthless queen gave him, to dry his cheeks,
A napkin steepèd in the harmless blood
Of sweet young Rutland, by rough Clifford slain;
And after many scorns, many foul taunts,
They took his head and on the gates of York
They set the same; and there it doth remain,
The saddest spectacle that e'er I viewed.

EDWARD
Sweet Duke of York, our prop to lean upon,
Now thou art gone, we have no staff, no stay.
70 O Clifford, boist'rous Clifford, thou hast slain
The flow'r of Europe for his chivalry;
And treacherously hast thou vanquished him,
For hand to hand he would have vanquished thee.
74 Now my soul's palace is become a prison.
Ah, would she break from hence, that this my body
Might in the ground be closèd up in rest.
For never henceforth shall I joy again;
Never, O never, shall I see more joy.

---

50 *Environèd* surrounded   51 *hope of Troy* i.e. Hector   59 *in high despite*
with great contempt   70 *boist'rous* savage   74 *soul's palace* i.e. body

RICHARD

    I cannot weep, for all my body's moisture

    Scarce serves to quench my furnace-burning heart;

    Nor can my tongue unload my heart's great burden,

    For selfsame wind that I should speak withal

    Is kindling coals that fires all my breast

    And burns me up with flames that tears would quench.

    To weep is to make less the depth of grief.

    Tears, then, for babes; blows and revenge for me!

    Richard, I bear thy name; I'll venge thy death

    Or die renownèd by attempting it.

EDWARD

    His name that valiant duke hath left with thee;

    His dukedom and his chair with me is left.

RICHARD

    Nay, if thou be that princely eagle's bird,   91

    Show thy descent by gazing 'gainst the sun;   92

    For chair and dukedom, throne and kingdom say,   93

    Either that is thine, or else thou wert not his.

       March. Enter Warwick, Marquess Montague, and

       their Army.

WARWICK

    How now, fair lords, what fare? What news abroad?

RICHARD

    Great Lord of Warwick, if we should recompt

    Our baleful news and at each word's deliverance   97

    Stab ponjards in our flesh till all were told,

    The words would add more anguish than the wounds.

    O valiant lord, the Duke of York is slain.

EDWARD

    O Warwick, Warwick, that Plantagenet

    Which held thee dearly as his soul's redemption

---

91 *bird* young   **92** *gazing 'gainst the sun* (Eagles, according to Pliny and many later writers, could gaze at the sun without blinking. The sun here may symbolize the king; the eagle may be an allusion to a Yorkist badge.) **93** *chair* (symbol of a duke's authority, as *throne* is of a king's)   **97** *baleful* deadly

Is by the stern Lord Clifford done to death.

WARWICK

Ten days ago I drowned these news in tears;
And now, to add more measure to your woes,
106   I come to tell you things sith then befallen.
After the bloody fray at Wakefield fought,
108   Where your brave father breathed his latest gasp,
Tidings, as swiftly as the posts could run,
110   Were brought me of your loss and his depart.
I, then in London, keeper of the king,
Mustered my soldiers, gathered flocks of friends,
113   [And very well appointed, as I thought,]
Marched toward Saint Albans to intercept the queen,
Bearing the king in my behalf along;
116   For by my scouts I was advertisèd
That she was coming with a full intent
To dash our late decree in parliament
Touching King Henry's oath and your succession.
Short tale to make, we at Saint Albans met,
Our battles joined, and both sides fiercely fought;
But whether 'twas the coldness of the king,
Who looked full gently on his warlike queen,
124   That robbed my soldiers of their heated spleen,
Or whether 'twas report of her success,
Or more than common fear of Clifford's rigor,
Who thunders to his captives blood and death,
I cannot judge; but to conclude with truth,
Their weapons like to lightning came and went;
Our soldiers', like the night owl's lazy flight
131   Or like an idle thresher with a flail,
Fell gently down, as if they struck their friends.
I cheered them up with justice of our cause,
With promise of high pay and great rewards;

106 *sith* since   108 *latest* last   110 *depart* death   113 *appointed* equipped
116 *advertisèd* informed   124 *spleen* spirit   131 *flail* an instrument for
threshing, a stout stick joined to a longer handle by a leather thong

But all in vain ; they had no heart to fight,
And we (in them) no hope to win the day ;
So that we fled : the king unto the queen ;
Lord George your brother, Norfolk, and myself,
In haste, post-haste, are come to join with you ; 139
For in the Marches here we heard you were, 140
Making another head to fight again. 141

EDWARD

Where is the Duke of Norfolk, gentle Warwick ?
And when came George from Burgundy to England ?

WARWICK

Some six miles off the duke is with the soldiers,
And for your brother, he was lately sent
From your kind aunt, Duchess of Burgundy, 146
With aid of soldiers to this needful war.

RICHARD

'Twas odds belike when valiant Warwick fled. 148
Oft have I heard his praises in pursuit,
But ne'er till now his scandal of retire. 150

WARWICK

Nor now my scandal, Richard, dost thou hear ;
For thou shalt know this strong right hand of mine
Can pluck the diadem from faint Henry's head
And wring the awful sceptre from his fist, 154
Were he as famous and as bold in war
As he is famed for mildness, peace, and prayer.

RICHARD

I know it well, Lord Warwick. Blame me not.
'Tis love I bear thy glories make me speak.

---

139 *post-haste* as speedily as post-riders **140** *Marches* borders (here, of
Wales) **141** *Making another head* gathering another force **146** *aunt . . .
Burgundy* (Isabel, Duchess of Burgundy, was a grand-daughter of John of
Gaunt and a distant cousin to Edward. Holinshed says that George and
Richard were sent for protection to the Duke of Burgundy after York's
death and remained with him until Edward was crowned.) **148** *'Twas
odds belike* no doubt the odds were heavily against him **150** *scandal of
retire* disgrace because of retreating **154** *awful* awe-inspiring

But in this troublous time what's to be done?
Shall we go throw away our coats of steel
And wrap our bodies in black mourning gowns,
162 Numb'ring our Ave-Maries with our beads?
Or shall we on the helmets of our foes
164 Tell our devotion with revengeful arms?
If for the last, say 'Ay,' and to it, lords.

WARWICK

Why, therefore Warwick came to seek you out,
And therefore comes my brother Montague.
Attend me, lords. The proud insulting queen,
169 With Clifford and the haught Northumberland,
170 And of their feather many moe proud birds,
171 Have wrought the easy-melting king like wax.
He swore consent to your succession,
His oath enrollèd in the parliament;
And now to London all the crew are gone,
To frustrate both his oath, and what beside
May make against the house of Lancaster.
Their power, I think, is thirty thousand strong.
Now if the help of Norfolk and myself
179 With all the friends that thou, brave Earl of March,
Amongst the loving Welshmen canst procure,
Will but amount to five-and-twenty thousand,
182 Why, via! to London will we march
And once again bestride our foaming steeds,
And once again cry 'Charge!' upon our foes,
But never once again turn back and fly.

RICHARD

Ay, now methinks I hear great Warwick speak.
187 Ne'er may he live to see a sunshine day
That cries 'Retire!' if Warwick bid him stay.

162 *Ave-Maries* Hail Maries (prayers to the Blessed Virgin)   164 *Tell our devotion* (1) count off our prayers, as on a rosary, (2) declare our love (ironically)   169 *haught* haughty   170 *moe* more   171 *wrought* worked on, persuaded; *easy-melting* soft-hearted, easily swayed   179 *Earl of March* i.e. Edward (his title before York's death; see l. 192)   182 *via* forward   187 *he* i.e. anyone

EDWARD

Lord Warwick, on thy shoulder will I lean,
And when thou fail'st (as God forbid the hour)
Must Edward fall, which peril heaven forfend.   191

WARWICK

No longer Earl of March, but Duke of York,
The next degree is England's royal throne;   193
For King of England shalt thou be proclaimed
In every borough as we pass along;
And he that throws not up his cap for joy
Shall for the fault make forfeit of his head.
King Edward, valiant Richard, Montague,
Stay we no longer, dreaming of renown,
But sound the trumpets and about our task.

RICHARD

Then, Clifford, were thy heart as hard as steel,
As thou hast shown it flinty by thy deeds,
I come to pierce it or to give thee mine.

EDWARD

Then strike up drums. God and Saint George for us!
        Enter a Messenger.

WARWICK

How now? What news?

MESSENGER

The Duke of Norfolk sends you word by me
The queen is coming with a puissant host,   207
And craves your company for speedy counsel.

WARWICK

Why, then it sorts. Brave warriors, let's away.   209
                Exeunt omnes.

*

191 *forfend* forbid   193 *degree* rank   207 *puissant* powerful   209 *sorts*
works out well

II, ii *Flourish. Enter the King [Henry], the Queen [Margaret], Clifford, Northumberland, and young Prince, with Drum and Trumpets.*

QUEEN MARGARET

Welcome, my lord, to this brave town of York.
Yonder's the head of that arch-enemy
That sought to be encompassed with your crown.
Doth not the object cheer your heart, my lord?

KING HENRY

5   Ay, as the rocks cheer them that fear their wrack.
To see this sight it irks my very soul.
Withhold revenge, dear God! 'Tis not my fault,
8   Nor wittingly have I infringed my vow.

CLIFFORD

9   My gracious liege, this too much lenity
And harmful pity must be laid aside.
To whom do lions cast their gentle looks?
Not to the beast that would usurp their den.
Whose hand is that the forest bear doth lick?
14   Not his that spoils her young before her face.
Who scapes the lurking serpent's mortal sting?
Not he that sets his foot upon her back.
The smallest worm will turn, being trodden on,
And doves will peck in safeguard of their brood.
19   Ambitious York did level at thy crown,
Thou smiling while he knit his angry brows.
He, but a duke, would have his son a king
22   And raise his issue like a loving sire;
Thou, being a king, blest with a goodly son,
Didst yield consent to disinherit him,
Which argued thee a most unloving father.
Unreasonable creatures feed their young;
And though man's face be fearful to their eyes,
Yet, in protection of their tender ones,

II, ii Before the walls of York   **5** *wrack* ruin   **8** *wittingly* knowingly   **9** *lenity* gentleness   **14** *spoils* destroys   **19** *level* aim   **22** *raise* promote

Who hath not seen them, even with those wings
Which sometime they have used with fearful flight,
Make war with him that climbed unto their nest,
Offering their own lives in their young's defense?
For shame, my liege. Make them your precedent.
Were it not pity that this goodly boy
Should lose his birthright by his father's fault
And long hereafter say unto his child,
'What my great-grandfather and grandsire got
My careless father fondly gave away'?   38
Ah, what a shame were this. Look on the boy,
And let his manly face, which promiseth
Successful fortune, steel thy melting heart
To hold thine own and leave thine own with him.

KING HENRY

Full well hath Clifford played the orator,
Inferring arguments of mighty force.   44
But, Clifford, tell me, didst thou never hear
That things ill got had ever bad success?
And happy always was it for that son   47
Whose father for his hoarding went to hell?   48
I'll leave my son my virtuous deeds behind,
And would my father had left me no more.
For all the rest is held at such a rate   51
As brings a thousandfold more care to keep
Than in possession any jot of pleasure.
Ah, cousin York, would thy best friends did know
How it doth grieve me that thy head is here.

QUEEN MARGARET

My lord, cheer up your spirits. Our foes are nigh,
And this soft courage makes your followers faint.   57
You promised knighthood to our forward son.   58
Unsheathe your sword and dub him presently.
Edward, kneel down.

38 *fondly* foolishly   44 *Inferring* adducing   47 *happy ... it* were things
always good   48 *for* because of   51 *rate* cost   57 *faint* faint-hearted   58
forward high-spirited, precocious

KING HENRY
  Edward Plantagenet, arise a knight,
  And learn this lesson : Draw thy sword in right.

PRINCE
  My gracious father, by your kingly leave,
64 I'll draw it as apparent to the crown
  And in that quarrel use it to the death.

CLIFFORD
66 Why, that is spoken like a toward prince.
    Enter a Messenger.

MESSENGER
  Royal commanders, be in readiness ;
  For with a band of thirty thousand men
69 Comes Warwick, backing of the Duke of York,
  And in the towns, as they do march along,
  Proclaims him king, and many fly to him.
72 Darraign your battle, for they are at hand.

CLIFFORD
  I would your highness would depart the field.
  The queen hath best success when you are absent.

QUEEN MARGARET
  Ay, good my lord, and leave us to our fortune.

KING HENRY
  Why, that's my fortune too. Therefore I'll stay.

NORTHUMBERLAND
  Be it with resolution, then, to fight.

PRINCE
  My royal father, cheer these noble lords
  And hearten those that fight in your defense.
80 Unsheathe your sword, good father. Cry 'Saint George !'
    March. Enter Edward, Warwick, Richard, Clarence,
    Norfolk, Montague, and Soldiers.

---

64 *apparent* heir apparent   **66** *toward* promising   **69** *backing of* in support of ; *Duke of York* i.e. Edward   **72** *Darraign your battle* deploy your forces **80** s.d. *Clarence* i.e. George (though George is not created Duke of Clarence until II, vi, 104, he is consistently termed Clarence in stage directions and speech-prefixes before then)

EDWARD

  Now, perjured Henry, wilt thou kneel for grace
  And set thy diadem upon my head,
  Or bide the mortal fortune of the field?   83

QUEEN MARGARET

  Go rate thy minions, proud insulting boy   84
  Becomes it thee to be thus bold in terms
  Before thy sovereign and thy lawful king?

EDWARD

  I am his king, and he should bow his knee.
  I was adopted heir by his consent;
  Since when, his oath is broke; for, as I hear,
  You that are king, though he do wear the crown,
  Have caused him by new act of parliament
  To blot out me and put his own son in.

CLIFFORD

  And reason too;
  Who should succeed the father but the son?

RICHARD

  Are you there, butcher? O, I cannot speak.

CLIFFORD

  Ay, Crookback, here I stand to answer thee,
  Or any he, the proudest of thy sort.   97

RICHARD

  'Twas you that killed young Rutland, was it not?

CLIFFORD

  Ay, and old York, and yet not satisfied.

RICHARD

  For God's sake, lords, give signal to the fight.

WARWICK

  What say'st thou, Henry? Wilt thou yield the crown?

QUEEN MARGARET

  Why, how now, long-tongued Warwick?
  Dare you speak?
  When you and I met at Saint Albans last,

---

83 *bide* await   84 *rate thy minions* berate your favorites   **97** *sort* gang

Your legs did better service than your hands.

WARWICK

Then 'twas my turn to fly, and now 'tis thine.

CLIFFORD

You said so much before, and yet you fled.

WARWICK

'Twas not your valor, Clifford, drove me thence.

NORTHUMBERLAND

No, nor your manhood that durst make you stay.

RICHARD

109   Northumberland, I hold thee reverently.
Break off the parley, for scarce I can refrain
The execution of my big-swol'n heart
Upon that Clifford, that cruel child-killer.

CLIFFORD

I slew thy father. Call'st thou him a child?

RICHARD

Ay, like a dastard and a treacherous coward,
As thou didst kill our tender brother Rutland.
But ere sun set I'll make thee curse the deed.

KING HENRY

Have done with words, my lords, and hear me speak.

QUEEN MARGARET

Defy them then, or else hold close thy lips.

KING HENRY

I prithee give no limits to my tongue.
I am a king, and privileged to speak.

CLIFFORD

My liege, the wound that bred this meeting here
Cannot be cured by words. Therefore be still.

RICHARD

Then, executioner, unsheathe thy sword.
124   By Him that made us all, I am resolved
125   That Clifford's manhood lies upon his tongue.

---

109 *reverently* in respect   **124** *resolved* convinced   **125** *Clifford's ...*
tongue i.e. he talks better than he fights

EDWARD

Say, Henry, shall I have my right, or no?
A thousand men have broke their fasts to-day
That ne'er shall dine unless thou yield the crown.

WARWICK

If thou deny, their blood upon thy head.   129
For York in justice puts his armor on.

PRINCE

If that be right which Warwick says is right,
There is no wrong, but everything is right.

RICHARD

Whoever got thee, there thy mother stands;   133
For well I wot thou hast thy mother's tongue.   134

QUEEN MARGARET

But thou art neither like thy sire nor dam,
But like a foul misshapen stigmatic,   136
Marked by the Destinies to be avoided,
As venom toads or lizards' dreadful stings.   138

RICHARD

Iron of Naples, hid with English gilt,   139
Whose father bears the title of a king
(As if a channel should be called the sea),   141
Sham'st thou not, knowing whence thou art extraught,   142
To let thy tongue detect thy base-born heart?

EDWARD

A wisp of straw were worth a thousand crowns,   144
To make this shameless callet know herself.   145
Helen of Greece was fairer far than thou,   146

129 *deny* refuse   133 *got* begot   134 *wot* know   136 *stigmatic* one branded (stigmatized) by deformity   138 *venom* venomous   139 *Iron ... gilt* i.e. you cheap Neapolitan, whose worthlessness is concealed by English gold (probably with punning allusion to Suffolk's 'guilt' in paying so high a price for her)   141 *channel* gutter   142 *Sham'st thou not* are you not ashamed; *extraught* extracted   144 *wisp of straw* (traditional mark of a scold)   145 *callet* lewd woman   146–48 *Helen ... Menelaus ... Agamemnon* (Paris of Troy abducted Helen, wife of Menelaus, King of Sparta, who was brother to Agamemnon, King of Mycenae; here Helen is the typical false woman and Menelaus the typical cuckold. There is an allusion to the belief that Prince Edward was not the son of Henry VI.)

Although thy husband may be Menelaus;
And ne'er was Agamemnon's brother wronged
By that false woman as this king by thee.
150 His father revelled in the heart of France,
And tamed the king, and made the Dauphin stoop;
152 And had he matched according to his state,
He might have kept that glory to this day;
But when he took a beggar to his bed
155 And graced thy poor sire with his bridal day,
Even then that sunshine brewed a show'r for him
157 That washed his father's fortunes forth of France
And heaped sedition on his crown at home.
159 For what hath broached this tumult but thy pride?
160 Hadst thou been meek, our title still had slept,
And we, in pity of the gentle king,
162 Had slipped our claim until another age.

CLARENCE
But when we saw our sunshine made thy spring
164 And that thy summer bred us no increase,
165 We set the axe to thy usurping root;
166 And though the edge hath something hit ourselves,
Yet know thou, since we have begun to strike,
We'll never leave till we have hewn thee down
169 Or bathed thy growing with our heated bloods.

EDWARD
And in this resolution I defy thee,
Not willing any longer conference,
172 Since thou denied'st the gentle king to speak.
Sound trumpets! Let our bloody colors wave,
And either victory, or else a grave!

---

150 *His father* i.e. Henry V   152 *he* i.e. Henry VI; *matched* wedded; *state*
worth, dignity   155 *graced ... day* i.e. did honor (grace) to him by
marrying his daughter   157 *of* from   159 *broached* started (literally, set
flowing)   160 *title* claim to the throne   162 *slipped* forgone   164 *increase*
harvest   165 *usurping* (because she is wife to Henry, regarded by the
Yorkists as a usurper)   166 *something* somewhat   169 *bathed* watered
172 *denied'st* forbade

QUEEN MARGARET
    Stay, Edward.

EDWARD
    No, wrangling woman, we'll no longer stay.
    These words will cost ten thousand lives this day.
                                        Exeunt omnes.

                      *

        Alarum. Excursions. Enter Warwick.   II, iii

WARWICK
    Forspent with toil, as runners with a race,   1
    I lay me down a little while to breathe;   2
    For strokes received and many blows repaid
    Have robbed my strong-knit sinews of their strength,
    And spite of spite needs must I rest awhile.   5
        Enter Edward, running.

EDWARD
    Smile, gentle heaven, or strike, ungentle death,
    For this world frowns, and Edward's sun is clouded.   7

WARWICK
    How now, my lord? What hap? What hope of good?   8
        Enter Clarence.

CLARENCE
    Our hap is loss, our hope but sad despair,
    Our ranks are broke and ruin follows us.
    What counsel give you? Whither shall we fly?

EDWARD
    Bootless is flight. They follow us with wings,   12
    And weak we are and cannot shun pursuit.   13
        Enter Richard.

RICHARD
    Ah, Warwick, why hast thou withdrawn thyself?

II, iii Fields near York (Towton)   s.d. *Alarum* trumpet call – 'to arms';
Excursions attacks and counter-attacks   1 *Forspent* utterly wearied   2
breathe rest   5 *spite of spite* come what may   7 *sun* i.e. good fortune (with
allusion to the Yorkist sun device)   8 *hap* fortune   12 *Bootless* worthless,
hopeless   13 *shun* avoid

15 Thy brother's blood the thirsty earth hath drunk,
16 Broached with the steely point of Clifford's lance;
And in the very pangs of death he cried,
Like to a dismal clangor heard from far,
'Warwick, revenge! Brother, revenge my death!'
So, underneath the belly of their steeds,
That stained their fetlocks in his smoking blood,
The noble gentleman gave up the ghost.

WARWICK

Then let the earth be drunken with our blood!
I'll kill my horse, because I will not fly.
Why stand we like soft-hearted women here,
26 Wailing our losses, whiles the foe doth rage,
27 And look upon, as if the tragedy
Were played in jest by counterfeiting actors?
Here on my knee I vow to God above
I'll never pause again, never stand still,
Till either death hath closed these eyes of mine
Or fortune given me measure of revenge.

EDWARD

O Warwick, I do bend my knee with thine
And in this vow do chain my soul to thine.
And ere my knee rise from the earth's cold face,
I throw my hands, mine eyes, my heart to thee,
Thou setter up and plucker down of kings,
38 Beseeching thee (if with thy will it stands)
That to my foes this body must be prey,
Yet that thy brazen gates of heaven may ope
And give sweet passage to my sinful soul.
Now, lords, take leave until we meet again,
Where'er it be, in heaven or in earth.

RICHARD

Brother, give me thy hand; and, gentle Warwick,

---

15 *Thy brother's blood* (a reference to the 'Bastard of Salisbury,' Warwick's half-brother, killed at Ferrybridge) 16 *Broached* set flowing 26 *whiles* while 27 *upon* on 38 *stands* agrees

Let me embrace thee in my weary arms.
I, that did never weep, now melt with woe
That winter should cut off our springtime so.

WARWICK

Away, away! Once more, sweet lords, farewell.

CLARENCE

Yet let us all together to our troops,
And give them leave to fly that will not stay,
And call them pillars that will stand to us;
And, if we thrive, promise them such rewards
As victors wear at the Olympian games.
This may plant courage in their quailing breasts;
For yet is hope of life and victory.
Forslow no longer! Make we hence amain!   56
                                    Exeunt.

    Excursions. Enter Richard [at one door] and   II, iv
    Clifford [at the other].

RICHARD

Now, Clifford, I have singled thee alone.   1
Suppose this arm is for the Duke of York,
And this for Rutland – both bound to revenge,
Wert thou environed with a brazen wall.   4

CLIFFORD

Now, Richard, I am with thee here alone.
This is the hand that stabbed thy father York,
And this the hand that slew thy brother Rutland!
And here's the heart that triumphs in their death
And cheers these hands that slew thy sire and brother
To execute the like upon thyself.
And so have at thee!
    They fight. Warwick comes. Clifford flies.

RICHARD

Nay, Warwick, single out some other chase,   12
For I myself will hunt this wolf to death.   *Exeunt.*

---

56 *Forslow* delay
II, iv   1 *singled* chosen one from the herd (a hunting term)   4 *environed*
surrounded   12 *chase* prey

II, v   *Alarum. Enter King Henry alone.*

KING HENRY

    This battle fares like to the morning's war,
    When dying clouds contend with growing light,
3   What time the shepherd, blowing of his nails,
    Can neither call it perfect day nor night.
    Now sways it this way, like a mighty sea
    Forced by the tide to combat with the wind;
    Now sways it that way, like the selfsame sea
    Forced to retire by fury of the wind.
    Sometime the flood prevails, and then the wind;
    Now one the better, then another best;
    Both tugging to be victors, breast to breast,
    Yet neither conqueror nor conquerèd.
13   So is the equal poise of this fell war.
14   Here on this molehill will I sit me down.
    To whom God will, there be the victory.
    For Margaret my queen, and Clifford too,
    Have chid me from the battle, swearing both
    They prosper best of all when I am thence.
    Would I were dead, if God's good will were so,
    For what is in this world but grief and woe?
    O God! methinks it were a happy life
22   To be no better than a homely swain;
    To sit upon a hill, as I do now,
24   To carve out dials quaintly, point by point,
    Thereby to see the minutes how they run –
    How many makes the hour full complete,
    How many hours brings about the day,
    How many days will finish up the year,
    How many years a mortal man may live;
    When this is known, then to divide the times –
    So many hours must I tend my flock,

II, v   **3** *of* on (for warmth)   **13** *fell* cruel   **14** *on this molehill* (see I, iv, 67n.)   **22** *swain* countryman   **24** *dials quaintly* sundials artfully (perhaps alluding to the shepherds' practise of cutting sundials in the turf of hillsides)

So many hours must I take my rest,
So many hours must I contemplate,   33
So many hours must I sport myself;   34
So many days my ewes have been with young,
So many weeks ere the poor fools will ean,   36
So many months ere I shall shear the fleece.
So minutes, hours, days, weeks, months, and years,
Passed over to the end they were created,   39
Would bring white hairs unto a quiet grave.
Ah, what a life were this! how sweet, how lovely!
Gives not the hawthorn bush a sweeter shade
To shepherds looking on their silly sheep   43
Than doth a rich embroidered canopy
To kings that fear their subjects' treachery?
O yes, it doth, a thousandfold it doth.
And to conclude, the shepherd's homely curds,
His cold thin drink out of his leather bottle,
His wonted sleep under a fresh tree's shade,   49
All which secure and sweetly he enjoys,
Is far beyond a prince's delicates,   51
His viands sparkling in a golden cup,
His body couchèd in a curious bed,   53
When care, mistrust, and treason waits on him.
        Alarum. Enter a Son that hath killed his father,
    at one door [bearing the body in his arms].

SON

Ill blows the wind that profits nobody.
This man whom hand to hand I slew in fight
May be possessèd with some store of crowns;   57
And I that, haply, take them from him now   58
May yet, ere night, yield both my life and them
To some man else, as this dead man doth me.
Who's this? O God! It is my father's face,

---

33 *contemplate* meditate, pray   34 *sport* amuse   36 *ean* give birth   39 *end
they* end for which they   43 *silly* innocent   49 *wonted* accustomed   51
delicates dainty foods   53 *curious* (1) elaborately wrought, (2) full of
cares   57 *crowns* money   58 *haply* by chance

62 Whom in this conflict I, unwares, have killed.
63 O heavy times, begetting such events.
64 From London by the king was I pressed forth;
My father, being the Earl of Warwick's man,
Came on the part of York, pressed by his master;
And I, who at his hands received my life,
Have by my hands of life bereavèd him.
Pardon me, God, I knew not what I did.
And pardon, father, for I knew not thee.
My tears shall wipe away these bloody marks;
And no more words till they have flowed their fill.

KING HENRY

O piteous spectacle, O bloody times!
Whiles lions war and battle for their dens,
75 Poor harmless lambs abide their enmity.
Weep, wretched man, I'll aid thee tear for tear;
And let our hearts and eyes, like civil war,
78 Be blind with tears and break o'ercharged with grief.

*Enter, at another door, a Father that hath killed
his son, bearing of his son.*

FATHER

Thou that so stoutly hast resisted me,
Give me thy gold, if thou hast any gold;
For I have bought it with an hundred blows.
But let me see. Is this our foeman's face?
Ah, no, no, no! It is mine only son!
Ah, boy, if any life be left in thee,
Throw up thine eye. See, see what show'rs arise,
Blown with the windy tempest of my heart
Upon thy wounds, that kills mine eye and heart.
O, pity, God, this miserable age.
89 What stratagems, how fell, how butcherly,
90 Erroneous, mutinous, and unnatural,
This deadly quarrel daily doth beget.

---

62 *unwares* unknowingly 63 *heavy* miserable 64 *pressed* impressed,
drafted 75 *abide* endure 78 *o'ercharged* overfilled 89 *stratagems*
bloody acts; *fell* cruel 90 *Erroneous* criminal

O boy! thy father gave thee life too soon,
And hath bereft thee of thy life too late.   93

KING HENRY
Woe above woe, grief more than common grief;
O that my death would stay these ruthful deeds!   95
O, pity, pity, gentle heaven, pity!
The red rose and the white are on his face,
The fatal colors of our striving houses.
The one his purple blood right well resembles;
The other his pale cheeks, methinks, presenteth.   100
Wither one rose, and let the other flourish.
If you contend, a thousand lives must wither.

SON
How will my mother for a father's death
Take on with me, and ne'er be satisfied.   104

FATHER
How will my wife for slaughter of my son
Shed seas of tears, and ne'er be satisfied.

KING HENRY
How will the country for these woeful chances
Misthink the king, and not be satisfied.   108

SON
Was ever son so rued a father's death?

FATHER
Was ever father so bemoaned his son?

KING HENRY
Was ever king so grieved for subject's woe?
Much is your sorrow; mine ten times so much.

SON
I'll bear thee hence, where I may weep my fill.
                                    [Exit with the body.]

FATHER
These arms of mine shall be thy winding sheet;
My heart, sweet boy, shall be thy sepulchre,

93 *late* recently   95 *ruthful* pitiful   100 *presenteth* symbolizes   104 *Take on* be profoundly distressed; *satisfied* comforted   108 *Misthink* misunderstand, blame

For from my heart thine image ne'er shall go.
My sighing breast shall be thy funeral bell;
118   And so obsequious will thy father be,
Even for the loss of thee, having no more,
120   As Priam was for all his valiant sons.
I'll bear thee hence, and let them fight that will,
For I have murdered where I should not kill.

Exit [with the body].

KING HENRY
123   Sad-hearted men, much overgone with care,
Here sits a king more woeful than you are.

*Alarums. Excursions. Enter the Queen [Margaret],
the Prince, and Exeter.*

PRINCE
Fly, father, fly! for all your friends are fled
126   And Warwick rages like a chafèd bull.
Away! for death doth hold us in pursuit.

QUEEN MARGARET
128   Mount you, my lord. Toward Berwick post amain.
Edward and Richard, like a brace of greyhounds
Having the fearful flying hare in sight,
With fiery eyes, sparkling for very wrath,
And bloody steel grasped in their ireful hands,
Are at our backs; and therefore hence amain.

EXETER
Away! for vengeance comes along with them.
Nay, stay not to expostulate; make speed!
Or else come after. I'll away before.

KING HENRY
Nay, take me with thee, good sweet Exeter.
Not that I fear to stay, but love to go
Whither the queen intends. Forward, away!   *Exeunt.*

---

118 *obsequious* dutiful in mourning   120 *Priam* king of Troy (whose fifty sons were killed defending the city)   123 *overgone* overcome   126 *chafèd* angry   128 *Berwick* Berwick-on-Tweed, Northumberland; *post amain* ride speedily

A loud alarum. Enter Clifford, wounded [with an   II, vi
arrow in his neck].

CLIFFORD

Here burns my candle out; ay, here it dies,
Which, whiles it lasted, gave King Henry light.   2
O Lancaster! I fear thy overthrow   3
More than my body's parting with my soul.
My love and fear glued many friends to thee,   5
And now I fall, thy tough commixture melts,   6
Impairing Henry, strength'ning misproud York.   7
[The common people swarm like summer flies;]
And whither fly the gnats but to the sun?   9
And who shines now but Henry's enemies?
O Phoebus, hadst thou never given consent   11
That Phaeton should check thy fiery steeds,   12
Thy burning car never had scorched the earth!   13
And, Henry, hadst thou swayed as kings should do,   14
Or as thy father and his father did,
Giving no ground unto the house of York,
They never then had sprung like summer flies;   17
I and ten thousand in this luckless realm
Had left no mourning widows for our death,
And thou this day hadst kept thy chair in peace.   20
For what doth cherish weeds but gentle air?   21
And what makes robbers bold but too much lenity?
Bootless are plaints and cureless are my wounds;   23
No way to fly, nor strength to hold out flight;
The foe is merciless and will not pity,
For at their hands I have deserved no pity.
The air hath got into my deadly wounds
And much effuse of blood doth make me faint.

II, vi   2 *whiles* while   3 *Lancaster* i.e. the house of Lancaster   5 *My ...
fear* the love and respect I commanded   6 *commixture* compound   7
Impairing weakening; *misproud* unjustly proud   9 *sun* (another allusion to
the Yorkist sun device)   11 *Phoebus* Phoebus Apollo, the sun   12 *Phaeton*
(see I, iv, 33n.); *check* manage   13 *car* chariot   14 *swayed* ruled   17
sprung multiplied   20 *chair* i.e. of state, throne   21 *cherish* foster   23
Bootless useless

Come, York and Richard, Warwick and the rest.
30   I stabbed your fathers' bosoms ; split my breast.
        [Faints.]
        Alarum and retreat. Enter Edward, Warwick,
        Richard, and Soldiers, Montague, and Clarence.

EDWARD

Now breathe we, lords. Good fortune bids us pause
And smooth the frowns of war with peaceful looks.
Some troops pursue the bloody-minded queen
That led calm Henry, though he were a king,
35   As doth a sail, filled with a fretting gust,
36   Command an argosy to stem the waves.
But thinks you, lords, the Clifford fled with them ?

WARWICK

No, 'tis impossible he should escape ;
For, though before his face I speak the words,
Your brother Richard marked him for the grave ;
And wheresoe'er he is, he's surely dead.
        Clifford groans [and dies].

EDWARD

Whose soul is that which takes her heavy leave ?

RICHARD

A deadly groan, like life and death's departing.

EDWARD

See who it is, and now the battle 's ended,
If friend or foe, let him be gently used.

RICHARD

46   Revoke that doom of mercy, for 'tis Clifford,
Who not contented that he lopped the branch
In hewing Rutland when his leaves put forth,
But set his murd'ring knife unto the root
From whence that tender spray did sweetly spring :
I mean our princely father, Duke of York.

WARWICK

From off the gates of York fetch down the head,

---

30 s.d. *retreat* a trumpet call – 'recall'   35 *fretting* (1) blowing in gusts, (2)
nagging   36 *argosy* large merchant ship   46 *doom* judgment

Your father's head, which Clifford placed there ;
Instead whereof let this supply the room.   54
Measure for measure must be answerèd.

EDWARD
Bring forth that fatal screech owl to our house,   56
That nothing sung but death to us and ours.
Now death shall stop his dismal threat'ning sound
And his ill-boding tongue no more shall speak.   59

WARWICK
I think his understanding is bereft.   60
Speak, Clifford, dost thou know who speaks to thee ?
Dark cloudy death o'ershades his beams of life,
And he nor sees, nor hears us what we say.   63

RICHARD
O, would he did ! and so, perhaps, he doth.
'Tis but his policy to counterfeit,   65
Because he would avoid such bitter taunts
Which in the time of death he gave our father.

CLARENCE
If so thou think'st, vex him with eager words.   68

RICHARD
Clifford, ask mercy, and obtain no grace.

EDWARD
Clifford, repent in bootless penitence.

WARWICK
Clifford, devise excuses for thy faults.

CLARENCE
While we devise fell tortures for thy faults.   72

RICHARD
Thou didst love York, and I am son to York.

EDWARD
Thou pitied'st Rutland ; I will pity thee.

---

54 *this* i.e. Clifford's head; *supply the room* take the place   **56** *screech owl* (a bird of ill omen)   **59** *ill-boding* foretelling ill   **60** *understanding* consciousness   **63** *nor ... nor* neither ... nor   **65** *policy* stratagem   **68** *eager* biting, bitter   **72** *fell* cruel

CLARENCE

75   Where's Captain Margaret, to fence you now?

WARWICK

76   They mock thee, Clifford. Swear as thou wast wont.

RICHARD

What, not an oath? Nay, then the world goes hard
When Clifford cannot spare his friends an oath.
I know by that he's dead; and, by my soul,
If this right hand would buy two hours' life,
That I (in all despite) might rail at him,
This hand should chop it off, and with the issuing blood
83   Stifle the villain whose unstanchèd thirst
York and young Rutland could not satisfy.

WARWICK

Ay, but he's dead. Off with the traitor's head
And rear it in the place your father's stands.
And now to London with triumphant march,
There to be crownèd England's royal king;
From whence shall Warwick cut the sea to France
And ask the Lady Bona for thy queen.
91   So shalt thou sinew both these lands together;
And, having France thy friend, thou shalt not dread
The scattered foe that hopes to rise again;
For though they cannot greatly sting to hurt,
95   Yet look to have them buzz to offend thine ears.
First will I see the coronation,
And then to Brittany I'll cross the sea
To effect this marriage, so it please my lord.

EDWARD

Even as thou wilt, sweet Warwick, let it be;
For in thy shoulder do I build my seat,
And never will I undertake the thing
Wherein thy counsel and consent is wanting.
Richard, I will create thee Duke of Gloucester;

---

75 *fence* protect   **76** *wont* accustomed   **83** *unstanchèd* unquenchable   **91**
sinew join (as if tied with sinew)   **95** *buzz* circulate scandal

And George, of Clarence. Warwick, as ourself,
Shall do and undo as him pleaseth best.

RICHARD

Let me be Duke of Clarence, George of Gloucester;
For Gloucester's dukedom is too ominous.   107

WARWICK

Tut, that's a foolish observation;   108
Richard, be Duke of Gloucester. Now to London
To see these honors in possession.   *Exeunt.*

*

Enter two Keepers with crossbows in their hands.   III, i

1. KEEPER

Under this thick-grown brake we'll shroud ourselves,   1
For through this laund anon the deer will come,   2
And in this covert will we make our stand,
Culling the principal of all the deer.   4

2. KEEPER

I'll stay above the hill, so both may shoot.

1. KEEPER

That cannot be; the noise of thy crossbow
Will scare the herd, and so my shoot is lost.
Here stand we both and aim we at the best;   8
And, for the time shall not seem tedious,   9
I'll tell thee what befell me on a day
In this self-place where now we mean to stand.   11

2. KEEPER

Here comes a man. Let's stay till he be past.
*Enter the King [Henry, disguised,] with a prayer
book.*

107 *too ominous* (because the three immediately preceding Dukes of
Gloucester had died violent deaths. These were Humphrey, in *2 Henry
VI*; Thomas of Woodstock, often referred to in *Richard II*; and Hugh
Spenser, a favorite of Edward II.)   108 *observation* comment
III, i A forest glade near Scottish border   s.d. *Keepers* gamekeepers   1
brake thicket   2 *laund* glade   4 *Culling* selecting   8 *at the best* as well as
we can   9 *for* so that   11 *self-place* same place

KING HENRY

13   From Scotland am I stol'n, even of pure love,
14   To greet mine own land with my wishful sight.
      No, Harry, Harry, 'tis no land of thine;
      Thy place is filled, thy sceptre wrung from thee,
      Thy balm washed off wherewith thou was anointed.
      No bending knee will call thee Caesar now,
19   No humble suitors press to speak for right:
20   No, not a man comes for redress of thee;
      For how can I help them, and not myself?

  1. KEEPER

22   Ay, here's a deer whose skin's a keeper's fee.
23   This is the quondam king. Let's seize upon him.

KING HENRY

      Let me embrace thee, sour adversity,
25   For wise men say it is the wisest course.

  2. KEEPER

      Why linger we? Let us lay hands upon him.

  1. KEEPER

      Forbear awhile. We'll hear a little more.

KING HENRY

      My queen and son are gone to France for aid;
      And, as I hear, the great commanding Warwick
      Is thither gone to crave the French king's sister
      To wife for Edward. If this news be true,
      Poor queen and son, your labor is but lost;
      For Warwick is a subtle orator
      And Lewis a prince soon won with moving words.
      By this account, then, Margaret may win him;
      For she's a woman to be pitied much.
37   Her sighs will make a batt'ry in his breast;
      Her tears will pierce into a marble heart;
      The tiger will be mild whiles she doth mourn,

---

13 *even of* precisely because of   14 *wishful* longing   19 *speak for right* beg
for justice   20 *of* from   22 *fee* perquisite   23 *quondam* former   25 *it* i.e.
accepting adversity   37 *batt'ry* breach

And Nero will be tainted with remorse   40
To hear and see her plaints, her brinish tears.   41
Ay, but she's come to beg; Warwick, to give;
She on his left side, craving aid for Henry;
He on his right, asking a wife for Edward.
She weeps, and says her Henry is deposed;
He smiles, and says his Edward is installed;
That she, poor wretch, for grief can speak no more,   47
While Warwick tells his title, smooths the wrong,   48
Inferreth arguments of mighty strength,   49
And in conclusion wins the king from her
With promise of his sister, and what else,   51
To strengthen and support King Edward's place.
O Margaret, thus 'twill be; and thou, poor soul,
Art then forsaken, as thou went'st forlorn.

2. KEEPER
Say, what art thou that talk'st of kings and queens?

KING HENRY
More than I seem, and less than I was born to:
A man at least, for less I should not be;
And men may talk of kings, and why not I?

2. KEEPER
Ay, but thou talk'st as if thou wert a king.

KING HENRY
Why, so I am in mind, and that's enough.

2. KEEPER
But if thou be a king, where is thy crown?

KING HENRY
My crown is in my heart, not on my head;
Not decked with diamonds and Indian stones,   63
Nor to be seen. My crown is called content;
A crown it is that seldom kings enjoy.

---

40 *Nero* (traditionally hard-hearted and cruel); *tainted* affected   **41** *brinish* salty   **47** *That* so that   **48** *tells his title* explains Edward's claim to the throne; *smooths* glosses over   **49** *Inferreth* adduces   **51** *and what else* i.e. and who knows what other promises   **63** *Indian stones* gems (probably pearls)

2. KEEPER

Well, if you be a king crowned with content,
Your crown content and you must be contented
To go along with us ; for, as we think,
You are the king King Edward hath deposed ;
And we his subjects, sworn in all allegiance,
Will apprehend you as his enemy.

KING HENRY

But did you never swear, and break an oath ?

2. KEEPER

No, never such an oath ; nor will not now.

KING HENRY

Where did you dwell when I was King of England ?

2. KEEPER

Here in this country where we now remain.

KING HENRY

I was anointed king at nine months old ;
My father and my grandfather were kings ;
And you were sworn true subjects unto me ;
And tell me then, have you not broke your oaths ?

1. KEEPER

No ;
81   For we were subjects but while you were king.

KING HENRY

Why, am I dead ? Do I not breathe a man ?
Ah, simple men, you know not what you swear.
Look, as I blow this feather from my face
And as the air blows it to me again,
Obeying with my wind when I do blow
And yielding to another when it blows,
Commanded always by the greater gust –
Such is the lightness of you common men.
90   But do not break your oaths ; for of that sin
My mild entreaty shall not make you guilty.
Go where you will, the king shall be commanded ;

---

81 *but* only

And be you kings. Command, and I'll obey.

1 . KEEPER
We are true subjects to the king, King Edward.

KING HENRY
So would you be again to Henry
If he were seated as King Edward is.

1 . KEEPER
We charge you, in God's name and the king's,
To go with us unto the officers.

KING HENRY
In God's name, lead. Your king's name be obeyed;
And what God will, that let your king perform;   *100*
And what he will, I humbly yield unto. —   *Exeunt.*

*

Enter King Edward, [Richard of] Gloucester,   III, ii
Clarence, Lady Grey [a widow].

KING EDWARD
Brother of Gloucester, at Saint Albans field
This lady's husband, Sir Richard Grey, was slain,   *2*
His lands then seized on by the conqueror.
Her suit is now to repossess those lands;
Which we in justice cannot well deny,
Because in quarrel of the house of York
The worthy gentleman did lose his life.

RICHARD
Your highness shall do well to grant her suit.
It were dishonor to deny it her.

KING EDWARD
It were no less; but yet I'll make a pause.

RICHARD *[aside to Clarence]*
Yea, is it so?

III, ii The royal palace in London   2 *Sir Richard Grey* (Lady Grey's
husband, actually Sir John, was killed at the second battle of St Albans,
where he fought for the Lancastrians. The facts are given correctly in
Richard III, I, iii, 126–29.)

I see the lady hath a thing to grant
Before the king will grant her humble suit.

CLARENCE [aside to Richard]

14   He knows the game. How true he keeps the wind.

RICHARD [aside to Clarence]

Silence.

KING EDWARD

Widow, we will consider of your suit;
And come some other time to know our mind.

WIDOW

18   Right gracious lord, I cannot brook delay.

19   May it please your highness to resolve me now,
And what your pleasure is shall satisfy me.

RICHARD [aside]

21   Ay, widow? Then I'll warrant you all your lands
An if what pleases him shall pleasure you.

23   Fight closer or, good faith, you'll catch a blow.

CLARENCE [aside to Richard]

I fear her not, unless she chance to fall.

RICHARD [aside to Clarence]

God forbid that, for he'll take vantages.

KING EDWARD

How many children hast thou, widow? Tell me.

CLARENCE [aside to Richard]

27   I think he means to beg a child of her.

RICHARD [aside to Clarence]

28   Nay, then, whip me; he'll rather give her two.

WIDOW

Three, my most gracious lord.

RICHARD [aside]

You shall have four if you'll be ruled by him.

---

14 keeps the wind hunts downwind, so as not to alarm the game   18 brook
endure   19 resolve me free me from uncertainty   21 warrant guarantee
23–25 Fight closer ... catch a blow ... fall ... vantages (all duelling terms,
here used with obvious double meaning)   27 beg ... her apply to her for a
wardship, a source of profit if the child were high-born (with bawdy overtones)   28 whip me (a mild imprecation; or perhaps, literally, for being so
childish as to think so)

KING EDWARD
'Twere pity they should lose their father's lands.

WIDOW
Be pitiful, dread lord, and grant it then.

KING EDWARD
Lords, give us leave. I'll try this widow's wit.   33

RICHARD *[aside]*
Ay, good leave have you; for you will have leave   34
Till youth take leave and leave you to the crutch.
          [Retires with Clarence.]

KING EDWARD
Now tell me, madam, do you love your children?

WIDOW
Ay, full as dearly as I love myself.

KING EDWARD
And would you not do much to do them good?

WIDOW
To do them good I would sustain some harm.

KING EDWARD
Then get your husband's lands, to do them good.

WIDOW
Therefore I came unto your majesty.

KING EDWARD
I'll tell you how these lands are to be got.

WIDOW
So shall you bind me to your highness' service.

KING EDWARD
What service wilt thou do me if I give them?   44

WIDOW
What you command that rests in me to do.

KING EDWARD
But you will take exceptions to my boon.   46

---

33 *give us leave* pardon us (i.e. please go away)   **34–35** *good leave ... have leave ... take leave ... leave you to* willing pardon ... take liberties ... bid farewell ... pass you on to (because you will be too old to be amorous)   **44** *service* (1) duty, (2) sexual attention   **46** *boon* request

WIDOW

47   No, gracious lord, except I cannot do it.

KING EDWARD

Ay, but thou canst do what I mean to ask.

WIDOW

Why, then I will do what your grace commands.

RICHARD *[aside to Clarence]*

50   He plies her hard, and much rain wears the marble.

CLARENCE *[aside to Richard]*

As red as fire? Nay then, her wax must melt.

WIDOW

Why stops my lord? Shall I not hear my task?

KING EDWARD

An easy task. 'Tis but to love a king.

WIDOW

That's soon performed, because I am a subject.

KING EDWARD

Why then, thy husband's lands I freely give thee.

WIDOW

I take my leave with many thousand thanks.

RICHARD *[aside to Clarence]*

The match is made. She seals it with a curtsy.

KING EDWARD

But stay thee. 'Tis the fruits of love I mean.

WIDOW

The fruits of love I mean, my loving liege.

KING EDWARD

Ay, but, I fear me, in another sense.

What love, think'st thou, I sue so much to get?

WIDOW

My love till death, my humble thanks, my prayers;

That love which virtue begs and virtue grants.

KING EDWARD

No, by my troth, I did not mean such love.

47 *except* unless   50 *plies* urges

WIDOW
  Why, then you mean not as I thought you did.

KING EDWARD
  But now you partly may perceive my mind.

WIDOW
  My mind will never grant what I perceive
  Your highness aims at, if I aim aright.   68

KING EDWARD
  To tell thee plain, I aim to lie with thee.

WIDOW
  To tell you plain, I had rather lie in prison.

KING EDWARD
  Why, then thou shalt not have thy husband's lands.

WIDOW
  Why, then mine honesty shall be my dower;   72
  For by that loss I will not purchase them.

KING EDWARD
  Therein thou wrong'st thy children mightily.

WIDOW
  Herein your highness wrongs both them and me.
  But, mighty lord, this merry inclination
  Accords not with the sadness of my suit.   77
  Please you dismiss me, either with ay or no.

KING EDWARD
  Ay, if thou wilt say ay to my request;
  No, if thou dost say no to my demand.

WIDOW
  Then, no, my lord. My suit is at an end.

RICHARD *[aside to Clarence]*
  The widow likes him not; she knits her brows.

CLARENCE *[aside to Richard]*
  He is the bluntest wooer in Christendom.

KING EDWARD *[aside]*
  Her looks doth argue her replete with modesty;

68 *aim* guess   72 *honesty* virtue   77 *sadness* seriousness

Her words doth show her wit incomparable;
All her perfections challenge sovereignty.
One way or other, she is for a king;
And she shall be my love, or else my queen. –
Say that King Edward take thee for his queen?

WIDOW

'Tis better said than done, my gracious lord.
I am a subject fit to jest withal,
But far unfit to be a sovereign.

KING EDWARD

93 Sweet widow, by my state I swear to thee
I speak no more than what my soul intends;
And that is, to enjoy thee for my love.

WIDOW

And that is more than I will yield unto.
I know I am too mean to be your queen,
And yet too good to be your concubine.

KING EDWARD

99 You cavil, widow. I did mean my queen.

WIDOW

'Twill grieve your grace my sons should call you father.

KING EDWARD

No more than when my daughters call thee mother.
Thou art a widow, and thou hast some children;
And, by God's Mother, I, being but a bachelor,
104 Have other some. Why, 'tis a happy thing
To be the father unto many sons.
Answer no more, for thou shalt be my queen.

RICHARD [aside to Clarence]

107 The ghostly father now hath done his shrift.

CLARENCE [aside to Richard]

108 When he was made a shriver, 'twas for shift.

93 *state* kingship 99 *cavil* make frivolous objections 104 *other some* some others 107 *ghostly father* i.e. confessor ('ghostly': spiritual); *done his shrift* finished hearing confession 108 *for shift* (1) as a trick to serve some purpose, (2) for the sake of a chemise (to say that a woman was 'shriven to her shift' was a common off-color joke meaning that she had been seduced)

KING EDWARD
  Brothers, you muse what chat we two have had.   109

RICHARD
  The widow likes it not, for she looks very sad.   110

KING EDWARD
  You'ld think it strange if I should marry her.

CLARENCE
  To who, my lord?

KING EDWARD   Why, Clarence, to myself.

RICHARD
  That would be ten days' wonder at the least.   113

CLARENCE
  That's a day longer than a wonder lasts.

RICHARD
  By so much is the wonder in extremes.

KING EDWARD
  Well, jest on, brothers. I can tell you both
  Her suit is granted for her husband's lands.
        Enter a Nobleman.

NOBLEMAN
  My gracious lord, Henry your foe is taken
  And brought your prisoner to your palace gate.

KING EDWARD
  See that he be conveyed unto the Tower.
  And go we, brothers, to the man that took him
  To question of his apprehension.   122
  Widow, go you along. Lords, use her honorably.
                    Exeunt. Manet Richard.

RICHARD
  Ay, Edward will use women honorably.
  Would he were wasted, marrow, bones, and all,
  That from his loins no hopeful branch may spring
  To cross me from the golden time I look for.   127

---

109 *muse* wonder   **110** *sad* serious   **113** *ten days' wonder* i.e. a most
marvellous thing (proverbially, a novelty attracts for only nine days)   **122**
question ... apprehension inquire about his capture   **127** *cross me from*
interfere with my attaining

And yet, between my soul's desire and me –
The lustful Edward's title burièd –
Is Clarence, Henry, and his son young Edward,
131   And all the unlooked-for issue of their bodies,
132   To take their rooms ere I can place myself.
133   A cold premeditation for my purpose.
Why, then I do but dream on sovereignty,
Like one that stands upon a promontory
And spies a far-off shore where he would tread,
137   Wishing his foot were equal with his eye,
And chides the sea that sunders him from thence,
139   Saying he'll lade it dry to have his way :
So do I wish the crown, being so far off ;
141   And so I chide the means that keeps me from it,
And so, I say, I'll cut the causes off,
143   Flattering me with impossibilities.
144   My eye 's too quick, my heart o'erweens too much,
Unless my hand and strength could equal them.
Well, say there is no kingdom then for Richard :
What other pleasure can the world afford ?
I'll make my heaven in a lady's lap
And deck my body in gay ornaments
150   And witch sweet ladies with my words and looks.
O miserable thought, and more unlikely
Than to accomplish twenty golden crowns.
Why, love forswore me in my mother's womb ;
154   And, for I should not deal in her soft laws,
She did corrupt frail nature with some bribe
To shrink mine arm up like a withered shrub ;
157   To make an envious mountain on my back,
Where sits deformity to mock my body ;
To shape my legs of an unequal size ;

131 *unlooked-for* unanticipated   132 *rooms* places   133 *cold premeditation* discouraging forecast   137 *equal with* as capable as   139 *lade* ladle, scoop 141 *means* obstacles   143 *me* myself   144 *o'erweens* presumes   150 *witch* bewitch   154 *for* so that   157 *envious* detested

To disproportion me in every part,
Like to a chaos, or an unlicked bear-whelp,   161
That carries no impression like the dam.   162
And am I then a man to be beloved?
O monstrous fault to harbor such a thought.
Then, since this earth affords no joy to me
But to command, to check, to o'erbear such   166
As are of better person than myself,   167
I'll make my heaven to dream upon the crown
And, whiles I live, t' account this world but hell
Until my misshaped trunk that bears this head
Be round impalèd with a glorious crown.   171
And yet I know not how to get the crown,
For many lives stand between me and home;   173
And I – like one lost in a thorny wood,
That rents the thorns and is rent with the thorns,
Seeking a way and straying from the way,
Not knowing how to find the open air
But toiling desperately to find it out –
Torment myself to catch the English crown;
And from that torment I will free myself
Or hew my way out with a bloody axe.
Why, I can smile, and murder whiles I smile,
And cry 'Content!' to that which grieves my heart,
And wet my cheeks with artificial tears,
And frame my face to all occasions.
I'll drown more sailors than the mermaid shall;   186
I'll slay more gazers than the basilisk;   187
I'll play the orator as well as Nestor,   188
Deceive more slily than Ulysses could   189

---

161 *chaos* unformed mass; *unlicked bear-whelp* (bear cubs were supposedly born as lumps of matter and licked into shape by their dams) **162** *impression* shape **166** *check* rebuke; *o'erbear* dominate **167** *of better person* more personable **171** *impalèd* encircled **173** *home* i.e. my goal **186** *mermaid* siren **187** *basilisk* a fabulous serpent whose look killed **188** *Nestor* aged Greek warrior at the siege of Troy, noted for his wisdom **189** *Ulysses* Greek warrior, subject of the *Odyssey*, noted for his craft

190 And, like a Sinon, take another Troy.
I can add colors to the chameleon,
192 Change shapes with Proteus for advantages,
193 And set the murderous Machiavel to school.
Can I do this, and cannot get a crown?
Tut, were it farther off, I'll pluck it down.   *Exit.*

*

III, iii   *Flourish. Enter Lewis the French King, his sister
Bona, his Admiral, called Bourbon; Prince Edward,
Queen Margaret, and the Earl of Oxford. Lewis
sits, and riseth up again.*

LEWIS
Fair Queen of England, worthy Margaret,
2 Sit down with us. It ill befits thy state
And birth that thou shouldst stand while Lewis doth sit.

QUEEN MARGARET
No, mighty King of France. Now Margaret
5 Must strike her sail, and learn awhile to serve
Where kings command. I was, I must confess,
7 Great Albion's queen in former golden days;
But now mischance hath trod my title down
And with dishonor laid me on the ground,
Where I must take like seat unto my fortune
And to my humble seat conform myself.

LEWIS
Why, say, fair queen, whence springs this deep despair?

QUEEN MARGARET
From such a cause as fills mine eyes with tears

190 *Sinon* the Greek who persuaded the Trojans to bring the Wooden
Horse into the city   192 *Proteus* a sea-deity who, when captured, changed
his shape; *for advantages* as my purpose dictates   193 *Machiavel* Machia-
velli, Italian political philosopher, known in England as an advocate of
guile and ruthlessness in the attainment of political objectives
III, iii The royal palace in France   2 *state* status   5 *strike her sail* lower
her sail (a mark of deference rendered at sea to a senior)   7 *Albion's*
England's

And stops my tongue, while heart is drowned in cares.

LEWIS

Whate'er it be, be thou still like thyself,   15
And sit thee by our side. *Seats her by him.* Yield not thy
   neck
To fortune's yoke – but let thy dauntless mind
Still ride in triumph over all mischance.
Be plain, Queen Margaret, and tell thy grief.
It shall be eased if France can yield relief.   20

QUEEN MARGARET

Those gracious words revive my drooping thoughts
And give my tongue-tied sorrows leave to speak.
Now therefore be it known to noble Lewis
That Henry, sole possessor of my love,
Is, of a king, become a banished man   25
And forced to live in Scotland a forlorn ;   26
While proud ambitious Edward Duke of York
Usurps the regal title and the seat
Of England's true anointed lawful king.
This is the cause that I, poor Margaret,
With this my son, Prince Edward, Henry's heir,
Am come to crave thy just and lawful aid ;
And if thou fail us, all our hope is done.
Scotland hath will to help, but cannot help ;
Our people and our peers are both misled,
Our treasure seized, our soldiers put to flight,
And (as thou seest) ourselves in heavy plight.

LEWIS

Renowned queen, with patience calm the storm
While we bethink a means to break it off.   39

QUEEN MARGARET

The more we stay, the stronger grows our foe.   40

LEWIS

The more I stay, the more I'll succor thee.

---

15 *be thou ... thyself* i.e. behave always in a way appropriate to your
greatness   **20** *France* the King of France   **25** *of* instead of   **26** *forlorn*
outcast   **39** *break it off* stop it   **40** *stay* delay

QUEEN MARGARET

42   O, but impatience waiteth on true sorrow.
And see where comes the breeder of my sorrow.
    Enter Warwick.

LEWIS

What's he approacheth boldly to our presence?

QUEEN MARGARET

Our Earl of Warwick, Edward's greatest friend.

LEWIS

Welcome, brave Warwick, what brings thee to France?
    He descends. She ariseth.

QUEEN MARGARET *[aside]*

Ay, now begins a second storm to rise;
For this is he that moves both wind and tide.

WARWICK

From worthy Edward, King of Albion,
My lord and sovereign and thy vowèd friend,
I come, in kindness and unfeignèd love,
First to do greetings to thy royal person,
And then to crave a league of amity,
And lastly to confirm that amity
With nuptial knot, if thou vouchsafe to grant
56   That virtuous Lady Bona, thy fair sister,
To England's king in lawful marriage.

QUEEN MARGARET *[aside]*

If that go forward, Henry's hope is done.

WARWICK *[speaking to Bona]*

And, gracious madam, in our king's behalf,
I am commanded, with your leave and favor,
Humbly to kiss your hand, and with my tongue
To tell the passion of my sovereign's heart;
Where fame, late ent'ring at his heedful ears,
Hath placed thy beauty's image and thy virtue.

QUEEN MARGARET

King Lewis, and Lady Bona, hear me speak

---

42 *waiteth on* attends   **56** *sister* i.e. sister-in-law

Before you answer Warwick. His demand
Springs not from Edward's well-meant honest love,
But from deceit, bred by necessity;
For how can tyrants safely govern home
Unless abroad they purchase great alliance?   70
To prove him tyrant this reason may suffice,
That Henry liveth still; but were he dead,
Yet here Prince Edward stands, King Henry's son.
Look, therefore, Lewis, that by this league and marriage
Thou draw not on thy danger and dishonor;
For though usurpers sway the rule awhile,   76
Yet heav'ns are just and time suppresseth wrongs.

WARWICK
Injurious Margaret!   78

PRINCE   And why not queen?

WARWICK
Because thy father Henry did usurp,
And thou no more art prince than she is queen.

OXFORD
Then Warwick disannuls great John of Gaunt,   81
Which did subdue the greatest part of Spain;   82
And after John of Gaunt, Henry the Fourth,
Whose wisdom was a mirror to the wisest;
And after that wise prince, Henry the Fifth,
Who by his prowess conquerèd all France.
From these our Henry lineally descends.

WARWICK
Oxford, how haps it in this smooth discourse
You told not how Henry the Sixth hath lost
All that which Henry the Fifth had gotten?
Methinks these peers of France should smile at that.
But for the rest: you tell a pedigree   92

---

76 *sway* exercise 78 *Injurious* insulting 81 *disannuls* cancels out 82
Which ... Spain (Gaunt did campaign in Spain, but his successes were
minor) 92–94 *you ... worth* i.e. the line you describe runs for sixty-two
years, a ridiculously short time upon which to base a claim sanctioned by
custom (*prescription*) to the wealth and honor of kingship

Of threescore and two years – a silly time
To make prescription for a kingdom's worth.

OXFORD

Why, Warwick, canst thou speak against thy liege,
Whom thou obeyèd'st thirty and six years,
And not bewray thy treason with a blush?

WARWICK

Can Oxford, that did ever fence the right,
99   Now buckler falsehood with a pedigree?
For shame! Leave Henry and call Edward king.

OXFORD

101   Call him my king by whose injurious doom
102   My elder brother, the Lord Aubrey Vere,
103   Was done to death? and more than so, my father,
Even in the downfall of his mellowed years,
When nature brought him to the door of death?
No, Warwick, no! While life upholds this arm,
This arm upholds the house of Lancaster.

WARWICK

And I the house of York.

LEWIS

Queen Margaret, Prince Edward, and Oxford,
Vouchsafe at our request to stand aside
While I use further conference with Warwick.
    They stand aloof.

QUEEN MARGARET

Heavens grant that Warwick's words bewitch him not.

LEWIS

Now, Warwick, tell me, even upon thy conscience,
Is Edward your true king? For I were loath
To link with him that were not lawful chosen.

WARWICK

Thereon I pawn my credit and mine honor.

---

99 *buckler* shield   **101** *injurious doom* unjust judgment   **102** *Lord Aubrey Vere* (Holinshed reports that in 1462 the 12th Earl of Oxford and Lord Aubrey Vere, his eldest son, were accused of treason and executed)   **103** *more than so* yet more

LEWIS
But is he gracious in the people's eye?

WARWICK
The more that Henry was unfortunate.

LEWIS
Then further: all dissembling set aside,
Tell me for truth the measure of his love
Unto our sister Bona.

WARWICK   Such it seems
As may beseem a monarch like himself.   122
Myself have often heard him say and swear
That this his love was an eternal plant,   124
Whereof the root was fixed in virtue's ground,
The leaves and fruit maintained with beauty's sun,
Exempt from envy, but not from disdain,   127
Unless the Lady Bona quit his pain.

LEWIS
Now, sister, let us hear your firm resolve.

BONA
Your grant, or your denial, shall be mine.   130
        (*Speaks to Warwick*)
Yet I confess that often ere this day,
When I have heard your king's desert recounted,   132
Mine ear hath tempted judgment to desire.

LEWIS
Then, Warwick, thus: our sister shall be Edward's,
And now forthwith shall articles be drawn
Touching the jointure that your king must make,   136
Which with her dowry shall be counterpoised.   137
Draw near, Queen Margaret, and be a witness
That Bona shall be wife to the English king.

---

122 *beseem* befit   **124** *eternal* i.e. heavenly   **127–8** *Exempt ... pain* i.e.
Edward's love will be free from the effects of sharp criticism (*envy*) of Lady
Bona (because of her coldness to his suit), but it will suffer from rejection
(*disdain*) unless she reward his passion for her (*quit his pain*)   **130** *grant*
concurrence   **132** *desert* merit   **136** *jointure* marriage settlement   **137**
counterpoised matched

PRINCE
To Edward, but not to the English king.

QUEEN MARGARET
Deceitful Warwick, it was thy device
By this alliance to make void my suit.
Before thy coming Lewis was Henry's friend.

LEWIS
And still is friend to him, and Margaret.
But if your title to the crown be weak,
As may appear by Edward's good success,
Then 'tis but reason that I be released
From giving aid which late I promisèd.
Yet shall you have all kindness at my hand
That your estate requires and mine can yield.

WARWICK
Henry now lives in Scotland at his ease,
Where having nothing, nothing can he lose.
153 And as for you yourself, our quondam queen,
You have a father able to maintain you,
And better 'twere you troubled him than France.

QUEEN MARGARET
Peace, impudent and shameless Warwick, peace,
Proud setter up and puller down of kings,
I will not hence till with my talk and tears
(Both full of truth) I make King Lewis behold
160 Thy sly conveyance and thy lord's false love;
161 For both of you are birds of selfsame feather.
        Post blowing a horn within.

LEWIS
Warwick, this is some post to us or thee.
        Enter the Post.

POST *[speaks to Warwick]*
My lord ambassador, these letters are for you,
Sent from your brother, Marquess Montague;

---

153 *quondam* former   160 *conveyance* trickery   161 s.d. *Post* dispatch-rider

 [To Lewis]
These from our king unto your majesty;
 [To Margaret]
And, madam, these for you: from whom I know not.
  They all read their letters.

OXFORD
 I like it well that our fair queen and mistress
 Smiles at her news, while Warwick frowns at his.

PRINCE
 Nay, mark how Lewis stamps as he were nettled.
 I hope all's for the best.

LEWIS
 Warwick, what are thy news? and yours, fair queen?

QUEEN MARGARET
 Mine such as fill my heart with unhoped joys.

WARWICK
 Mine full of sorrow and heart's discontent.

LEWIS
 What? Has your king married the Lady Grey?
 And now, to soothe your forgery and his,   175
 Sends me a paper to persuade me patience?
 Is this th' alliance that he seeks with France?
 Dare he presume to scorn us in this manner?

QUEEN MARGARET
 I told your majesty as much before.
 This proveth Edward's love and Warwick's honesty.

WARWICK
 King Lewis, I here protest in sight of heaven
 And by the hope I have of heavenly bliss
 That I am clear from this misdeed of Edward's —
 No more my king, for he dishonors me,
 But most himself, if he could see his shame.
 Did I forget that by the House of York
 My father came untimely to his death?   187

---

175 *forgery* deceit 187 *My ... death* (according to the chronicles,
Salisbury, Warwick's father, was captured by the Lancastrians at Wakefield and beheaded, as was York)

188   Did I let pass th' abuse done to my niece?
189   Did I impale him with the regal crown?
      Did I put Henry from his native right?
191   And am I guerdoned at the last with shame?
      Shame on himself, for my desert is honor;
      And to repair my honor, lost for him,
      I here renounce him and return to Henry.
      My noble queen, let former grudges pass,
      And henceforth I am thy true servitor.
      I will revenge his wrong to Lady Bona
      And replant Henry in his former state.

QUEEN MARGARET
      Warwick, these words have turned my hate to love,
      And I forgive and quite forget old faults
      And joy that thou becom'st King Henry's friend.

WARWICK
      So much his friend, ay, his unfeignèd friend,
      That, if King Lewis vouchsafe to furnish us
      With some few bands of chosen soldiers,
      I'll undertake to land them on our coast
      And force the tyrant from his seat by war.
      'Tis not his new-made bride shall succor him.
      And as for Clarence, as my letters tell me,
      He's very likely now to fall from him
210   For matching more for wanton lust than honor
      Or than for strength and safety of our country.

BONA
      Dear brother, how shall Bona be revenged
      But by thy help to this distressèd queen?

QUEEN MARGARET
      Renownèd prince, how shall poor Henry live
      Unless thou rescue him from foul despair?

BONA
      My quarrel and this English queen's are one.

---

188 *Did ... niece* (Holinshed reports that Edward 'would have defloured'
Warwick's 'daughter or his neece')   189 *impale him* encircle his brow
191 *guerdoned* rewarded   210 *matching* marrying

WARWICK
> And mine, fair Lady Bona, joins with yours.

LEWIS
> And mine with hers and thine and Margaret's.
> Therefore, at last, I firmly am resolved
> You shall have aid.

QUEEN MARGARET
> Let me give humble thanks for all at once.

LEWIS
> Then, England's messenger, return in post
> And tell false Edward, thy supposèd king,
> That Lewis of France is sending over masquers   224
> To revel it with him and his new bride.
> Thou seest what's passed. Go fear thy king withal.   226

BONA
> Tell him, in hope he'll prove a widower shortly,
> I'll wear the willow garland for his sake.   228

QUEEN MARGARET
> Tell him my mourning weeds are laid aside
> And I am ready to put armor on.

WARWICK
> Tell him from me that he hath done me wrong
> And therefore I'll uncrown him ere't be long.
> There's thy reward. Be gone.   *Exit Post.*

LEWIS   But, Warwick,
> Thou and Oxford, with five thousand men,
> Shall cross the seas and bid false Edward battle;
> And as occasion serves, this noble queen
> And prince shall follow with a fresh supply.
> Yet, ere thou go, but answer me one doubt:
> What pledge have we of thy firm loyalty?

WARWICK
> This shall assure my constant loyalty,
> That if our queen and this young prince agree,

---

224 *masquers* participants in a courtly dramatic performance or revel
(ironically)   **226** *fear* frighten; *withal* with it   **228** *willow garland* (symbol
of rejected love)

242   I'll join mine eldest daughter, and my joy,
        To him forthwith in holy wedlock bands.

QUEEN MARGARET

244   Yes, I agree, and thank you for your motion.
        Son Edward, she is fair and virtuous.
        Therefore delay not; give thy hand to Warwick
        And, with thy hand, thy faith irrevocable
        That only Warwick's daughter shall be thine.

PRINCE

        Yes, I accept her, for she well deserves it,
        And here to pledge my vow I give my hand.
                He gives his hand to Warwick.

LEWIS

        Why stay we now? Those soldiers shall be levied,
        And thou, Lord Bourbon, our High Admiral,
253   Shall waft them over with our royal fleet.
        I long till Edward fall by war's mischance
        For mocking marriage with a dame of France.
                        Exeunt. Manet Warwick.

WARWICK

        I came from Edward as ambassador,
        But I return his sworn and mortal foe.
        Matter of marriage was the charge he gave me,
        But dreadful war shall answer his demand.
260   Had he none else to make a stale but me?
        Then none but I shall turn his jest to sorrow.
        I was the chief that raised him to the crown
        And I'll be chief to bring him down again;
        Not that I pity Henry's misery,
        But seek revenge on Edward's mockery.   *Exit.*

*

242 *eldest daughter* (actually his younger daughter, Anne, as his elder
daughter, Isabella, is to marry Clarence. In the chronicles, Isabella and
Clarence are already married at this time.)   244 *motion* offer   253 *waft*
transport by water   260 *stale* dupe

Enter Richard, Clarence, Somerset, and Montague.   IV, i

RICHARD
Now tell me, brother Clarence, what think you
Of this new marriage with the Lady Grey?
Hath not our brother made a worthy choice?

CLARENCE
Alas, you know 'tis far from hence to France,
How could he stay till Warwick made return?   5

SOMERSET
My lords, forbear this talk. Here comes the king.
    Flourish. Enter King Edward, Lady Grey [as
    Queen Elizabeth], Pembroke, Stafford, Hastings.
    Four stand on one side and four on the other.

RICHARD
And his well-chosen bride.

CLARENCE
I mind to tell him plainly what I think.   8

KING EDWARD
Now, brother of Clarence, how like you our choice,
That you stand pensive, as half malcontent?   10

CLARENCE
As well as Lewis of France or the Earl of Warwick,
Which are so weak of courage and in judgment
That they'll take no offense at our abuse.   13

KING EDWARD
Suppose they take offense without a cause:
They are but Lewis and Warwick; I am Edward,
Your king and Warwick's, and must have my will.

RICHARD
And shall have your will, because our king.
Yet hasty marriage seldom proveth well.

KING EDWARD
Yea, brother Richard, are you offended too?

RICHARD
Not I.

IV, i The royal palace in London   5 *stay* wait   8 *mind* intend   10
malcontent one disgusted with the world   13 *abuse* insult

No, God forbid that I should wish them severed
Whom God hath joined together. Ay, and 'twere pity
To sunder them that yoke so well together.

KING EDWARD

24   Setting your scorns and your mislike aside,
Tell me some reason why the Lady Grey
Should not become my wife and England's queen.
And you too, Somerset, and Montague,
Speak freely what you think.

CLARENCE

Then this is mine opinion, that King Lewis
Becomes your enemy for mocking him
About the marriage of the Lady Bona.

RICHARD

And Warwick, doing what you gave in charge,
Is now dishonorèd by this new marriage.

KING EDWARD

What if both Lewis and Warwick be appeased
35   By such invention as I can devise?

MONTAGUE

Yet, to have joined with France in such alliance
Would more have strengthened this our commonwealth
'Gainst foreign storms than any home-bred marriage.

HASTINGS

Why, knows not Montague that of itself
England is safe, if true within itself?

MONTAGUE

But the safer when 'tis backed with France.

HASTINGS

'Tis better using France than trusting France.
Let us be backed with God, and with the seas,
Which he hath giv'n for fence impregnable,
And with their helps only defend ourselves.
In them and in ourselves our safety lies.

---

24 *mislike* displeasure   35 *invention* plan

CLARENCE

    For this one speech Lord Hastings well deserves
    To have the heir of the Lord Hungerford.

KING EDWARD

    Ay, what of that ? It was my will and grant.
    And for this once my will shall stand for law.

RICHARD

    And yet methinks your grace hath not done well
    To give the heir and daughter of Lord Scales
    Unto the brother of your loving bride.   53
    She better would have fitted me or Clarence;
    But in your bride you bury brotherhood.

CLARENCE

    Or else you would not have bestowed the heir
    Of the Lord Bonville on your new wife's son   57
    And leave your brothers to go speed elsewhere.   58

KING EDWARD

    Alas, poor Clarence ! Is it for a wife
    That thou art malcontent ? I will provide thee.

CLARENCE

    In choosing for yourself you showed your judgment,
    Which being shallow, you shall give me leave
    To play the broker in mine own behalf;   63
    And to that end I shortly mind to leave you.

KING EDWARD

    Leave me or tarry, Edward will be king
    And not be tied unto his brother's will.

QUEEN ELIZABETH

    My lords, before it pleased his majesty
    To raise my state to title of a queen,
    Do me but right, and you must all confess
    That I was not ignoble of descent,
    And meaner than myself have had like fortune.
    But as this title honors me and mine,

---

53 *brother ... bride* i.e. Lord Rivers   57 *son* i.e. Sir Thomas Grey,
Marquess Dorset   58 *go speed* prosper (for themselves)   63 *broker* agent

73   So your dislikes, to whom I would be pleasing,
74   Doth cloud my joys with danger and with sorrow.

KING EDWARD

My love, forbear to fawn upon their frowns.
What danger or what sorrow can befall thee
So long as Edward is thy constant friend
And their true sovereign, whom they must obey?
Nay, whom they shall obey, and love thee too,
Unless they seek for hatred at my hands;
Which if they do, yet will I keep thee safe,
And they shall feel the vengeance of my wrath.

RICHARD [aside]

I hear; yet say not much, but think the more.
        Enter a Post.

KING EDWARD

Now, messenger, what letters or what news
From France?

POST

My sovereign liege, no letters, and few words,
But such as I, without your special pardon,
Dare not relate.

KING EDWARD

89   Go to, we pardon thee. Therefore, in brief,
90   Tell me their words as near as thou canst guess them.
What answer makes King Lewis unto our letters?

POST

92   At my depart these were his very words:
'Go tell false Edward, thy supposèd king,
That Lewis of France is sending over masquers
To revel it with him and his new bride.'

KING EDWARD

96   Is Lewis so brave? Belike he thinks me Henry.
But what said Lady Bona to my marriage?

POST

These were her words, uttered with mild disdain:

73 *dislikes* disapproval   74 *danger* apprehension   89 *Go to* all right, don't
worry   90 *guess* approximate   92 *depart* departure   96 *Belike* perhaps

'Tell him, in hope he'll prove a widower shortly,
I'll wear the willow garland for his sake.'

KING EDWARD
I blame not her. She could say little less.
She had the wrong. But what said Henry's queen?
For I have heard that she was there in place.   103

POST
'Tell him,' quoth she, 'my mourning weeds are done
And I am ready to put armor on.'

KING EDWARD
Belike she minds to play the Amazon.
But what said Warwick to these injuries?

POST
He, more incensed against your majesty
Than all the rest, discharged me with these words:
'Tell him from me that he hath done me wrong,
And therefore I'll uncrown him ere 't be long.'

KING EDWARD
Ha! durst the traitor breathe out so proud words?
Well, I will arm me, being thus forewarned.
They shall have wars and pay for their presumption.
But say, is Warwick friends with Margaret?

POST
Ay, gracious sovereign. They are so linked in friendship
That young Prince Edward marries Warwick's daughter.

CLARENCE [aside]
Belike the elder; Clarence will have the younger. –   118
Now, brother king, farewell, and sit you fast;
For I will hence to Warwick's other daughter,
That, though I want a kingdom, yet in marriage   121
I may not prove inferior to yourself.
You that love me and Warwick, follow me.
                    Exit Clarence, and Somerset follows.

RICHARD [aside]
Not I.

103 *in place* present   118 *Belike ... younger* (see III, iii, 242n.)   121 *want*
lack

My thoughts aim at a further matter. I
Stay not for the love of Edward but the crown.

KING EDWARD

Clarence and Somerset both gone to Warwick?
Yet am I armed against the worst can happen;
And haste is needful in this desp'rate case.
Pembroke and Stafford, you in our behalf
131   Go levy men and make prepare for war.
They are already, or quickly will be landed.
Myself in person will straight follow you.

                   Exeunt Pembroke and Stafford.

But ere I go, Hastings and Montague,
Resolve my doubt. You twain, of all the rest,
Are near to Warwick by blood and by alliance.
Tell me if you love Warwick more than me.
If it be so, then both depart to him;
139   I rather wish you foes than hollow friends.
But if you mind to hold your true obedience,
Give me assurance with some friendly vow,
142   That I may never have you in suspect.

MONTAGUE

So God help Montague as he proves true.

HASTINGS

And Hastings as he favors Edward's cause.

KING EDWARD

Now, brother Richard, will you stand by us?

RICHARD

Ay, in despite of all that shall withstand you.

KING EDWARD

Why, so! then am I sure of victory.
Now therefore let us hence, and lose no hour
Till we meet Warwick with his foreign power.   *Exeunt.*

*

131 *prepare* preparation   139 *hollow* empty, i.e. untrustworthy   142
suspect suspicion

Enter Warwick and Oxford in England with French   IV, ii
Soldiers.

WARWICK

Trust me, my lord, all hitherto goes well.

The common people by numbers swarm to us.
  Enter Clarence and Somerset.

But see where Somerset and Clarence comes.

Speak suddenly, my lords, are we all friends?

CLARENCE

Fear not that, my lord.

WARWICK

Then, gentle Clarence, welcome unto Warwick;

And welcome, Somerset. I hold it cowardice

To rest mistrustful where a noble heart

Hath pawned an open hand in sign of love.   9

Else might I think that Clarence, Edward's brother,

Were but a feignèd friend to our proceedings.

But welcome, sweet Clarence. My daughter shall be
  thine.

And now what rests but, in night's coverture,   13

Thy brother being carelessly encamped,

His soldiers lurking in the towns about,   15

And but attended by a simple guard,

We may surprise and take him at our pleasure?

Our scouts have found the adventure very easy;

That as Ulysses and stout Diomede   19

With sleight and manhood stole to Rhesus' tents

And brought from thence the Thracian fatal steeds,

So we, well covered with the night's black mantle,

At unawares may beat down Edward's guard

And seize himself. I say not, slaughter him,

For I intend but only to surprise him.   25

IV, ii Fields near Warwick **9** *pawned* pledged **13** *rests* remains; *in
night's coverture* under cover of night **15** *lurking* idling **19–21** *That ...
steeds* (The oracle predicted that Troy would not fall if the horses of
Rhesus, king of Thrace, grazed on the Trojan plain. To prevent their
doing so, Ulysses and Diomedes captured them on a night raid.) **25**
surprise capture

You that will follow me to this attempt,
Applaud the name of Henry with your leader.
        They all cry 'Henry!'
28 Why then, let's on our way in silent sort.
For Warwick and his friends, God and Saint George!
                                Exeunt.

∗

IV, iii   *Enter three Watchmen, to guard King Edward's tent.*

1. WATCHMAN
Come on, my masters. Each man take his stand.
2 The king by this is set him down to sleep.

2. WATCHMAN
What, will he not to bed?

1. WATCHMAN
Why, no; for he hath made a solemn vow
Never to lie and take his natural rest
Till Warwick or himself be quite suppressed.

2. WATCHMAN
To-morrow then belike shall be the day,
If Warwick be so near as men report.

3. WATCHMAN
But say, I pray, what nobleman is that
That with the king here resteth in his tent?

1. WATCHMAN
'Tis the Lord Hastings, the king's chiefest friend.

3. WATCHMAN
O, is it so? But why commands the king
That his chief followers lodge in towns about him,
While he himself keeps in the cold field?

2. WATCHMAN
'Tis the more honor, because more dangerous.

3. WATCHMAN
16 Ay, but give me worship and quietness.

28 *sort* manner
IV, iii Edward's camp near Warwick   2 *this* i.e. this time   16 *worship* a
place of dignity

I like it better than a dangerous honor.
If Warwick knew in what estate he stands,   18
'Tis to be doubted he would waken him.   19

1. WATCHMAN
Unless our halberds did shut up his passage.

2. WATCHMAN
Ay! wherefore else guard we his royal tent
But to defend his person from night-foes?
> *Enter Warwick, Clarence, Oxford, Somerset, and*
> *French Soldiers, silent all.*

WARWICK
This is his tent; and see where stand his guard.
Courage, my masters, honor now or never!
But follow me, and Edward shall be ours.

1. WATCHMAN Who goes there?

2. WATCHMAN Stay, or thou diest!
> *Warwick and the rest cry all 'Warwick! Warwick!'*
> *and set upon the Guard, who fly, crying 'Arm! arm!',*
> *Warwick and the rest following them.*
> *The Drum playing and Trumpet sounding, enter*
> *Warwick, Somerset, and the rest, bringing [Edward]*
> *the King out in his gown, sitting in a chair.*
> *Richard and Hastings flies over the stage.*

SOMERSET
What are they that fly there?

WARWICK
Richard and Hastings. Let them go. Here is the duke.

KING EDWARD
The duke? Why, Warwick, when we parted
Thou called'st me king.

WARWICK   Ay, but the case is altered.   31
When you disgraced me in my embassade,   32
Then I degraded you from being king,
And come now to create you Duke of York.
Alas, how should you govern any kingdom

18 *estate* condition   19 *doubted* feared   31 *the case is altered* things have
changed (a proverbial expression)   32 *embassade* embassy

That know not how to use ambassadors,
Nor how to be contented with one wife,
Nor how to use your brothers brotherly,
Nor how to study for the people's welfare,
40 Nor how to shroud yourself from enemies?

KING EDWARD

Yea, brother of Clarence, art thou here too?
42 Nay, then I see that Edward needs must down.
Yet, Warwick, in despite of all mischance,
44 Of thee thyself, and all thy complices,
Edward will always bear himself as king.
Though Fortune's malice overthrow my state,
47 My mind exceeds the compass of her wheel.

WARWICK

Then, for his mind, be Edward England's king,
        Takes off his crown.
But Henry now shall wear the English crown
And be true king indeed, thou but the shadow.
My Lord of Somerset, at my request
See that forthwith Duke Edward be conveyed
53 Unto my brother, Archbishop of York.
When I have fought with Pembroke and his fellows,
I'll follow you and tell what answer
Lewis and the Lady Bona send to him.
Now for a while farewell, good Duke of York.

KING EDWARD

What fates impose, that men must needs abide;
59 It boots not to resist both wind and tide.
        They lead him out forcibly. Exeunt.

OXFORD

What now remains, my lords, for us to do
But march to London with our soldiers?

WARWICK

Ay, that's the first thing that we have to do,

---

40 *shroud* conceal, protect 42 *needs must down* must necessarily be put
down 44 *complices* accomplices 47 *compass* circumference 53 *Archbishop of York* i.e. George Nevil 59 *boots not* is no use

To free King Henry from imprisonment
And see him seated in the regal throne.
                    Exit [Warwick with the rest].

*

                Enter Rivers and Lady Grey [as Queen Elizabeth].   IV, iv

RIVERS
    Madam, what makes you in this sudden change?

QUEEN ELIZABETH
    Why, brother Rivers, are you yet to learn
    What late misfortune is befall'n King Edward?

RIVERS
    What? Loss of some pitched battle against Warwick?

QUEEN ELIZABETH
    No, but the loss of his own royal person.

RIVERS
    Then is my sovereign slain?

QUEEN ELIZABETH
    Ay, almost slain, for he is taken prisoner,
    Either betrayed by falsehood of his guard
    Or by his foe surprised at unawares;
    And, as I further have to understand,
    Is new committed to the Bishop of York,   11
    Fell Warwick's brother, and by that our foe.   12

RIVERS
    These news, I must confess, are full of grief.
    Yet, gracious madam, bear it as you may;
    Warwick may lose, that now hath won the day.

QUEEN ELIZABETH
    Till then fair hope must hinder life's decay.
    And I the rather wean me from despair
    For love of Edward's offspring in my womb.
    This is it that makes me bridle passion
    And bear with mildness my misfortune's cross.

IV, iv The royal palace in London   11 *new* recently; *Bishop* i.e. archbishop   12 *Fell* cruel; *by that* i.e. because of that relationship

Ay, ay, for this I draw in many a tear

22   And stop the rising of bloodsucking sighs,
Lest with my sighs or tears I blast or drown
King Edward's fruit, true heir to th' English crown.

RIVERS

25   But, madam, where is Warwick then become?

QUEEN ELIZABETH

I am informèd that he comes toward London
To set the crown once more on Henry's head.
Guess thou the rest. King Edward's friends must down.

29   But, to prevent the tyrant's violence
(For trust not him that hath once broken faith),
I'll hence forthwith unto the sanctuary,
To save, at least, the heir of Edward's right.
There shall I rest secure from force and fraud.
Come, therefore, let us fly while we may fly.
If Warwick take us, we are sure to die.   *Exeunt*.

*

IV, v   *Enter Richard, Lord Hastings, and Sir William*
              Stanley.

RICHARD

Now, my Lord Hastings and Sir William Stanley,
Leave off to wonder why I drew you hither

3   Into this chiefest thicket of the park.
Thus stands the case: you know our king, my brother,
Is prisoner to the bishop here, at whose hands
He hath good usage and great liberty;
And often, but attended with weak guard,

8   Comes hunting this way to disport himself.

9   I have advertisèd him by secret means
That if about this hour he make this way

---

22 *bloodsucking sighs* (sighing was supposed to waste the heart's blood, which explains why *hope* can *hinder life's decay* [l. 16]) 25 *become* gone 29 *prevent* forestall
IV, v The Archbishop of York's park 3 *chiefest* largest 8 *disport* amuse 9 *advertised* notified

Under the color of his usual game,   11
He shall here find his friends with horse and men
To set him free from his captivity.
   Enter King Edward and a Huntsman with him.

HUNTSMAN
This way, my lord, for this way lies the game.

KING EDWARD
Nay, this way, man, see where the huntsmen stand.
Now, brother of Gloucester, Lord Hastings, and the rest,
Stand you thus close to steal the bishop's deer?   17

RICHARD
Brother, the time and case requireth haste.
Your horse stands ready at the park corner.

KING EDWARD
But whither shall we then?

HASTINGS
To Lynn, my lord.   21

KING EDWARD And ship from thence to Flanders?

RICHARD
Well guessed, believe me; for that was my meaning.

KING EDWARD
Stanley, I will requite thy forwardness.   23

RICHARD
But wherefore stay we? 'Tis no time to talk.

KING EDWARD
Huntsman, what say'st thou? Wilt thou go along?

HUNTSMAN
Better do so than tarry and be hanged.

RICHARD
Come then, away. Let's ha' no more ado.

KING EDWARD
Bishop, farewell. Shield thee from Warwick's frown
And pray that I may repossess the crown. *Exeunt.*

*

11 *Under ... game* i.e. as though he were merely hunting   17 *close*
hidden   21 *Lynn* i.e. King's Lynn, on the Norfolk coast   23 *forwardness*
zeal

IV, vi   *Flourish. Enter King Henry the Sixth, Clarence,*
Warwick, Somerset, young Henry [Earl of
Richmond], Oxford, Montague, and Lieutenant
[of the Tower].

KING HENRY

Master lieutenant, now that God and friends
Have shaken Edward from the regal seat
And turned my captive state to liberty,
My fear to hope, my sorrows unto joys,
5   At our enlargement what are thy due fees?

LIEUTENANT

Subjects may challenge nothing of their sovereigns;
But if an humble prayer may prevail,
I then crave pardon of your majesty.

KING HENRY

For what, lieutenant? for well using me?
Nay, be thou sure I'll well requite thy kindness
For that it made my imprisonment a pleasure;
Ay, such a pleasure as incagèd birds
Conceive when, after many moody thoughts,
At last by notes of household harmony
They quite forget their loss of liberty.
But, Warwick, after God, thou set'st me free,
And chiefly therefore I thank God and thee;
He was the author, thou the instrument.
Therefore, that I may conquer fortune's spite
By living low, where fortune cannot hurt me,
And that the people of this blessèd land
22   May not be punished with my thwarting stars,
Warwick, although my head still wear the crown,
I here resign my government to thee,
For thou art fortunate in all thy deeds.

IV, vi The Tower of London   s.d. *Lieutenant* Deputy Warden   5
enlargement release; *fees* (due because prisoners who could afford it were
charged for special quarters and food)   22 *thwarting stars* stars (instru-
ments of fortune) whose influence impedes happiness and success

WARWICK

    Your grace hath still been famed for virtuous,   26
    And now may seem as wise as virtuous
    By spying and avoiding fortune's malice,
    For few men rightly temper with the stars.   29
    Yet in this one thing let me blame your grace,
    For choosing me when Clarence is in place.   31

CLARENCE

    No, Warwick, thou art worthy of the sway,   32
    To whom the heavens in thy nativity
    Adjudged an olive branch and laurel crown,
    As likely to be blest in peace and war ;
    And therefore I yield thee my free consent.

WARWICK

    And I choose Clarence only for Protector.   37

KING HENRY

    Warwick and Clarence, give me both your hands.
    Now join your hands, and with your hands your hearts,
    That no dissension hinder government.
    I make you both Protectors of this land,
    While I myself will lead a private life
    And in devotion spend my latter days,
    To sin's rebuke and my Creator's praise.

WARWICK

    What answers Clarence to his sovereign's will ?

CLARENCE

    That he consents, if Warwick yield consent,
    For on thy fortune I repose myself.

WARWICK

    Why then, though loath, yet must I be content.
    We'll yoke together, like a double shadow
    To Henry's body, and supply his place ;   50
    I mean, in bearing weight of government,
    While he enjoys the honor and his ease.

---

26 *still* always   29 *temper . . . stars* i.e. come to terms with their fate   31 *in place* here   32 *sway* rule   37 *only* alone

And, Clarence, now then it is more than needful
Forthwith that Edward be pronounced a traitor
And all his lands and goods be confiscate.

CLARENCE
What else ? And that succession be determined.

WARWICK
Ay, therein Clarence shall not want his part.

KING HENRY
But with the first of all your chief affairs,
Let me entreat (for I command no more)
60   That Margaret your queen and my son Edward
Be sent for, to return from France with speed ;
For till I see them here, by doubtful fear
My joy of liberty is half eclipsed.

CLARENCE
It shall be done, my sovereign, with all speed.

KING HENRY
My Lord of Somerset, what youth is that
Of whom you seem to have so tender care ?

SOMERSET
67   My liege, it is young Henry, Earl of Richmond.

KING HENRY
Come hither, England's hope. *Lays his hand on his head.*
    If secret powers
69   Suggest but truth to my divining thoughts,
This pretty lad will prove our country's bliss.
His looks are full of peaceful majesty,
His head by nature framed to wear a crown,
His hand to wield a sceptre, and himself
Likely in time to bless a regal throne.
Make much of him, my lords ; for this is he
Must help you more than you are hurt by me.
    Enter a Post.

WARWICK
What news, my friend ?

67 *Henry* (the future Henry VII ; at his accession to the throne the Wars of
the Roses finally ceased)   69 *divining* foretelling the future

POST
> That Edward is escapèd from your brother
> And fled, as he hears since, to Burgundy.   79

WARWICK
> Unsavory news! But how made he escape?

POST
> He was conveyed by Richard Duke of Gloucester   81
> And the Lord Hastings, who attended him   82
> In secret ambush on the forest side
> And from the bishop's huntsmen rescued him;
> For hunting was his daily exercise.

WARWICK
> My brother was too careless of his charge.
> But let us hence, my sovereign, to provide
> A salve for any sore that may betide.   88
>   *Exeunt. Manent Somerset, Richmond, and Oxford.*

SOMERSET
> My lord, I like not of this flight of Edward's,
> For doubtless Burgundy will yield him help
> And we shall have more wars before't be long.
> As Henry's late presaging prophecy
> Did glad my heart with hope of this young Richmond,
> So doth my heart misgive me, in these conflicts
> What may befall him, to his harm and ours.
> Therefore, Lord Oxford, to prevent the worst,
> Forthwith we'll send him hence to Brittany
> Till storms be past of civil enmity.

OXFORD
> Ay, for if Edward repossess the crown,
> 'Tis like that Richmond with the rest shall down.

SOMERSET
> It shall be so; he shall to Brittany.
> Come therefore, let's about it speedily.   *Exeunt.*

*

79 *he* i.e. your brother, the Archbishop of York   81 *conveyed* secretly
carried away   82 *attended* waited for   88 *betide* develop

IV, vii   *Flourish. Enter [King] Edward, Richard, Hastings,*
           and Soldiers [a troop of Hollanders].

KING EDWARD

Now, brother Richard, Lord Hastings, and the rest,
Yet thus far Fortune maketh us amends
And says that once more I shall interchange
4   My wanèd state for Henry's regal crown.
Well have we passed and now repassed the seas
And brought desirèd help from Burgundy.
What then remains, we being thus arrived
8   From Ravenspurgh haven before the gates of York,
But that we enter, as into our dukedom?

RICHARD

The gates made fast! Brother, I like not this.
11   For many men that stumble at the threshold
Are well foretold that danger lurks within.

KING EDWARD

13   Tush, man, abodements must not now affright us;
By fair or foul means we must enter in,
For hither will our friends repair to us.

HASTINGS

My liege, I'll knock once more to summon them.
        Enter [aloft], on the walls, the Mayor of York and his
        Brethren [the Aldermen].

MAYOR

My lords, we were forewarnèd of your coming
And shut the gates for safety of ourselves;
For now we owe allegiance unto Henry.

KING EDWARD

But, Master Mayor, if Henry be your king,
Yet Edward at the least is Duke of York.

MAYOR

True, my good lord. I know you for no less.

IV, vii Before the walls of York   4 *wanèd* faded, declined   8 *Ravenspurgh*
(on the Yorkshire coast, at the mouth of the River Humber)   11 *stumble at*
the threshold (a sign of bad luck)   13 *abodements* omens

KING EDWARD

    Why, and I challenge nothing but my dukedom,   23
    As being well content with that alone.

RICHARD *[aside]*

    But when the fox hath once got in his nose,
    He'll soon find means to make the body follow.

HASTINGS

    Why, Master Mayor, why stand you in a doubt?
    Open the gates. We are King Henry's friends.

MAYOR

    Ay, say you so? The gates shall then be opened.
        He descends [with the Aldermen].

RICHARD

    A wise stout captain, and soon persuaded.

HASTINGS

    The good old man would fain that all were well,   31
    So 'twere not long of him; but being entered,   32
    I doubt not, I, but we shall soon persuade
    Both him and all his brothers unto reason.
        Enter [below] the Mayor, [bringing the keys in
        his hand,] and two Aldermen.

KING EDWARD

    So, Master Mayor. These gates must not be shut
    But in the night or in the time of war.
    What, fear not, man, but yield me up the keys;
        Takes his keys.
    For Edward will defend the town and thee
    And all those friends that deign to follow me.   39
        March. Enter Montgomery with Drum and Soldiers.

RICHARD

    Brother, this is Sir John Montgomery,   40
    Our trusty friend, unless I be deceived.

---

23 *challenge* claim   31 *would fain* desires   32 *So . . . him* as long as he
bears no responsibility   39 *deign* are willing   40 *Sir John Montgomery*
(called Sir Thomas in the Chronicles, which report that he met Edward at
Nottingham after the securing of York)

KING EDWARD
 Welcome, Sir John ; but why come you in arms ?

MONTGOMERY
 To help King Edward in his time of storm,
 As every loyal subject ought to do.

KING EDWARD
 Thanks, good Montgomery. But we now forget
 Our title to the crown and only claim
 Our dukedom till God please to send the rest.

MONTGOMERY
 Then fare you well, for I will hence again.
 I came to serve a king and not a duke.
50 Drummer, strike up, and let us march away.
      The Drum begins to march.

KING EDWARD
 Nay, stay, Sir John, awhile, and we'll debate
 By what safe means the crown may be recovered.

MONTGOMERY
 What talk you of debating ? In few words,
 If you'll not here proclaim yourself our king,
 I'll leave you to your fortune and be gone
 To keep them back that come to succor you.
57 Why shall we fight, if you pretend no title ?

RICHARD
58 Why, brother, wherefore stand you on nice points ?

KING EDWARD
 When we grow stronger, then we'll make our claim ;
 Till then 'tis wisdom to conceal our meaning.

HASTINGS
61 Away with scrupulous wit ! Now arms must rule.

RICHARD
 And fearless minds climb soonest unto crowns.
63 Brother, we will proclaim you out of hand ;
64 The bruit thereof will bring you many friends.

---

50 s.d. *march* i.e. commence beating a march   **57** *pretend* claim   **58** *nice
points* minor details   **61** *wit* reasoning   **63** *out of hand* immediately   **64**
bruit news

KING EDWARD

   Then be it as you will; for 'tis my right,
   And Henry but usurps the diadem.

MONTGOMERY

   Ay, now my sovereign speaketh like himself
   And now will I be Edward's champion.   68

HASTINGS

   Sound trumpet. Edward shall be here proclaimed.
   Come, fellow soldier, make thou proclamation.
     Flourish. Sound.

SOLDIER 'Edward the Fourth, by the grace of God, King
   of England and France, and Lord of Ireland, etc.'   72

MONTGOMERY

   And whosoe'er gainsays King Edward's right,
   By this I challenge him to single fight.
     Throws down his gauntlet.

ALL Long live Edward the Fourth!

KING EDWARD

   Thanks, brave Montgomery, and thanks unto you all.
   If fortune serve me I'll requite this kindness.
   Now for this night let's harbor here in York,
   And when the morning sun shall raise his car   79
   Above the border of this horizon,
   We'll forward towards Warwick and his mates;
   For well I wot that Henry is no soldier.   82
   Ah, froward Clarence, how evil it beseems thee 83
   To flatter Henry and forsake thy brother.
   Yet, as we may, we'll meet both thee and Warwick.
   Come on, brave soldiers. Doubt not of the day,
   And that once gotten, doubt not of large pay.
       Exeunt [as into the city].

*

68 *champion* defender   **72** *etc.* (the soldier adds the conventional titles of
the monarch)   **79** *car* chariot   **82** *wot* know   **83** *froward* perverse,
refractory

IV, viii   *Flourish. Enter the King [Henry], Warwick,*
Montague, Clarence, Oxford, and Exeter.

WARWICK

1   What counsel, lords ? Edward from Belgia,

2   With hasty Germans and blunt Hollanders,
     Hath passed in safety through the narrow seas

4   And with his troops doth march amain to London,
     And many giddy people flock to him.

OXFORD

     Let's levy men and beat him back again.

CLARENCE

     A little fire is quickly trodden out,

8   Which, being suffered, rivers cannot quench.

WARWICK

     In Warwickshire I have true-hearted friends,
     Not mutinous in peace, yet bold in war.

11   Those will I muster up ; and thou, son Clarence,
     Shalt stir up in Suffolk, Norfolk, and in Kent
     The knights and gentlemen to come with thee.
     Thou, brother Montague, in Buckingham,
     Northampton, and in Leicestershire shalt find
     Men well inclined to hear what thou command'st.
     And thou, brave Oxford, wondrous well beloved,
     In Oxfordshire shalt muster up thy friends.
     My sovereign, with the loving citizens,
     Like to his island girt in with the ocean
     Or modest Dian circled with her nymphs,
     Shall rest in London till we come to him.
     Fair lords, take leave and stand not to reply.
     Farewell, my sovereign.

KING HENRY

25   Farewell, my Hector and my Troy's true hope.

IV, viii The Bishop of London's palace **1** *Belgia* the Netherlands **2**
hasty rash, quick-tempered; *blunt* merciless **4** *amain* speedily **8** *suffered*
tolerated **11** *son* i.e. son-in-law **25** *my Troy's* (because London [New
Troy] was supposedly founded by Brutus, legendary grandson of the
Trojan hero Aeneas)

CLARENCE
>In sign of truth I kiss your highness' hand.

KING HENRY
>Well-minded Clarence, be thou fortunate.

MONTAGUE
>Comfort, my lord, and so I take my leave.

OXFORD *[kisses Henry's hand]*
>And thus I seal my truth and bid adieu.

KING HENRY
>Sweet Oxford, and my loving Montague,
>And all at once, once more a happy farewell.   31

WARWICK
>Farewell, sweet lords. Let's meet at Coventry.
>>*Exeunt [all but King Henry and Exeter].*

KING HENRY
>Here at the palace will I rest awhile.
>Cousin of Exeter, what thinks your lordship?
>Methinks the power that Edward hath in field
>Should not be able to encounter mine.

EXETER
>The doubt is that he will seduce the rest.   37

KING HENRY
>That's not my fear. My meed hath got me fame.   38
>I have not stopped mine ears to their demands
>Nor posted off their suits with slow delays.   40
>My pity hath been balm to heal their wounds,
>My mildness hath allayed their swelling griefs,
>My mercy dried their water-flowing tears.
>I have not been desirous of their wealth
>Nor much oppressed them with great subsidies,   45
>Nor forward of revenge, though they much erred.   46
>Then why should they love Edward more than me?
>No, Exeter, these graces challenge grace;

---

31 *at once* together   37 *doubt* fear   38 *meed* rewards given for merit, generosity   40 *posted off* treated lightly, postponed   45 *subsidies* taxes 46 *forward of* eager for

And when the lion fawns upon the lamb,
The lamb will never cease to follow him.
            Shout within, 'A Lancaster ! A Lancaster !'

EXETER

Hark, hark, my lord ! what shouts are these ?
            Enter [King] Edward and his Soldiers [, with
            Richard].

KING EDWARD

52   Seize on the shamefaced Henry, bear him hence,
        And once again proclaim us King of England.
        You are the fount that makes small brooks to flow.
        Now stops thy spring ; my sea shall suck them dry
        And swell so much the higher by their ebb.
        Hence with him to the Tower. Let him not speak.
                Exit [Guard] with King Henry [and Exeter].
        And, lords, toward Coventry bend we our course,
59   Where peremptory Warwick now remains.
60   The sun shines hot, and if we use delay,
        Cold biting winter mars our hoped-for hay.

RICHARD

62   Away betimes, before his forces join,
        And take the great-grown traitor unawares.
        Brave warriors, march amain toward Coventry. *Exeunt.*

                            *

V, i   *Enter [aloft] Warwick, the Mayor of Coventry,*
            two Messengers, and others, upon the walls.

WARWICK

Where is the post that came from valiant Oxford ?
How far hence is thy lord, mine honest fellow ?

1. MESSENGER

3   By this at Dunsmore, marching hitherward.

52 *shamefaced* shamefast, modest   59 *peremptory* overbearing   60–61
The sun ... hay i.e. we should make hay while the sun shines   62 *betimes* at
once
V, i Before the walls of Coventry   3 *Dunsmore* Dunsmore Heath, between
Coventry and Daventry

WARWICK
  How far off is our brother Montague?
  Where is the post that came from Montague?
2. MESSENGER
  By this at Daintry, with a puissant troop.   6
      Enter Somervile [aloft].
WARWICK
  Say, Somervile, what says my loving son?
  And by thy guess how nigh is Clarence now?
SOMERVILE
  At Southam I did leave him with his forces   9
  And do expect him here some two hours hence.
WARWICK
  Then Clarence is at hand. I hear his drum.
SOMERVILE
  It is not his, my lord. Here Southam lies.   12
  The drum your honor hears marcheth from Warwick.
WARWICK
  Who should that be? Belike unlooked-for friends.   14
SOMERVILE
  They are at hand, and you shall quickly know.
      March. Flourish. Enter [below, King] Edward,
      Richard, and Soldiers.
KING EDWARD
  Go, trumpet, to the walls, and sound a parle.   16
RICHARD
  See how the surly Warwick mans the wall.
WARWICK
  O unbid spite! Is sportful Edward come?   18
  Where slept our scouts or how are they seduced
  That we could hear no news of his repair?   20

6 *Daintry* i.e. Daventry, about twenty miles southeast of Coventry; *puissant* strong 9 *Southam* (about ten miles southeast of Coventry) 12–13 *It . . . Warwick* (the city of Warwick lies southwest of Coventry; the earl has slightly mistaken his directions, as Somervile points out) 14 *Belike* no doubt 16 *parle* parley, a trumpet call requesting a truce for conference 18 *unbid* uninvited, unwelcome; *sportful* lascivious 20 *repair* approach

KING EDWARD

Now, Warwick, wilt thou ope the city gates,
Speak gentle words, and humbly bend thy knee.
Call Edward king and at his hands beg mercy,
And he shall pardon thee these outrages.

WARWICK

Nay, rather, wilt thou draw thy forces hence,
Confess who set thee up and plucked thee down,
Call Warwick patron, and be penitent?
And thou shalt still remain the Duke of York.

RICHARD

I thought at least he would have said 'the king';
Or did he make the jest against his will?

WARWICK

Is not a dukedom, sir, a goodly gift?

RICHARD

Ay, by my faith, for a poor earl to give;
33   I'll do thee service for so good a gift.

WARWICK

'Twas I that gave the kingdom to thy brother.

KING EDWARD

Why, then 'tis mine, if but by Warwick's gift.

WARWICK

36   Thou art no Atlas for so great a weight;
And, weakling, Warwick takes his gift again,
And Henry is my king, Warwick his subject.

KING EDWARD

But Warwick's king is Edward's prisoner;
And, gallant Warwick, do but answer this:
What is the body when the head is off?

RICHARD

42   Alas that Warwick had no more forecast,

---

33 *do thee service* accept you as my feudal overlord (ironically)   36 *Thou
... Atlas* i.e. you cannot bear (Atlas, a Titan, supported the world on his
shoulders)   42 *forecast* forethought

But, whiles he thought to steal the single ten,   43
The king was slily fingered from the deck.
You left poor Henry at the bishop's palace
And ten to one you'll meet him in the Tower.

KING EDWARD

'Tis even so. Yet you are Warwick still.

RICHARD

Come, Warwick, take the time. Kneel down, kneel   48
    down.
Nay, when? Strike now, or else the iron cools.   49

WARWICK

I had rather chop this hand off at a blow
And with the other fling it at thy face
Than bear so low a sail to strike to thee.   52

KING EDWARD

Sail how thou canst, have wind and tide thy friend,
This hand, fast wound about thy coal-black hair,
Shall, whiles thy head is warm and new cut off,
Write in the dust this sentence with thy blood:
'Wind-changing Warwick now can change no more.'   57
    Enter Oxford, with Drum and Colors.

WARWICK

O cheerful colors, see where Oxford comes.

OXFORD

Oxford, Oxford, for Lancaster!
    [Exeunt Oxford and his men as into the city.]

RICHARD

The gates are open; let us enter too.

KING EDWARD

So other foes may set upon our backs.   61
Stand we in good array, for they no doubt
Will issue out again and bid us battle.   63

---

43 *single ten* mere ten (the ten, highest of the plain cards, is worth having,
but not in comparison with the king)   48 *take the time* seize the opportunity   49 *Nay, when* (an exclamation indicating impatience)   52 *bear ...
thee* (see III, iii, 5n.)   57 *Wind-changing* i.e. fickle, inconstant   61 *So* if
so   63 *bid* offer

If not, the city being but of small defense,
65 We'll quickly rouse the traitors in the same.
        [Enter Oxford aloft.]

WARWICK
    O, welcome, Oxford, for we want thy help.
        Enter Montague, with Drum and Colors.

MONTAGUE
    Montague, Montague, for Lancaster!
            [Exeunt Montague and his men as into the city.]

RICHARD
    Thou and thy brother both shall buy this treason
    Even with the dearest blood your bodies bear.

KING EDWARD
    The harder matched, the greater victory.
    My mind presageth happy gain and conquest.
        Enter Somerset, with Drum and Colors.

SOMERSET
    Somerset, Somerset, for Lancaster!
            [Exeunt Somerset and his men as into the city.]

RICHARD
73 Two of thy name, both Dukes of Somerset,
    Have sold their lives unto the house of York;
    And thou shalt be the third, if this sword hold.
        Enter Clarence, with Drum and Colors.

WARWICK
    And lo where George of Clarence sweeps along,
    Of force enough to bid his brother battle;
    With whom an upright zeal to right prevails
    More than the nature of a brother's love.
    Come, Clarence, come; thou wilt, if Warwick call.
        *[Sound a parle and Richard and Clarence whisper
        together.]*

65 *rouse ... in* drive ... from (a hunting term)   73 *Two ... name* (The
Somerset being addressed is Edmund, the 4th duke. His elder brother,
Henry Beaufort, 3rd duke, was executed after the Battle of Hexham, 1464,
though his defection from Edward is described in IV, i and ii as taking
place in 1470. Their father, Edmund, 2nd duke, was killed at St Albans,
1445; it is his head that Richard flings down at I, i, 16.)

CLARENCE
>   Father of Warwick, know you what this means?
>   *[Takes his red rose out of his hat.]*
>   Look here, I throw my infamy at thee.
>   I will not ruinate my father's house,
>   Who gave his blood to lime the stones together,   84
>   And set up Lancaster. Why, trowest thou, Warwick,   85
>   That Clarence is so harsh, so blunt, unnatural,   86
>   To bend the fatal instruments of war
>   Against his brother and his lawful king?
>   Perhaps thou wilt object my holy oath.   89
>   To keep that oath were more impiety
>   Than Jephtha when he sacrificed his daughter.   91
>   I am so sorry for my trespass made
>   That, to deserve well at my brother's hands,
>   I here proclaim myself thy mortal foe,
>   With resolution, wheresoe'er I meet thee
>   (As I will meet thee if thou stir abroad),
>   To plague thee for thy foul misleading me.
>   And so, proud-hearted Warwick, I defy thee
>   And to my brother turn my blushing cheeks.
>   Pardon me, Edward, I will make amends;
>   And, Richard, do not frown upon my faults,
>   For I will henceforth be no more unconstant.   102

KING EDWARD
>   Now welcome more, and ten times more beloved,
>   Than if thou never hadst deserved our hate.

RICHARD
>   Welcome, good Clarence. This is brotherlike.

WARWICK
>   O passing traitor, perjured and unjust.   106

KING EDWARD
>   What, Warwick, wilt thou leave the town and fight?
>   Or shall we beat the stones about thine ears?

---

84 *lime* cement 85 *trowest thou* do you believe 86 *blunt* unfeeling 89
object raise as an objection 91 *Jephtha* (see Judges xi, 30–40) 102
unconstant fickle, disloyal 106 *passing* surpassing

WARWICK
Alas, I am not cooped here for defense.
110   I will away towards Barnet presently
And bid thee battle, Edward, if thou dar'st.
KING EDWARD
Yes, Warwick, Edward dares and leads the way.
Lords, to the field. Saint George and victory!

Exeunt [King Edward and his company below,
Warwick and his company aloft]. March.
[Enter below as out of the city] Warwick and
his company [and] follows [King Edward].

*

V, ii   *Alarum and excursions. Enter [King] Edward,*
bringing forth Warwick wounded.

KING EDWARD
So, lie thou there! Die thou, and die our fear!
2   For Warwick was a bug that feared us all.
Now, Montague, sit fast. I seek for thee,
That Warwick's bones may keep thine company.   *Exit.*
WARWICK
Ah, who is nigh? Come to me, friend or foe,
And tell me who is victor, York or Warwick.
Why ask I that? My mangled body shows,
My blood, my want of strength, my sick heart shows,

110 *Barnet* (about ten miles north of London and seventy-five miles southeast of Coventry. At IV, viii the dramatist had departed from the historical order of events: in mid-March, 1471, from York [IV, vii] Edward had moved south to Coventry, to which Warwick had withdrawn. Here the Yorkist army invited battle. When Warwick declined, Edward continued south, occupying the town of Warwick, whence he doubled back to Coventry to challenge the Lancastrian forces once more. When Warwick again refused, Edward marched south, capturing London and Henry VI on April 11, this time with the Lancastrians following. By April 13 Warwick had reached Barnet, where early the next day he encountered the Yorkist army, which had marched north from London. Because he put Henry's capture [IV, viii] out of its historical sequence, the dramatist is here forced to treat Barnet as though it lay adjacent to Coventry.)
V, ii Fields near Coventry (Barnet)   2 *bug* goblin; *feared* frightened

That I must yield my body to the earth
And, by my fall, the conquest to my foe.
Thus yields the cedar to the axe's edge,   11
Whose arms gave shelter to the princely eagle,   12
Under whose shade the ramping lion slept,   13
Whose top-branch overpeered Jove's spreading tree   14
And kept low shrubs from winter's powerful wind.
These eyes, that now are dimmed with death's black veil,
Have been as piercing as the midday sun
To search the secret treasons of the world.
The wrinkles in my brows, now filled with blood,
Were likened oft to kingly sepulchres;
For who lived king but I could dig his grave?
And who durst smile when Warwick bent his brow?
Lo now my glory smeared in dust and blood;
My parks, my walks, my manors that I had,
Even now forsake me; and of all my lands
Is nothing left me but my body's length.
Why, what is pomp, rule, reign, but earth and dust?
And, live we how we can, yet die we must.
     Enter Oxford and Somerset.

SOMERSET

Ah, Warwick, Warwick, wert thou as we are,
We might recover all our loss again.
The queen from France hath brought a puissant power.   31
Even now we heard the news. Ah, couldst thou fly!

WARWICK

Why, then I would not fly. Ah, Montague,
If thou be there, sweet brother, take my hand
And with thy lips keep in my soul awhile.
Thou lov'st me not; for, brother, if thou didst,
Thy tears would wash this cold congealèd blood

---

11 *cedar* (symbol of pre-eminence)   **12–13** *eagle ... lion* (the allusion may be general, i.e. 'royal creatures'; or it may be intended specifically, through the identification of the men with their emblems: i.e. 'eagle': Richard of York, as perhaps at II, i, 92, and 'lion': Henry VI, three rampant lions being represented on his royal arms)   **13** *ramping* rampant   **14** *overpeered* overlooked; *Jove's ... tree* i.e. the oak   **31** *puissant* strong

That glues my lips and will not let me speak.
Come quickly, Montague, or I am dead.

SOMERSET

Ah, Warwick, Montague hath breathed his last,
41 And to the latest gasp cried out for Warwick
And said, 'Commend me to my valiant brother.'
And more he would have said, and more he spoke,
Which sounded like a cannon in a vault,
45 That mought not be distinguished ; but at last
I well might hear, delivered with a groan,
'O, farewell, Warwick!'

WARWICK

Sweet rest his soul. Fly, lords, and save yourselves ;
For Warwick bids you all farewell, to meet in heaven.
   [Dies.]

OXFORD

Away, away, to meet the queen's great power.
                  Here they bear away his body. Exeunt.

V, iii   *Flourish. Enter King Edward in triumph ;*
            with Richard, Clarence, and the rest.

KING EDWARD

Thus far our fortune keeps an upward course
And we are graced with wreaths of victory ;
But in the midst of this bright-shining day
I spy a black, suspicious, threat'ning cloud
That will encounter with our glorious sun
Ere he attain his easeful western bed.
I mean, my lords, those powers that the queen
8 Hath raised in Gallia have arrived our coast
And, as we hear, march on to fight with us.

CLARENCE

A little gale will soon disperse that cloud
And blow it to the source from whence it came.
Thy very beams will dry those vapors up,
13 For every cloud engenders not a storm.

41 *latest* final   45 *mought* might
V, iii   8 *Gallia* France   13 *engenders* begets

RICHARD

   The queen is valued thirty thousand strong,
   And Somerset, with Oxford, fled to her.
   If she have time to breathe, be well assured   16
   Her faction will be full as strong as ours.

KING EDWARD

   We are advertised by our loving friends   18
   That they do hold their course toward Tewkesbury.
   We, having now the best at Barnet field,   20
   Will thither straight, for willingness rids way ;   21
   And as we march our strength will be augmented
   In every county as we go along.
   Strike up the drum. Cry 'Courage !' and away.   *Exeunt.*

*

   Flourish. March. Enter the Queen [Margaret],   V, iv
   young [Prince] Edward, Somerset, Oxford, and
   Soldiers.

QUEEN MARGARET

   Great lords, wise men ne'er sit and wail their loss
   But cheerly seek how to redress their harms.   2
   What though the mast be now blown overboard,
   The cable broke, the holding anchor lost,
   And half our sailors swallowed in the flood ?
   Yet lives our pilot still. Is't meet that he
   Should leave the helm and, like a fearful lad,
   With tearful eyes add water to the sea
   And give more strength to that which hath too much,
   Whiles, in his moan, the ship splits on the rock,   10
   Which industry and courage might have saved ?
   Ah, what a shame, ah, what a fault were this.
   Say Warwick was our anchor. What of that ?
   And Montague our topmast. What of him ?

16 *breathe* i.e. gather her strength   18 *advertised* notified   20 *having ...*
best having now overcome   21 *rids way* i.e. decreases the distance
V, iv Fields near Tewkesbury   2 *cheerly* cheerfully   10 *in* at

15   Our slaught'red friends the tackles. What of these?
      Why, is not Oxford here, another anchor?
      And Somerset, another goodly mast?
18   The friends of France our shrouds and tacklings?
      And, though unskillful, why not Ned and I
20   For once allowed the skillful pilot's charge?
      We will not from the helm, to sit and weep,
      But keep our course (though the rough wind say no)
23   From shelves and rocks that threaten us with wrack.
      As good to chide the waves as speak them fair.
      And what is Edward but a ruthless sea?
      What Clarence but a quicksand of deceit?
      And Richard but a ragged fatal rock?
      All these the enemies to our poor bark.
      Say you can swim – alas, 'tis but a while,
      Tread on the sand – why there you quickly sink,
      Bestride the rock – the tide will wash you off
      Or else you famish: that's a threefold death.
      This speak I, lords, to let you understand,
34   If case some one of you would fly from us,
      That there's no hoped-for mercy with the brothers
      More than with ruthless waves, with sands and rocks.
      Why, courage then, what cannot be avoided
      'Twere childish weakness to lament or fear.

PRINCE
      Methinks a woman of this valiant spirit
      Should, if a coward heard her speak these words,
      Infuse his breast with magnanimity
42   And make him, naked, foil a man-at-arms.
      I speak not this as doubting any here;
      For did I but suspect a fearful man,
45   He should have leave to go away betimes,

---

15 *tackles* lines and pulleys for raising sail (running rigging)   18 *shrouds* lines bracing the mast (standing rigging); *tacklings* fittings and similar equipment   20 *charge* responsibility (i.e. to guide the ship)   23 *shelves* sandbanks; *wrack* wreck, ruin   34 *If* in   42 *foil a man-at-arms* defeat an armed man   45 *betimes* immediately

Lest in our need he might infect another
And make him of like spirit to himself.
If any such be here (as God forbid!)
Let him depart before we need his help.

OXFORD
Women and children of so high a courage,
And warriors faint? Why, 'twere perpetual shame.
O brave young prince, thy famous grandfather   52
Doth live again in thee. Long mayst thou live
To bear his image and renew his glories.

SOMERSET
And he that will not fight for such a hope,
Go home to bed, and, like the owl by day,
If he arise, be mocked and wondered at.

QUEEN MARGARET
Thanks, gentle Somerset; sweet Oxford, thanks.

PRINCE
And take his thanks that yet hath nothing else.
    Enter a Messenger.

MESSENGER
Prepare you, lords; for Edward is at hand,
Ready to fight. Therefore be resolute.

OXFORD
I thought no less. It is his policy
To haste thus fast, to find us unprovided.   63

SOMERSET
But he's deceived; we are in readiness.

QUEEN MARGARET
This cheers my heart, to see your forwardness.   65

OXFORD
Here pitch our battle; hence we will not budge.   66
    Flourish and march. Enter [King] Edward, Richard,
    Clarence, and Soldiers.

KING EDWARD
Brave followers, yonder stands the thorny wood

---

52 *grandfather* i.e. Henry V   63 *unprovided* unprepared   65 *forwardness*
zeal   66 *pitch our battle* deploy our forces

Which, by the heavens' assistance and your strength,
Must by the roots be hewn up yet ere night.
I need not add more fuel to your fire,
71   For well I wot ye blaze to burn them out.
Give signal to the fight, and to it, lords!

QUEEN MARGARET
Lords, knights and gentlemen, what I should say
74   My tears gainsay; for every word I speak,
Ye see I drink the water of my eye.
Therefore, no more but this: Henry, your sovereign,
Is prisoner to the foe, his state usurped,
His realm a slaughterhouse, his subjects slain,
His statutes cancelled, and his treasure spent;
And yonder is the wolf that makes this spoil.
You fight in justice. Then, in God's name, lords,
82   Be valiant and give signal to the fight.

*Alarum [to the battle: they fight]; retreat [and King
Edward and his company fly, driven out by Queen
Margaret and her company]. Excursions [and the
chambers be discharged, and re-enter King Edward
and his company, making a great shout and cry
'A York, a York'; and then the Queen Margaret,
Prince, Oxford, and Somerset are taken].   Exeunt.*

V, v   *Flourish. Enter [King] Edward, Richard, [with
Soldiers guarding] Queen [Margaret as prisoner],
Clarence, [with Soldiers guarding] Oxford,
Somerset [as prisoners].*

KING EDWARD
1   Now here a period of tumultuous broils.
2   Away with Oxford to Hames Castle straight.
For Somerset, off with his guilty head!
Go bear them hence. I will not hear them speak.

---

71 *wot* know   74 *gainsay* forbid   82 s.d. *chambers* saluting cannon (to
simulate ordnance)
V, v   1 *period* full stop   2 *Hames Castle* i.e. Hanmes Castle, near Calais
(where Oxford was confined after his capture in 1474, three years later than
Tewkesbury)

OXFORD

For my part, I'll not trouble thee with words.

SOMERSET

Nor I, but stoop with patience to my fortune.

Exeunt [Oxford and Somerset, guarded].

QUEEN MARGARET

So part we sadly in this troublous world

To meet with joy in sweet Jerusalem.   8

KING EDWARD

Is proclamation made that who finds Edward

Shall have a high reward, and he his life?

RICHARD

It is. And lo where youthful Edward comes.

Enter [Soldiers, with] the Prince.

KING EDWARD

Bring forth the gallant; let us hear him speak.

What? Can so young a thorn begin to prick?

Edward, what satisfaction canst thou make   14

For bearing arms, for stirring up my subjects,

And all the trouble thou hast turned me too?

PRINCE

Speak like a subject, proud ambitious York!

Suppose that I am now my father's mouth;

Resign thy chair, and where I stand kneel thou,

Whilst I propose the selfsame words to thee

Which, traitor, thou wouldst have me answer to.

QUEEN MARGARET

Ah, that thy father had been so resolved.

RICHARD

That you might still have worn the petticoat   23

And ne'er have stol'n the breech from Lancaster.   24

PRINCE

Let Aesop fable in a winter's night.   25

8 *Jerusalem* i.e. Heaven, the New Jerusalem   14 *satisfaction* recompense
23 *still* always   24 *breech* breeches   25–26 *Let … place* i.e. you lie about
the relationship between my mother and father (with a gibe at Richard, for
Aesop was supposedly stunted and deformed)

26   His currish riddles sorts not with this place.

RICHARD
By heaven, brat, I'll plague ye for that word.

QUEEN MARGARET
Ay, thou wast born to be a plague to men.

RICHARD
For God's sake take away this captive scold.

PRINCE
Nay, take away this scolding crook-back rather.

KING EDWARD
31   Peace, willful boy, or I will charm your tongue.

CLARENCE
32   Untutored lad, thou art too malapert.

PRINCE
I know my duty ; you are all undutiful.
Lascivious Edward, and thou perjured George,
And thou misshapen Dick, I tell ye all
I am your better, traitors as ye are,
And thou usurp'st my father's right and mine.

KING EDWARD
38   Take that, the likeness of this railer here.
        Stabs him.

RICHARD
39   Sprawl'st thou ? Take that, to end thy agony.
        Richard stabs him.

CLARENCE
And there's for twitting me with perjury.
        Clarence stabs him.

QUEEN MARGARET
O, kill me too !

RICHARD
42   Marry, and shall.

---

26 *currish* mean, cynical; *sorts not* are not appropriate   31 *charm your tongue* i.e. silence you ('charm': cast a spell upon)   32 *malapert* impertinent   38 *this railer* i.e. Queen Margaret   39 *Sprawl'st thou* do you struggle in your death-throes   42 *Marry, and shall* I will indeed ('marry': by the Virgin Mary)

Offers to kill her.

KING EDWARD

  Hold, Richard, hold ; for we have done too much.

RICHARD

  Why should she live to fill the world with words ?

KING EDWARD

  What ? Doth she swoon ? Use means for her recovery.

RICHARD

  Clarence, excuse me to the king my brother.
  I'll hence to London on a serious matter ;
  Ere ye come there, be sure to hear some news.   48

CLARENCE What ? what ?

RICHARD The Tower, the Tower.   *Exit.*

QUEEN MARGARET

  O Ned, sweet Ned, speak to thy mother, boy.
  Canst thou not speak ? O traitors ! murderers !
  They that stabbed Caesar shed no blood at all,
  Did not offend, nor were not worthy blame,
  If this foul deed were by, to equal it.   55
  He was a man ; this (in respect) a child,   56
  And men ne'er spend their fury on a child.
  What's worse than murderer, that I may name it ?
  No, no, my heart will burst an if I speak.
  And I will speak, that so my heart may burst.
  Butchers and villains, bloody cannibals,
  How sweet a plant have you untimely cropped.
  You have no children, butchers ; if you had,
  The thought of them would have stirred up remorse ;
  But if you ever chance to have a child,
  Look in his youth to have him so cut off
  As, deathsmen, you have rid this sweet young prince.   67

KING EDWARD

  Away with her ! Go bear her hence perforce !

QUEEN MARGARET

  Nay, never bear me hence, dispatch me here.

48 *be sure to* be confident that you will   55 *equal* compare with   56 *in respect* by comparison   67 *rid* killed

Here sheathe thy sword, I'll pardon thee my death.
What, wilt thou not? Then, Clarence, do it thou.

CLARENCE

By heaven, I will not do thee so much ease.

QUEEN MARGARET

Good Clarence, do! Sweet Clarence, do thou do it!

CLARENCE

Didst thou not hear me swear I would not do it?

QUEEN MARGARET

75   Ay, but thou usest to forswear thyself.
'Twas sin before, but now 'tis charity.
What, wilt thou not? Where is that devil's butcher,
78   Hard-favored Richard? Richard, where art thou?
79   Thou art not here. Murder is thy almsdeed.
80   Petitioners for blood thou ne'er put'st back.

KING EDWARD

Away, I say. I charge ye bear her hence.

QUEEN MARGARET

So come to you and yours as to this prince.

Exit Queen [Margaret, guarded].

KING EDWARD

Where's Richard gone?

CLARENCE

84   To London, all in post; and, as I guess,
To make a bloody supper in the Tower.

KING EDWARD

He's sudden if a thing comes in his head.
87   Now march we hence, discharge the common sort
With pay and thanks, and let's away to London
And see our gentle queen how well she fares.
90   By this, I hope, she hath a son for me.

Exit [King Edward with his company].

*

75 *thou . . . to forswear* you have the habit of forswearing   78 *Hard-favored*
grim in appearance   79 *almsdeed* charity   80 *Petitioners . . . back* you
never turn away those who ask for blood   84 *post* haste   87 *common sort*
ordinary soldiers   90 *this* this time

Enter [King] Henry the Sixth and Richard, with the   V, vi
Lieutenant in the Tower.

RICHARD

Good day, my lord. What, at your book so hard?   1

KING HENRY

Ay, my good lord – 'my lord' I should say rather.
'Tis sin to flatter. 'Good' was little better.
'Good Gloucester' and 'good devil' were alike,
And both preposterous. Therefore, not 'good lord.'   5

RICHARD

Sirrah, leave us to ourselves; we must confer.
                    [Exit Lieutenant.]

KING HENRY

So flies the reckless shepherd from the wolf;   7
So first the harmless sheep doth yield his fleece,
And next his throat unto the butcher's knife.
What scene of death hath Roscius now to act?   10

RICHARD

Suspicion always haunts the guilty mind;
The thief doth fear each bush an officer.

KING HENRY

The bird that hath been limèd in a bush   13
With trembling wings misdoubteth every bush;   14
And I, the hapless male to one sweet bird,   15
Have now the fatal object in my eye
Where my poor young was limed, was caught, and killed.

RICHARD

Why, what a peevish fool was that of Crete   18
That taught his son the office of a fowl.
And yet, for all his wings, the fool was drowned.

V, vi The Tower of London   1 *book* (of devotions)   5 *preposterous* unnatural   7 *reckless* heedless   10 *Roscius* famous Roman actor (died 62 B.C.),
supposed by the Elizabethans to be a tragedian   13 *limèd* caught with bird-
lime   14 *misdoubteth* suspects   15 *male* father; *bird* chick   18–25 *fool . . .
life* (Daedalus wished to escape from Crete, having been imprisoned there
by King Minos. He devised wings for himself and his son Icarus, fastening
them on with wax. The father flew to safety, but Icarus rose too near the
sun; the heat melted the wax, and Icarus fell into the sea and drowned.)

KING HENRY

I, Daedalus; my poor boy, Icarus;
Thy father, Minos, that denied our course;
The sun that seared the wings of my sweet boy,
Thy brother Edward; and thyself, the sea
25 Whose envious gulf did swallow up his life.
Ah, kill me with thy weapon, not with words.
27 My breast can better brook thy dagger's point
Than can my ears that tragic history.
But wherefore dost thou come? Is't for my life?

RICHARD

Think'st thou I am an executioner?

KING HENRY

A persecutor I am sure thou art.
If murdering innocents be executing,
Why, then thou art an executioner.

RICHARD

Thy son I killed for his presumption.

KING HENRY

Hadst thou been killed when first thou didst presume,
Thou hadst not lived to kill a son of mine.
And thus I prophesy, that many a thousand
38 Which now mistrust no parcel of my fear,
And many an old man's sigh and many a widow's,
40 And many an orphan's water-standing eye –
Men for their sons, wives for their husbands,
42 Orphans for their parents' timeless death –
Shall rue the hour that ever thou wast born.
The owl shrieked at thy birth, an evil sign;
45 The night crow cried, aboding luckless time;
Dogs howled and hideous tempest shook down trees;
47 The raven rooked her on the chimney's top,
48 And chattering pies in dismal discords sung.

---

25 *envious gulf* hateful gullet   27 *brook* tolerate   38 *mistrust no parcel* do
not suspect any part   40 *water-standing* full of tears   42 *timeless* untimely   45 *night crow* nightjar or owl; *aboding* foreboding   47 *rooked her*
squatted   48 *pies* magpies

Thy mother felt more than a mother's pain,
And yet brought forth less than a mother's hope,
To wit, an indigested and deformèd lump,
Not like the fruit of such a goodly tree.
Teeth hadst thou in thy head when thou wast born,
To signify thou cam'st to bite the world ;
And, if the rest be true which I have heard,
Thou cam'st –

RICHARD

I'll hear no more. Die, prophet, in thy speech.
    Stabs him.
For this (amongst the rest) was I ordained.

KING HENRY

Ay, and for much more slaughter after this.
O, God forgive my sins and pardon thee.
    Dies.

RICHARD

What ? Will the aspiring blood of Lancaster
Sink in the ground ? I thought it would have mounted.
See how my sword weeps for the poor king's death.
O may such purple tears be always shed   64
From those that wish the downfall of our house.
If any spark of life be yet remaining,
Down, down to hell, and say I sent thee thither,
    Stabs him again.
I, that have neither pity, love, nor fear.
Indeed 'tis true that Henry told me of ;
For I have often heard my mother say
I came into the world with my legs forward.
Had I not reason, think ye, to make haste
And seek their ruin that usurped our right ?
The midwife wondered, and the women cried,
'O, Jesus bless us ! He is born with teeth !'
And so I was ; which plainly signified
That I should snarl and bite and play the dog.

64 *purple* i.e. bloody

Then, since the heavens have shaped my body so,
79   Let hell make crook'd my mind to answer it.
I have no brother, I am like no brother;
And this word 'love,' which greybeards call divine,
Be resident in men like one another,
And not in me. I am myself alone.
Clarence, beware. Thou keep'st me from the light;
85   But I will sort a pitchy day for thee;
86   For I will buzz abroad such prophecies
That Edward shall be fearful of his life;
And then, to purge his fear, I'll be thy death.
King Henry and the prince his son are gone.
Clarence, thy turn is next, and then the rest,
Counting myself but bad till I be best.
I'll throw thy body in another room
And triumph, Henry, in thy day of doom.

                                  Exit [with the body].

                    ∗

V, vii   *Flourish. Enter King [Edward], Queen [Elizabeth],*
               Clarence, Richard, Hastings, Nurse [with the young
               Prince], and Attendants.

KING EDWARD
Once more we sit in England's royal throne,
Repurchased with the blood of enemies.
3   What valiant foemen, like to autumn's corn,
Have we mowed down in tops of all their pride.
Three Dukes of Somerset, threefold renowned
6   For hardy and undoubted champions;
7   Two Cliffords, as the father and the son;
And two Northumberlands – two braver men
9   Ne'er spurred their coursers at the trumpet's sound;

79 *answer* accord with   85 *sort* seek out (as being befitting); *pitchy* black   86 *buzz* whisper (scandal)
V, vii The royal palace in London   3 *corn* wheat   6 *undoubted* fearless
7 *as* to wit   9 *coursers* war horses

With them, the two brave bears, Warwick and   10
   Montague,
That in their chains fettered the kingly lion
And made the forest tremble when they roared.
Thus have we swept suspicion from our seat   13
And made our footstool of security.
Come hither, Bess, and let me kiss my boy.
Young Ned, for thee thine uncles and myself
Have in our armors watched the winter's night,   17
Went all afoot in summer's scalding heat,
That thou mightst repossess the crown in peace;
And of our labors thou shalt reap the gain.

RICHARD *[aside]*
I'll blast his harvest, if your head were laid;   21
For yet I am not looked on in the world.   22
This shoulder was ordained so thick to heave,
And heave it shall some weight or break my back.
Work thou the way, and thou shalt execute.   25

KING EDWARD
Clarence and Gloucester, love my lovely queen,
And kiss your princely nephew, brothers both.

CLARENCE
The duty that I owe unto your majesty
I seal upon the lips of this sweet babe.   29

QUEEN ELIZABETH
Thanks, noble Clarence; worthy brother, thanks.

RICHARD
And that I love the tree from whence thou sprang'st
Witness the loving kiss I give the fruit.
   [Aside]
To say the truth, so Judas kissed his master
And cried 'All hail!' when as he meant all harm.

---

10 *bears* (the bear was the emblem of the Nevils)   **13** *suspicion* apprehension   **17** *watched* stayed awake during   **21** *laid* laid down (dead)   **22** *looked on* respected   **25** *thou ... thou* (he indicates his head and his arm or shoulder)   **29** *seal* pledge

KING EDWARD
Now am I seated as my soul delights,
Having my country's peace and brothers' loves.

CLARENCE
What will your grace have done with Margaret?
Reignier, her father, to the King of France
Hath pawned the Sicils and Jerusalem,
And hither have they sent it for her ransom.

KING EDWARD
41   Away with her, and waft her hence to France.
And now what rests but that we spend the time
43   With stately triumphs, mirthful comic shows,
Such as befits the pleasure of the court?
Sound drums and trumpets! Farewell sour annoy!
For here I hope begins our lasting joy.   *Exeunt omnes.*

---

41 *waft* convoy   43 *triumphs* festivities

APPENDIX A:
GENEALOGICAL CHARTS

These charts do not attempt to be complete records of the families included, but they cite all the descendants of Edward III who are of consequence (by presence or parenthood) in these two plays and they mention every person of quality in the two lists of dramatis personae with the exception of the following:

PART TWO

William de la Pole, Duke of Suffolk. Not of royal blood, despite his claim in Part II, IV, i, 50–51.

Lord Say. Sir James Fiennes, Lord Say and Sele, Treasurer of England (d. 1450).

Sir Humphrey Stafford and William Stafford. These brothers appear to have been kinsmen of the Earls of Stafford.

Vaux. Presumably Sir William Vaux (d. 1471).

Sir Matthew Gough. A military man, friend of the Lord Scales.

PART THREE

Earl of Pembroke. Sir William Herbert (d. 1469). Not of royal blood.

Lord Stafford. Sir Humphrey Stafford, Earl of Devon (d. 1469).

Sir John and Sir Hugh Mortimer. These brothers are thought to be illegitimate sons of an unidentified Mortimer.

Sir John Montgomery. Called Sir Thomas in Holinshed (d. 1495).

Somerville. Not identified.

In the charts the names of persons in the plays of the two tetralogies are printed in italics. The order of the names does not necessarily indicate the order of birth.

NOTES TO PAGE 278

1. Though Thomas died in 1426, Shakespeare has evidently retained him for Part Three.
2. Part Two; Part Three, I, i, 16.
3. Part Three; these have been combined: Henry is in Act IV, Edmund in Act V.
4. Part Three, I, i, i, 7.

NOTES TO PAGE 279

1. Called Sir Richard at Part Three, III, ii, 2.
2. Sister of Edmund, 5th Earl of Stafford.
3. Mentioned Part Three, I, i, 4.
4. The personality depicted is historically that of his brother John.
5. Died 1461; it is possible, but unlikely, that his son is intended.
6. The guardian of Eleanor Cobham, called John in Part Two.
7. And from 1464 to 1470, Earl of Northumberland.
8. Betrothed to Edward, son of Henry VI, but not married. Shakespeare has reversed the ages of Isabel and Anne.

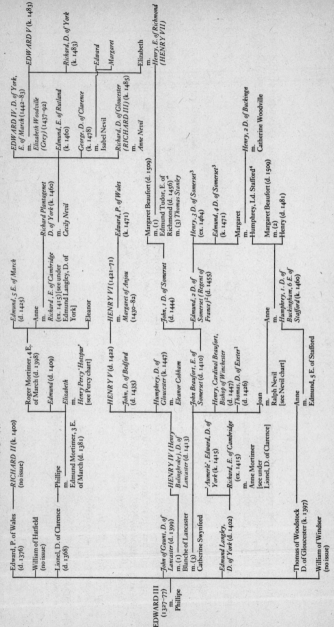

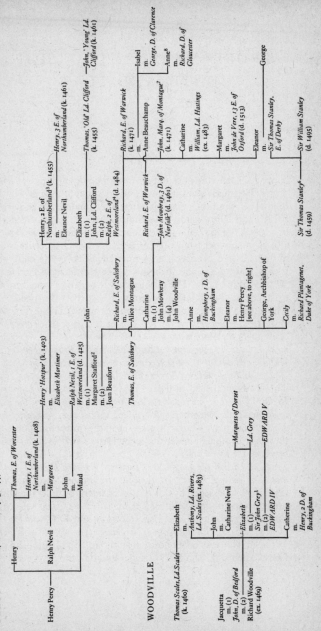

PERCY-NEVIL (for notes see page 277)

APPENDIX B:
PROBLEMS OF AUTHORSHIP, DATE, AND TEXT

Among scholars the question of the authorship of *2* and *3 Henry VI* has long been a vexing one. The inclusion of the plays in the folio of 1623 indicates that Heminge and Condell, Shakespeare's friends and fellow-actors who compiled the volume, considered him to have been their author. However, as these same compilers also included at least one play, *Henry VIII*, which is generally admitted to have been written jointly by Shakespeare and John Fletcher, the degree of Shakespeare's involvement in the Henry VI plays is left open. The problem is further complicated by the existence of two different versions of both Part Two and Part Three. Part Two first appeared in quarto in 1594 as *The First part of the Contention betwixt the two famous Houses of York and Lancaster, with the death of the good Duke Humphrey : And the banishment and death of the Duke of Suffolke, and the Tragicall end of the proud Cardinall of Winchester, with the notable Rebellion of Iacke Cade : And the Duke of Yorkes first claime unto the Crowne* ; Part Three was published in octavo in 1595 as *The true Tragedie of Richard Duke of Yorke, and the death of good King Henrie the Sixt, with the whole contention betweene the two Houses Lancaster and Yorke.* Both plays were reprinted separately in 1600, and in 1619 they were combined under the general title *The Whole Contention betweene the two Famous Houses, Lancaster and Yorke. With the Tragicall ends of the good Duke Humfrey, Richard Duke of Yorke, and King Henrie the sixt.* In the folio of 1623 these two early versions were superseded by new texts, considerably fuller than their predecessors, under the titles *The second Part of Henry the Sixt, with the death of the Good Duke Humfrey* and *The third Part of Henry the Sixt, with the death of the Duke of Yorke.*

The first critic to take a position on the authorship problem was Lewis Theobald, who in 1734 suggested that the plays were not entirely by Shakespeare. Dr Johnson disputed Theobald's position, claiming the plays to be wholly Shakespearean. A more extensive early analysis was that of Edmond Malone in *A Dissertation on the Three Parts of Henry VI* (1787). Here Malone (who had previously supported the opposite view) argued (1) that the plays were originally the work of other dramatists, revised or rewritten by Shakespeare because their "inferior parts are not merely unequal to the rest . . . but of quite a different complexion from the inferior parts" of Shakespeare's recognized work; (2) that the quarto and octavo editions of the plays represented the original versions and the folio editions the Shakespearean revisions; and (3) that a complaint by Robert Greene in 1592 pointed clearly to the fact that Shakespeare had plagiarized from Greene in writing the plays. The complaint appeared in Greene's *Groats-worth of Wit*, addressed to three of Greene's literary associates – presumably Marlowe, Nashe, and Peele – warning them against relying on the good faith of actors:

Base minded men, all three of you, if by my miserie you be not warnd: for unto none of you (like mee) sought those burres [the actors] to cleave: those Puppets (I meane) that spake from our mouths, those Anticks garnisht in our colours. Is it not strange, that I, to whom they all have beene beholding: is it not like that you, to whome they all have beene beholding, shall (were yee in that case as I am now) bee both at once of them forsaken: Yes trust them not: for there is an upstart Crow, beautified with our feathers, that with his *Tygers hart wrapt in a Players hyde*, supposes he is as well able to bombast out a blanke verse as the best of you: and beeing an absolute *Johannes fac totum*, is in his owne conceit the onely Shake-scene in a countrey . . . whilest you may, seeke you better Maisters.

Malone interpreted this complaint as Greene's retaliation for the hard treatment that he – an educated man – had received from ignorant and callous players who had made their fortunes by parroting his lines while he lay dying in penury. Greene singled out one player who was so presumptuous as to attempt to write plays and, specifically, to rewrite a play on Henry VI written by Greene himself. This "Shake-scene" was Shakespeare: the "Tygers hart wrapt in a Players hyde" was Greene's parody of Shakespeare's "tiger's heart wrapped in a woman's hide" (*3 Henry VI*, I, iv, 137), a phrase, according to Malone, stolen from Greene.

Malone's view of the evidence, though often questioned, was not supplanted until in 1929 Professor Peter Alexander and in 1930 Miss Madeleine Doran, working independently in Great

Britain and America, reached the conclusion that the quarto and octavo editions were not early plays by Greene or others but were versions of the folio texts which had been derived chiefly by actors writing down (or dictating to a scribe) what they could remember of parts they had learned for performances of Shakespeare's plays. The two scholars demonstrated that the 1594 and 1595 editions bore marks regularly accepted as denoting texts memorially reconstructed for sale to a printer or for use in the provinces by an acting company that did not have access to the official prompt-book. The 1594 and 1595 texts thus, though earlier in date of publication than those of 1623, were later in the line of transmission; so far from being early drafts revised and improved into the folio versions, they were versions derived from the folio texts and mutilated in the process. Professor Alexander explained Greene's charge against "Shake-scene" not as one of plagiarism but as one of presumptuous conceit; Greene indicated by the quotation of the line no more than that Shakespeare was the author of *Henry VI*, Part Three (and hence of Part Two). Thus it was argued that the existence of the differing versions could no longer be used as evidence bearing on the question of authorship.

This interpretation of the evidence was accepted in the 1930's and 1940's by one after another of the leading Shakespearean critics. Malone's belief that the 1594 and 1595 editions represented the work of Greene and others while the folio represented the Shakespearean revisions is now conceded by most critics to have been erroneous. On the other hand, the repudiation of Malone's other points on authorship and plagiarism has not received complete assent.

This fact is effectively represented by the appearance in the 1950's of editions of the plays in the two chief British series of Shakespeare, one editor supporting Greene, Nashe, and Peele as joint authors of work revised by Shakespeare, the other supporting Shakespeare as sole author.

John Dover Wilson in his editions of 1951 and 1952 in the Cambridge New Shakespeare supports Malone's belief that Greene was charging Shakespeare with misappropriation of Greene's material. Wilson does so by pointing to Greene's other uses of Aesop's fable of the "upstart Crow, beautified with our feathers," which all refer to literary plagiarism, the vice with which the allusion was conventionally associated. Working solely with the folio versions, Wilson analyzes the two plays and the writings of Greene, Nashe, and Peele. On the basis of "common verbal parallels, . . . syntactical peculiarities, little mannerisms and tricks of style, proverbial phrases, . . . classical or other allusions, and clichés of various types," Wilson concludes that Greene was responsible for the plotting of the two Parts and for the verse (with perhaps a little help from Peele in Part Three) and that Nashe was responsible for the prose of the Jack Cade scenes. Shakespeare revised throughout with varying degrees of thoroughness.

Andrew S. Cairncross in his edition of 1957 in the New Arden series rejects this position by arguing that the offensive plagiarism was not wholesale but only the re-use of particular allusions or occasional bits and pieces of material. He sees the verbal and stylistic parallels as an inconclusive demonstration of joint authorship; they can be explained as the work of a young author deliberately copying the devices and mannerisms of men who have practiced the craft before him. Cairncross argues for sole Shakespearean authorship and derives the difficulties and inconsistencies in the plays from two causes. The first of these is external to transmission – the requirement of the official censor that many passages be rewritten so as not to give offense to authority. The second is textual – the use of the early version in the printing of the late. These two explanations are both fresh suggestions in the argument; their evaluation will follow in the years to come.

Both Wilson and Cairncross took for granted Alexander's and Miss Doran's demonstrations of memorial reconstruction as the method of origin of *The Contention* and *The True Tragedy*, but this matter has been recently re-opened by C. T. Prouty, who, in a study of *The Contention and Shakespeare's 2 Henry VI* (1954), argues for a return to Malone's theory of revision. While Prouty's thesis has received little support from other scholars, its very existence proves the continuing uncertainty over the textual history of the plays. And, as if the authorship question were not sufficiently troublesome, there is also disagreement about the date of composition of the two Parts, a matter linked not only with authorship but also with the date of composition of the plays which adjoin them, *1 Henry VI* and *Richard III*.

The Diary of Philip Henslowe, who had financial interests in the Elizabethan theatre, records that in March, 1592, Lord Strange's Men performed a play called *Harey the vj*, and beside the entry is the notation "ne," which presumably means that the play was new and being presented for the first time. Because in the same year Thomas Nashe in *Pierce Pennilesse* referred to a current play featuring the exploits of Talbot, the hero of the wars in France, and because Talbot has a significant role in Shakespeare's *1 Henry VI*, it is tempting to identify *1 Henry VI* with the play mentioned by Nashe as well as with *Harey the vj*. One difficulty with this interpretation of the evidence is that *Harey the vj* definitely belonged to Strange's Men while the other plays in the series belonged to Pembroke's Men, at least at some period in their history. *Harey the vj* may thus have no direct bearing on the problems related to Shakespeare's Henry VI plays, and Nashe's allusion may have been either to a lost *Harey the vj* or to *1 Henry VI*.

The anterior date of the Henry VI plays, it has recently been argued, can be fixed by the registering for publication in December, 1589, of Books I–III of Spenser's *The Faerie Queene*, for *1 Henry VI* shows the influence of this work in several places, and their posterior date by the publication in 1591 of a play called *The Troublesome Raigne of King John*, which seems to draw some of its language from other dramatic works, including *Richard III*, generally agreed to be the last in Shakespeare's series to be written. As Greene died on September 3, 1592, his parody of the line from *3 Henry VI* proves the existence of the play by that date. Within these limits, 1590 has been assigned as the approximate date of composition of both *2* and *3 Henry VI*. There are some, however, who, while willing to accept a date of 1589, 1590, or 1591 for *2* and *3 Henry VI*, feel that *Harey the vj* was probably *1 Henry VI*; if Henslowe's "ne" means "new" in 1592, then it would follow that the plays were not written sequentially but *1 Henry VI* after *2* and *3 Henry VI*, although it may later have been revised to make it fit into the first place in the series. Supporting this line of reasoning is the fact that Talbot, who looms large in *1 Henry VI*, is ignored in *2* and *3*, even being omitted from Gloucester's list of those who suffered in France (*2 Henry VI*, I, i, 78–87).

Although scholars cannot as yet agree on precise dates for *2* and *3 Henry VI*, there is no question of the fact that Shakespeare had a hand in them very early in his career, about the same time as his writing of *Titus Andronicus* and *The Comedy of Errors* and possibly before. There is, moreover, general agreement that even if he was not the sole author of the two history plays, Shakespeare exercised the dominant force in shaping them into their present form, and that he worked on them sequentially and meant them to be considered as related, even though both plays are sufficiently self-contained to be performed separately. Thus we are probably not far off the mark in speaking of them as though their conception and execution were altogether his while silently acknowledging the possibility that he worked from earlier plays.

The present edition is based on the assumption that *The First Part of the Contention* and *The True Tragedie* are versions of the two Parts memorially reconstructed by actors. Hence they possess little authority for the text of the dialogue, but in disclosing details of performance they solve some theatrical problems which seem to have been left by Shakespeare to the discretion of the dramatic company. Their stage directions have therefore been generously incorporated in square brackets into this text, but where these directions offer a staging clearly not intended by the folio text, they have been ignored.

The folio versions give indications of having been printed from authorial manuscript, and on them the present editions are based. Two brief passages in the folio (Part Two, IV, v, 1 – IV, vi, 6; Part Three, IV, ii, 1–18) would seem to have been printed directly from the quarto versions of 1619, perhaps because the manuscript was illegible. For the present editions, the folio versions have been corrected and emended by reference to the quarto and octavo, and the following lines have been admitted to supply omissions in the folio: Part Two, IV, i, 48; Part Three, II, i, 113; II, vi, 8. The collation of the folio by Mr Charlton Hinman has disclosed three substantive press variants, all in Part Three, V, vii, 25–42; these have been printed in the corrected readings.

The folio preserves in stage directions and speech-prefixes the names of five or six "bit" actors: Part Two, IV, ii, 1–28, the two Rebels are named Bevis and John Holland; IV, vii, 7, 14, the Rebel is named John (see l. 9); IV, vii, 20, the Rebel with the Lord Say is named George (presumably Bevis' Christian name); IV, ii, 99–106, the Messenger is named Michael (possibly an actor's name); Part Three, I, ii, 47 s.d. and 49, the Messenger is named Gabriel (Gabriel Spencer); III, i, the two Keepers are named Sinklo and Humfrey (John Sinklo and Humfrey Jeffes). The present edition substitutes dramatic designations for each of the above in both stage directions and speech-prefixes as indicated in the following list of emendations, which includes all substantive departures from the copy text. The adopted reading in italics is followed by the folio reading in roman.

2 HENRY VI

I, i, 176 *Protector* (Q) Protectors   177, 211 s.d. *Exeunt* (Eds) Exit   254 *in* (F2) in in

I, ii, 37 *Westminster*; (This ed.) Westminster,   40 *diadem* – (This ed.) Diadem.

I, iii, 6 *1. Petitioner* (F4) Peter   13 *For* (Wordsworth) To   29 *master was* (Warburton) Mistresse was   39 s.d. *Exeunt* (Eds) Exit   98 *helm.* (Eds) Helme. Exit.   140 *would* (Q) could

I, iv, 15 *silence* (Q) silent   23 *Asnath* (Cairncross) Asmath   60 *te* (Warburton) Omitted   61 *posse* (Eds) posso

II, i, 48 *Cardinal* (Theobald) Cardinall,   106 *Alban* (F3) Albones   130 *his* (Q) it,

II, ii, 45 *son* (Rowe) Omitted   46 *son* (Theobald) Sonnes Sonne

II, iii, 3 *sins* (Theobald) sinne   30 *helm* (Steevens) Realme

III, i, s.d. (order of entrance in procession is from Q; the order in F is King, Queen, Cardinal, Suffolk, York, Buckingham, Salisbury, Warwick)   211 *strains* (Vaughan) strayes   260 *treasons* (Hudson) Reasons

III, ii, 14 s.d. *Somerset* (Eds) Suffolke, Somerset   26 *Meg* (Capell) Nell   79, 100, 120 *Margaret* (Rowe) Elianor   116 *witch* (Theobald) watch   332 *turn* (Rowe) turnes   385 *sorrow's* (This ed.) sorrowes

IV, i, s.d. (characters other than Lieutenant and Suffolk listed from Q; F reads 'and others')   48 *Jove ... I?* (Q) Omitted   50 *Suffolk* (before l. 51 in F)   71 *Suffolk* (Alexander) Sir   72 *Lieutenant* (Alexander) Lord   86 mother's bleeding (Rowe) Mother-bleeding   94 *are* (Rowe) and   118 *Paene* (Malone) Pine   133 *Suffolk* (before l. 134 in F)   142 s.d. *Exeunt* (Eds) Exit

IV, ii, s.d. *two Rebels* (This ed.) Bevis, and Iohn Holland   1–28 *1. Rebel, 2. Rebel* (This ed.) Bevis, Hol.   31 *fall* (F4) faile   92 *an* (F2) a   98 s.d., 99, 101, 106 *Messenger* (This ed.) Michael   124 *this :* (Eds) this

IV, iv, 43 *hate* (F2) hateth   58 *be* (F2) Omitted   59 *Say* (Q) Omitted

IV, vi, 11 *Messenger* (This ed.) Dicke

IV, vii, 7, 14 2. *Rebel* (This ed.) Iohn   9 *Weaver* (Cairncross)
Smith   20 s.d. *First Rebel* (This ed.) George   63–64 *hands,* /
But (Johnson conj.; Rann) hands? / Kent   76 *1. Rebel* (This
ed.) George   82 *caudle* (F4) Candle   *pap with a* (Farmer conj.;
Cairncross) the help of   119 s.d. *two* (Q) one

IV, viii, 12 *rebel* (Singer) rabble

IV, ix, 33 *calmed* (F4) calme

IV, x, 19 *waning* (Rowe) warning   56 *God* (Q) Ioue

V, i, 109 *these* (Theobald) thee   111 *sons* (Q) sonne   113 *for* (F2)
of   194 *or* (Rowe) and   196 *Thou* (Cairncross) You   201
house's (F2) housed

V, ii, 28 *oeuvres* (Eds) eumenes

V, iii, 1 *Old* (Q) Of   29 *faith* (Q) hand

3 HENRY VI

I, i, 14 *cousin* (as in O at I, ii, 1, 36, 55) Brother   69 *Exeter* (O)
Westm   83 *and* (F2) Omitted   105 *Thy* (O) My   201 s.d.
(after l. 205 in F)   205 s.d. *Sennet* (followed by 'Here they come
down' in F)   259 *with* (F2) Omitted   261 *from* (O) to

I, ii, 4 *cousin* (as in O at I, ii, 1, 36, 55) Brother   36 *Cousin* (O)
Brother   47 s.d. *a Messenger* (O) Gabriel   49 *Messenger* (O)
Gabriel   55 *cousin* (O) Brother   60 *Cousin* (O) Brother

I, iv, 50 *buckle* (O) buckler

II, i, 113 *And ... thought* (O) Omitted   131 *an idle* (O) a lazie

II, ii, 89 *Since* (Eds) Cla. Since   116 sun set (O) Sunset   133
Richard (O) War

II, iii, 49 *all together* (Rowe) altogether

II, v, 37 *months* (Rowe) yeares   54 s.d. *door* (followed by 'and a
Father that hath kill'd his Sonne at another doore' in F)   78 s.d.
Enter ... son (replaces 'Enter Father, bearing of his Sonne' in
F)   79 *hast* (F3) hath   119 *Even* (Capell) Men

II, vi, 6 *commixture* (O) Commixtures   8 *The ... flies* (O) Omitted
42 *Edward* (O) Rich   43 *Richard* (O) Omitted   44 *Edward. See
who it is , and* (Capell) See who it is. / Ed. And   60 *his* (F2) is

III, i, s.d. *two Keepers* (O) Sinklo, and Humfrey   1–97 *1. Keeper,
2. Keeper* (Malone) Sink., Hum.   24 *thee ... adversity* (Dyce)
the ... Adversaries   55 *that* (O) Omitted

III, ii, 3 *lands* (O) Land   123 *honorably* (O) honourable

III, iii, 124 *eternal* (O) externall   156 *peace* (F2) Omitted   161 s.d.
  (after l. 160 in F)   228 *I'll* (O) I
IV, i, 93 *thy* (O) the
IV, ii, 15 *towns* (Theobald) Towne
IV, iii, s.d. *King Edward's* (Eds) the Kings   59 s.d. (after l. 57 in F)
IV, v, 4 *stands* (F2) stand   8 *Comes* (F2) Come   21 *King Edward*
  (Wilson) Omitted   *ship* (F2) shipt
IV, vi, 55 *be* (Malone) Omitted   88 s.d. *Manent* (Eds) Manet
IV, viii, s.d. *Exeter* (Capell) Somerset   6 *Oxford* (O) King
V, i, 78 *an* (Rowe) in
V, iv, 27 *ragged* (Rowe) raged
V, v, 50 *The* (O) Omitted   77 *butcher* (O) butcher Richard
V, vi, s.d. *in the Tower* (O) on the Walles*
V, vii, 5 *renowned* (Rowe) Renowne   25 *and* (corrected F) add
  (uncorrected F)   *and thou* (O) and that   27 *kiss* (corrected F)
  'tis (uncorrected F)   30 *Queen Elizabeth* (O) Cla   *Thanks* (F3)
  Thanke   38 *Reignier* (Rowe) Reynard   42 *rests* (corrected F)
  tests (uncorrected F)

---

* Stage directions throughout have indicated the use of the usual facilities
of an Elizabethan stage with the exception of a "discovery" recess. The rear
stage gallery has several times been used to represent the walls of a city, or an
elevated gallery. Only in the present instance does the folio direction locate
the action "on the Walles" when there is no simultaneous and related action
on the stage proper. The location given in the octavo "in the Tower" suggests that this scene, too, was played on the stage proper, with the locale
given in the author's script regarded as literary and not theatrical.